BEST NEWSPAPER WRITING 1985

The Poynter Institute also publishes:
Best Newspaper Writing 1984
Best Newspaper Writing 1983
The Adversary Press
Believing the News
Making Sense of the News

Best Newspaper Writing 1979-1982 are now out of print.

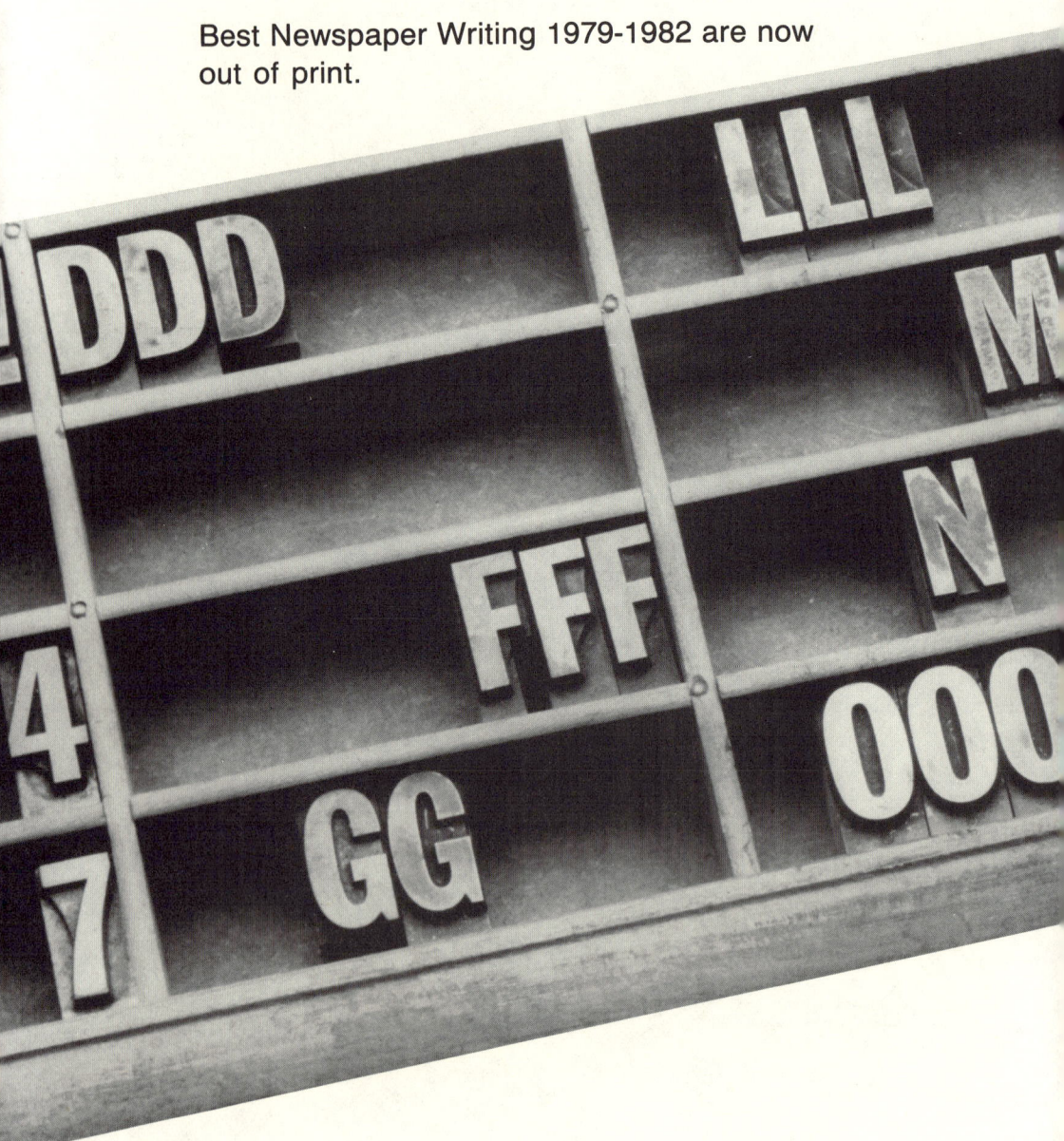

BEST NEWSPAPER WRITING 1985

Library of Congress Cataloging in Publication Data

Best Newspaper Writing, 1979 -
　　St. Petersburg, Fla., Modern Media Institute Annual
"Winners, the American Society of Newspaper
Editors' competition," Editor: 1979 - , Roy Peter Clark

Key Title: Best Newspaper Writing, ISSN 0195-895X

1. Journalism—Competitions.   I. Clark, Roy Peter.   II. Modern Media Institute.   III. American Society of Newspaper Editors.

PN4726.B38　　　　081　　　　80-646604
ISBN 0-935742-10-7

Copyright © 1985 by The Poynter Institute for Media Studies
Post Office Box 31266, St. Petersburg, Florida

All rights reserved.
No part of this publication may
be reproduced in any form or by
any means without permission
in writing from the publisher.

Printed in the United States of America

　　Copies of Best Newspaper Writing 1985 are available for $7.95 each from The Poynter Institute. The Institute offers discounts for purchases of 20 or more copies of the same title. Please write for details.

To the memory of Richard G. Gray

About this book

AUGUST 1985

If newspapers are a first rough draft of history, as one editor has said, then this book is devoted to the notion that such instant histories should be marked by literary grace as well as factual reliability.

This is Volume VII of *Best Newspaper Writing,* which increasingly since 1979 has been bought by students, teachers and professionals as an indispensable text on clear, effective and graceful use of the language.

As in past years, *Best Newspaper Writing 1985* is a joint venture of the American Society of Newspaper Editors, The Poynter Institute for Media Studies of St. Petersburg, Florida, and Dr. Roy Peter Clark, the Institute's associate director and editor of this series of books.

Seven years ago, the ASNE made better newspaper writing one of its principal long-range goals. The following year it inaugurated a contest to select the best writing in several categories from papers in the U.S. and Canada and to reward the writers with $1,000 prizes. The Institute volunteered to spread the gospel of good writing by publishing the winning entries along with Clark's notes, commentaries and interviews with the winning writers. That was *Best Newspaper Writing 1979,* which is now sold out and becoming a collector's item.

Each year the winners are chosen by a panel of ASNE editors which meets in St. Petersburg for several days to screen nearly 500 entries in four categories. The 1985 categories were deadline and non-deadline writing, commentary and editorial writing.

Fifteen editors, under the chairmanship of Arnold Rosenfeld, editor of the Austin, Texas,

American-Statesman, made up the 1985 Writing Awards Board. They are:

Don E. Carter, formerly of Knight-Ridder Newspapers

Anthony Day, *Los Angeles Times*

Meg Greenfield, *Washington Post*

John C. Quinn, *USA Today*

Eugene C. Patterson, *St. Petersburg Times*

James A. Clendinen, formerly of the *Tampa Tribune*

William Hosokawa, formerly of *The Denver Post*

David Laventhol, *Newsday,* New York

Don Shoemaker, *The Miami Herald*

Robert Bartley, *The Wall Street Journal*

Mary Ann Dolan, *Los Angeles Herald Examiner*

Albert Fitzpatrick, Knight-Ridder Newspapers

Dan A. Martin, *The Times Herald,* Port Huron, Michigan

Ross Mackenzie, *News Leader,* Richmond, Virginia

Dr. Clark was one of the first newspaper writing coaches and has been a national leader in the growing movement to make American newspapers more readable, more interesting and more accurate. Trained as a Chaucer scholar at the State University of New York, he came to the *St. Petersburg Times* in 1977 on leave from the English faculty at Auburn University for what was supposed to be a one-year sabbatical as a newsroom writing coach. The one year turned into two, the coach turned into a staff writer and then he joined The Poynter Institute (then known as Modern Media Institute) to direct its Writing Center. He conducts frequent writing seminars for newspaper professionals and for advanced liberal arts students seeking careers in journalism. He also works with high school students, including many minority students, college journalism teachers, high school newspaper advisors and their student editors. At a time when many despair that "kids just can't write anymore," he has developed a pilot program for fourth and fifth graders which has had remarkable success in teaching elementary school children not only to write well—but to love writing.

Clark's center is one of four at the Institute which instruct students, teachers and professionals in writing, graphics, management and ethics.

Beginning in 1985, Clark was joined on the faculty of the Writing Center by Dr. Donald K. Fry, who had been a mentor and colleague at the State University of New York at Stony Brook. Fry, a graduate of Duke University and the University of California at Berkeley, is a distinguished scholar of early English and also an outstanding teacher of contemporary writing. He joins Clark as co-editor of this year's edition of *Best Newspaper Writing*.

Founded in 1975 by the late Nelson Poynter, chairman of the *St. Petersburg Times* and its Washington affiliate, *Congressional Quarterly,* the Institute was bequeathed controlling stock in the Times Publishing Co. in 1978. It invests its dividends in projects such as this book, its four teaching centers and other educational and research projects, all of which seek the same goal: to raise levels of excellence in newspapers and the communications media generally.

Robert J. Haiman, President
The Poynter Institute

Acknowledgments

Atlanta Journal and Constitution and John Carman
Greensboro News & Record and Greta Tilley
Kansas City Times and Howard Goodman
Los Angeles Times and Jim Murray
Newsday and Murray Kempton
Philadelphia Daily News and Richard Aregood
The Post Standard, Syracuse, and Jonathan Bor
Providence Journal-Bulletin and Mark Patinkin
The Wall Street Journal and Daniel Henninger

Book design by Billie M. Keirstead
Portraits by Jack Barrett
Cover photo by Dick Dickinson Photography

Contents

Introduction	xii
Greta Tilley Non-Deadline Writing	1
Jonathan Bor Deadline Writing	67
A New Shape for the News	90
Murray Kempton Commentary	97
Richard Aregood Editorial Writing	137
Finalists:	
Daniel Henninger	174
Mark Patinkin	186
John Carman	217
Jim Murray	234
The 'Jedi' Murder Howard Goodman	244
Good Newspaper Writing	275
1985 Finalists	281
Former ASNE Winners	282

Introduction

MAY 1985

I enjoy attending national conventions of the American Society of Newspaper Editors (ASNE), not to slurp pistachio soup with newspaper bigshots, but to see Greta Tilley, a reporter for the *Greensboro* (N.C.) *News & Record.* Greta will argue with me about this, but she is one of the best newspaper writers in America. For the second time in three years she has won an ASNE Distinguished Writing Award. Given the politics of contests, that is a magnificient achievement.

During a panel discussion at the ASNE convention in Washington in April 1985, Greta revealed the secret of her success. During the writing process, she sucks on lemon-flavored cough drops. This must represent the mildest form of chemical dependency in the history of newspaper writing. I envisioned the editors in the audience lugging home cases of lemon cough drops to get the creative juices flowing among their dry-throated troops. If Tilley wins this award a third time, they should enshrine her cough drops in the Smithsonian, next to Jake Garn's spacesuit and Ronald Reagan's hair.

Sitting beside Tilley on the dais was Richard Aregood of the *Philadelphia Daily News,* a man whose very name is an ungrammatical sentence. To me, Aregood is a legend before his own time. In my file rests an old editorial titled "Yes, the Chair," urging the execution of a murderer. The first line is seared on my brain: "It's about time for Leonard Edwards to take the Hot Squat." Aregood concludes this notorious masterpiece with the horribly ambiguous imperative: "Fry him." (In a healthier age, Aregood might have written "Broil him.") Richard Aregood makes all other editorial writers look like...well, editorial writers.

Next to Aregood sat a bearded young man named Jonathan Bor of the Syracuse *Post-Standard,* who threatens to bring some zest and bravado back into deadline writing. Bor was applauded for a story on a heart transplant that manages to be both dramatic and tightly written. Bor fills his story with wonderful details: a yellowed, diseased heart plopped into a stainless steel bowl, and a new heart shipped across country in a beer cooler. The story behind the story is that Bor, after a day and a half of reporting and 48 hours without sleep, wrote his narrative on deadline in 90 minutes. Made the first edition.

Not present for the morning's discussion was the winner for commentary, Murray Kempton, who was, appropriately enough, off writing commentary. Kempton has been doing that so well for papers like the *New York World-Telegram,* the *New York Post,* and now *Newsday,* that he has earned George Will's praise as "the best columnist the United States has ever produced." His historical memory from 40 years of reporting and his literary elegance have gained for him an honored position among his peers. Gary Wills writes that "Kempton, alone among his contemporaries, has made an art form of the newspaper column. These pieces have their exits and their entrances; they are disciplined, paced, *constructed* things. More is said in their 800-1,000 words, by way of epigram, allusion, disturbing juxtaposition, and haunting conclusion, than most men say in books."

The total volume of copy entered into the ASNE contest on behalf of these winning writers is less than 30 photocopied pages. Only Greta Tilley produced stories that required a jump inside the paper. That has left us the wonderful opportunity of sharing with readers the work of four other ASNE finalists. We even had room to include the work of a writer not entered in the competition, a story that by every definition of good journalism deserves recognition and discussion.

The writers interviewed for this collection seek the standard rewards for excellent work: freedom to pursue their own ideas, the time to do it right, collaborative support from good editors, and prominent display in the newspaper.

These are writers of superior talent, but at the ASNE convention I argued that talent is never enough, that relationships, working conditions, leadership, opportunity, and innovation all count. The overriding question, I argued, is one of "climate control": How do reporters and editors create an environment in which good work is encouraged, recognized, and rewarded? I offered these suggestions:

• Reporters and editors at newspapers need to know in specific terms how they are doing. The most common complaint among journalists, especially young ones, is that they get no "feedback," an electronically unpleasant word, but the one they most often use. Writers want a chance to collaborate with good editors and receive constructive criticism of their work.

• Most journalists want and need a periodic opportunity to express their goals and aspirations to their editors. Such conversations help editors make important personnel decisions, matching the best person with the right job. Too often, when such conversations do not take place, journalists fulfill their aspirations by moving to another paper, or out of newspapering.

• Criticism of work should be horizontal as well as vertical. When criticism comes from one direction only, the top down, workers come to resent what they describe as "the golden shower," a euphemism for being pissed on from above. Journalists must be involved in organized efforts to improve the paper. Copy desks, for example, can engage in regular critiques of the paper with all desk editors participating.

• The habitual nature of journalism causes staleness and burnout. Variety of opportunity and new challenges keep workers fresh and productive. Good editors struggle against the forces of institutional inertia. A beat reporter can be encouraged to write an occasional feature story. The education writer chained to the school board can be encouraged to get into the classroom. Beats can be rotated. Copy editors can be encouraged to write book reviews.

• All workers need to feel involved in the quest for better story ideas. At too many papers, most ideas come from assignments, press releases, or the competition. Many ideas should come from reporters on the street and close to the action. They should also come from copy editors, the publisher's children, clerks, librarians, summer interns and readers. Most ideas surface casually, but organized brainstorming sessions and analyses of coverage help.

Good leaders inspire conversations on how to perfect the craft and improve the paper. Talking about writing helps the staff understand what editors are looking for and what reporters are trying to accomplish. Such talk gets important issues on the table and helps journalists develop a critical vocabulary for describing their work. These discussions can be organized or occur spontaneously. Reporters and editors can discuss changes in a story. Writers can exchange stories and help each other.

• Editors have a special responsibility to share learning materials with reporters and desk editors. Each year the study of journalism generates a significant body of books, articles and reports that can be used to improve the work of journalists. Too often, these are routed to top editors and then chucked. Editors need to develop creative ways to get the hay down where the goats can get it.

• More and more newspapers conduct in-house seminars on special topics. These show commitment on the part of management to help journalists improve. They energize the staff and renew the drive toward excellence. They can be conducted on specific topics selected by the staff, such as headline writing, leads, photojournalism, design, ethics, libel, etc.

• Outside experts can help, but it is crucial to cultivate your own expertise. Relieve your best teaching editors of clerical or bureaucratic responsibilities so they can spend time working with writers. Turn attention and resources toward the training of editors to make them more concerned with the values of writers and with the needs of readers.

• Newspapers must find ways to encourage and nurture reporters and editors laboring in bureaus. More and more bureaus exist, and they are breeding grounds for discontent. Many bureau journalists feel unfulfilled and look forward to the day they can leave the hinterlands to come downtown. The work of bureau reporters is edited at a distance. Communication comes over the telephone. The *St. Petersburg Times* sent some of its best reporters and editors into the bureaus to conduct a continuing series of workshops. For the first time, the best people in the main office got a chance to get to know the folks in the bureau and open some lines of communication and support.

• Reporters and copy editors are traditionally suspicious of each other. It helps if both groups understand in specific terms what is expected of them. Copy editors, especially, need to have their important responsibilities spelled out. Are they free to improve a story in any way? Can they rewrite a lead in ways that affect the writer's style? Do they have a responsibility to check changes with the writer or the assigning editor? How are changes explained to the writer, and by whom? It helps if all workers understand and agree on a protocol.

• It is easier to hire an excellent writer or editor than to train one. Editors must devote more time and creative energy to the recruitment and retention of talented workers.

• Improving the newspaper is the special responsibility of editors, the climate-control officers of the newsroom, but must be shared by all who work for the paper. In the absence of enlightened leadership, reporters and low-level editors can spark reform movements and sneak good work into bad newspapers. You don't need a memo from the boss to get something going. Read this book and pass it on to a friend.

Roy Peter Clark
St. Petersburg, Fla.

BEST NEWSPAPER WRITING 1985

Greta Tilley
Non-Deadline Writing

GRETA TILLEY, 38, was graduated from the University of South Carolina in 1968 with a degree in journalism. She joined the staff of the *Greensboro* (N.C.) *Record* in 1969 to do the Hot Line (question-and-answer) column. She moved on to write obituaries, civic club announcements and, when time permitted, feature stories. She then covered police, county government, and the consumer beat. She left the paper to free-lance from 1976 to 1979, but returned to write features for the now-merged *News & Record* staff. She is the only person to win an ASNE Distinguished Writing Award twice.

Dix offers a refuge for the mentally ill

APRIL 29, 1984

Nothing could prepare Greta Tilley for what she saw behind the walls of a state mental institution, although the administrators of Dorothea Dix Hospital tried.

The director, Dr. Granville Tolley, agreed to open the doors for two weeks and show things as they are. Because of state law, patient anonymity was promised.

The staff spoke frankly. They said to expect the unexpected. They told her not to turn her back on anyone. They said not everything she heard would be true.

She went in with her eyes and heart open, and came out with the story. Here, then, is a six-part series that presents life as it is on Dix Hill, from the first hollow laughter in the morning to the last song in the Rose Room.

RALEIGH—They say spring is the best time to visit Dix Hill.

Dogwoods are blooming, the oaks are fat with leaves, the crabapple trees full and bright.

As in the story books, the campus turns into a fairy kingdom before the eyes behind the locked windows and becomes a sedative that doesn't have to be shot into a vein or swallowed with water.

This complementary dose of medicine may or may not help. When you are sick, beauty can inspire. It can also hurt.

People who live at Dorothea Dix Hospital are sick. They are the hard-core sick.

They are people who have tried to get well and did for a while, people who have tried and did not, and people too sick to try at all.

They are the people the communities couldn't handle or didn't want after a mental health movement in the Kennedy years stripped state institutions of patients.

They have been diagnosed as severely depressed or manic-depressed or mentally retarded, schizophrenic with chemical disorders, psychotic with severe personality disorders, delusional and dangerous to strangers and themselves.

Life has dealt them a mean lot because their minds aren't the only resources they have lost. They have lost money if they had it to lose, they have lost jobs, they have lost husbands, wives, children, friends and a place to go. They have lost a chance for the good life, and are struggling for a lousy existence. Some have even lost that.

Lucy has lived on Dix Hill 21 years. Her dull blue eyes and puffy face show she reached 43 the hard way. Her legs are bare on a cool day. Red rouge accents the pock marks on her cheeks.

"I go home and have to come back 'cause I can't live in society," she says, "I get three meals a day, don't go hungry, don't freeze, have a bed to sleep in and a warm place to stay and medical care. I couldn't afford it on the outside."

The last time the doctor told Lucy she could try again, she broke a perfume bottle and cut her wrist and face with the glass.

Her home, Dorothea Dix Hospital, is a complex of renovated buildings on 1,354 state-owned acres just off Western Boulevard in southwestern Raleigh. North Carolina State University fronts it by a block. Central Prison brings up the rear.

Downtown is just a look away, yet the city belongs to another world. In the city, people are coping with problems. On Dix Hill, the ability to cope has slipped away.

A lean man is stalking the bare cement floors on a ward of older people who have lost the privilege of functioning for themselves. He guards his territory like an agitated animal and will strike at anyone who enters. It takes two people to hold him while another feeds him meals. No one knows why his brain has burned out or how long it will be before he walks the rest of himself away.

A fragile little woman stands in a corridor with her face against the wall. She has been frozen this way for hours. A nurse puts an arm around her and asks why she is standing there.

"I don't know," the woman says, not moving. "I just have to."

The nurse guides her toward a chair in the day room and tells her to sit.

"She's catatonic," she says "She'd stay in the same position for days if someone didn't make her move."

A wrinkled woman in jogging shoes and one sock takes a key from around her neck and opens her home, a narrow, neat room with drawn curtains and two single beds. On top of one is Holly, the stuffed doll she sleeps with at night. She has a roommate, but doesn't know her name. She says she has lived on Dix Hill since her teens. She begs for a cigarette.

A woman writhes on a bed in a dark room, her hospital gown and knees curled against her chest. Raw screams do not unlock her torment. She has entered the manic cycle of her depression, the nurse says. Medicine doesn't help. Technicians force liquids into her mouth so she won't dehydrate. Reflexes swallow for her.

These are some of the things happening all the time. And there is always the background music: the shuffle of drug-slowed footsteps, the tangle of drug-slurred tongues, the tics, the jerks, the moans, the rattling of phlegmed coughs, the curses, the hollow laughter.

Perhaps Dorothea Lynde Dix was haunted by the laughter on a frigid Sunday morning in 1841 as she left a jailhouse in Cambridge, Mass.

She had come to teach a Sunday School class and, after the lesson, asked to inspect the dungeon. She found insane prisoners chained naked in cells without heat.

This sight ignited a passion to crusade for the mentally ill, and Dix traveled the country to uncover injustices more extreme than those in the Cambridge jail.

She found poor people with mental problems being auctioned by communities to labor for the highest bidder. The insane didn't feel heat or cold, she was told, and weren't given protection from either. They were treated more like animals than humans.

In North Carolina, she found the mentally ill jammed into jails and workhouses. As she had in other states, Dix appealed to the legislature to build a hospital for the insane. The men who ruled in Raleigh believed $100,000 could be put to more profitable use and turned down the pale nurse with chronic lung trouble.

Then chance delivered Dix to the Mansion House Hotel in the capital city. She heard about an ill woman in another room and offered to care for her. The patient turned out to be the wife of powerful legislator James C. Dobbin. Before Mrs. Dobbin died, she asked her husband to rally the "asylum bill."

By 1856, Dix Hill Asylum, named after Dix's grandfather, became the first public mental hospital in North Carolina. One hundred years later the institution was rededicated to the woman who had dedicated her life to the desolate people inside.

Howard Johnson came to work on campus before the last name change. The Second World War had not yet ended, and he wanted a job with decent wages that didn't scrimp on benefits. His brother picked him up one night and delivered him to Dix Hill.

Those are the days Johnson misses. Consolidation hadn't emptied half the buildings, shoved everything to one side of the railroad tracks and squeezed everyone together like sardines.

No one needed to orchestrate media blitzes and marches to the capitol steps to keep the hospital from closing. Dix Hill would always be around.

Johnson, a burly man close with words, circles the campus in a green 1972 Dodge pickup with exterminating equipment in back and summons the past.

He doesn't remember the big iron gates being closed from the 1940s to the 1960s except during the prison riots, but if they ever had rusted shut, it might have taken a while to notice. Dix was a self-contained island of dirt streets where people lived together as a family.

Everything needed to run the hospital was produced inside. Patients farmed food and livestock on the rich red soil in Dix Hill's back yard, and made furniture and clothing.

In the evenings, Johnson could rock on the front porch of the house he rented from the hospital, look through the pecan trees and watch the stoplight change downtown.

"Right there was what they called the old epileptic colony," he says. "They dropped like flies all day and night because there wasn't any medicine for seizures."

He drives by the research center, one of 10 in the country, where patients hungry for relief sign themselves in for experimental treatment by psychiatrists exploring chemical imbalances in mental illness.

He passes the buildings where teen-agers, confused and angry at life's rules or lack of them, are looking for a future. Willie M., who became a symbol for violent, disturbed children in North Carolina, once stayed there.

He parks next to the barred windows and barbed-wire fences of Spruill Building, the forensic unit where criminal defendants are tested for competency. James Hutchins, executed in March, was found competent there.

Barbara Gardner, the tiny, dark-haired nurse in charge, calls Spruill the safest place at Dix.

"But technicians tell me they used to come in in the morning and fight 'til they went home, and second shift would take over the fighting at night."

Howard Johnson remembers. He worked in Spruill when they called it the building for the criminally insane. He couldn't count the times his clothes were ripped off. His thumb was broken in a fight, and he was knocked in the head by a spittoon.

"Just something to do, that's all," he says. "He just didn't like my looks. You need a lot of patience to work in the hospital. A short temper just don't do any good. You got to remember, these people aren't here 'cause they want to be. You've got to look after them. You've got to make it so they will like it. Some never do, but you've got to try to make it easier for them, anyway."

Johnson didn't see dungeons or people in leg chains. He did see straitjackets.

"I'm sure you couldn't find one on Dix Hill now," he says. "It was made from a real heavy canvas cloth, impossible to tear, and it had laces in the back. You put a fella in there and the long arms were all closed up and on the end was a leather strap and buckle.

"You'd wrap the arms around and fasten the belt in back. You could walk or run but couldn't use your arms. They'd be pulling their ears and picking their eyes out. So when they got into what they called a spell, they were put in a straitjacket."

He has pulled up to an open, hilly piece of land wrapped in a chain link fence. The wind cuts across the yellowed grass that first supported woods, then a city landfill until room ran out.

Johnson's broad steps press into the damp ground as he follows a line of flat concrete markers sunken into a hill. He stops at one and leans down to read the small aluminum letters.

"State Hospital, Raleigh." He can't make out the number next to the words. "Jenni - - - - - - . Pasquotank County." He spits and rubs it across the date. "1913."

"If they sink down too much they haul dirt in and try to keep it level," he says. "They keep it up after a fashion.

"Instead of being put in a vault the body was put in a wooden box. They weren't the finest coffins but I've seen worse, too. The state furnished 'em. I myself helped bury two or three out there a long time ago. It's been several years ago since the last one was buried.

"I have known families to come to request to see where their people were buried. I'd get the records and look 'em up and go show 'em.

"The majority buried out there didn't have any folks to claim 'em, or if they did they were ashamed of 'em and wouldn't. It used to be a very deep stigma to someone, being in an insane asylum."

Johnson drives the Dodge to the vacant Kirby Building a few yards away. Before consolidation last December, hard-to-handle patients were locked upstairs on the management ward. Things sometimes got rough.

"Over there's a recreation area for patients," he says. "They can amuse themselves and get exercise, too."

Johnson is looking toward a locked section of chain-link fence behind the Kirby Building and next to the cemetery. Inside are eight swings like those in elementary school yards, a basketball goal and a shuffleboard court.

No one is playing.

Observations and questions

1) Study the organization of Greta Tilley's opening story. Discuss how she organizes the following elements: setting and atmosphere, key characters, hospital history, and hospital structure.

2) The writer gets the most out of simple words. She tells readers that spring is the "best time" to visit Dix Hill. Study those two words in context. Do you detect a tinge of irony, that even the "best time" is not a "good time"?

3) How does Tilley use this first story as a general introduction to her series? What elements in the narrative are picked up in subsequent stories? What major themes are defined?

4) Tilley names some patients, such as Lucy. But she refers to others as "a lean man" or "a fragile little woman." Consider the different functions played by the named and unnamed characters throughout the series.

5) Dix Hill is a place of patients and workers. Tilley focuses on one group and then the other, at times showing them relating or interacting. Consider how Tilley uses this shift of focus to reveal the special environment of this hospital.

6) Tilley ends with the sentence "No one is playing." Discuss the effect of this sentence on readers, and study Tilley's use of short sentences throughout these stories.

When drugs fail, shocks can ease the torment

APRIL 30, 1984

RALEIGH—The clock above Anthony's head says 11 past eight.

It's morning. Anthony hasn't eaten or drunk since midnight.

He is strapped to a blue-sheeted hospital bed on wheels. Close by are two psychiatrists, two nurse anesthetists, one psychiatric nurse and two technicians.

"One-ten over 64," the psychiatric nurse says through the hiss of the blood pressure machine. She puts her fingers against Anthony's pulse.

"Sixty. After his treatment the last time he had a bit of a temp, so we need to watch that."

Anthony wears a medium Afro, a full mustache and a blue hospital gown. His tall, strong frame fills the skinny bed.

His bare feet, propped on a pillow, stick out from the end of the sheet covering his body. His eyes are half closed. A stethoscope rests on his stomach.

The technicians have just rolled him from the admissions ward, where he has lived for four months, to a small, clean room in the medical/surgery unit.

Thirty minutes before, he got an injection of atropine to dry his saliva.

In 17 minutes, 140 volts of electrical current will be shot into his brain.

This is Anthony's seventh treatment. He will have one more to go.

When the mental health center in his county sent him to Dorothea Dix Hospital, he couldn't talk, wouldn't eat and didn't respond. His chart described him as catatonic. Drugs didn't help.

Anthony's depression could be coming from a chemical abnormality or stress, or both.

The psychiatrist assigned to his case, Dr. Joe Mazzaglia, asked him to try electroshock therapy. He explained that an electrically induced grand mal seizure would release chemical substances in the brain that could jolt life back into his system.

Anthony gave a reluctant yes.

Shock treatments were introduced to mental institutions 50 years ago. The reception wasn't pleasant.

Late-night horror reruns aren't far off in capturing those early scenes. A poor, washed-out patient is buckled to the bed. A zealous doctor hooks him to a little black box, and zap. The convulsing and screams begin.

Two Italians named Cerletti and Bini invented the machine that uses house current to stimulate the brain electrically. Before that, psychiatrists were provoking seizures chemically. This didn't work well.

"You could give a patient a pill at 6 o'clock in the morning," says Dr. Sal Cefalu, "and the seizure might not happen until three that afternoon. It could be bad if nobody was around to help."

Cefalu, a Louisiana-born psychiatrist with two decades on Dix Hill, has been giving electroconvulsive therapy (ECT) for years.

"The first time, I was an extern in a state hospital in New Orleans," he says. "There was this woman on the ward. She moaned, groaned, lay on the sofa, wouldn't eat. She was notified she was going to get shock treatment.

"It scared the hell out of me because they didn't get medication back then. But after three or four times the lady was eating and talking and seemed to be so in control."

Psychiatrists practicing in the 1940s and 1950s say they gave shock treatments all day long. They know people who accumulated up to 400 without being harmed.

Cefalu started practicing on Dix Hill when 3,000 patients boarded there.

"All we took was that little black box and an oxygen mask and we'd go from ward to ward," he says. "We would have people trained to hold certain joints to keep down fractures. In the early days, fractures are what happened the most.

"Then we began throwing in EKGs to make sure the heart was OK. If we had those done and the patients fasted at midnight, we'd go from ward to ward, put you in bed, give the treatment, watch you three to five minutes, get you up and feed you breakfast.

"We'd give up to 50 or 60 a day, usually on Monday, Wednesday and Friday. I did see on occasion some get two shocks a day. Raging maniacs or people extremely suicidal."

Mental illness is an elusive disease, and the right diagnosis is critical. Trends change.

During the heyday of ECT, doctors were liberal in labeling schizophrenics. Since people with epilepsy had no symptoms of schizophrenia, they reasoned, electrically induced seizures might help.

Doctors don't consider electroshock for schizophrenics anymore unless other treatments have failed. They do use it for some cases of extreme depression.

Anthony is the only one of 700 patients at Dix this week taking shock therapy.

"With ECT and depression you can rehabilitate a patient so much more quickly," Cefalu says. "You could get them back to work in four to six weeks, whereas some depressions could last four to six years. In that time you could lose your family and your job, and live in an institution forever."

Two things happened to demote the little black box.

Doctors discovered medicines such as Thorazine can tranquilize raging nerves.

Social reformers stormed into mental hospitals and turned down the electric current.

"There was so much opposition to ECT," Cefalu says. "You get patients who had it years ago who say, 'Why did you do that to me?'"

He digs out a letter from his desk postmarked Modesto, Calif.

"Dear Dr. Cefalu,

"I have been mad at you for years for giving me shock treatments. Why did I have to take them? I bet if you ever had just one, you'd never give another. They're terrible and they hurt.

"The Bible says to forgive and I am sorry I was so mad at you. I hope you will be OK and happy from now on. I hope you will never give any more treatments. Those things are horrible. They are not lasting for they continually have to be repeated. A hug and a kiss can make one feel better than a shock treatment can.

"I am getting old now. My hair is turning white. I saw my mother today. Why didn't you want me to see her?"

The procedure has been refined. Patients are put to sleep so they won't feel the pain of a grand mal seizure. The chemical atropine dries the saliva, which can cause choking.

Anectine, a muscle relaxer, paralyzes the muscles and softens the convulsion.

Treatments aren't given to competent patients unless they agree.

Guardians make the decision for patients the court has ruled to be incapable of thinking for themselves.

"Probably no more than 2 or 3 percent of the people would seek electroshock," Cefalu says. "You won't find it in fancy mental health programs. Somewhere along the line somebody must have died. The mortality rate is one-tenth of a percent, but it can happen, and you always have to tell people that."

Twenty-three psychiatrists see patients on Dix Hill. Two give ECT. That's exactly the number of malpractice policies the state has budgeted.

A decade ago, insurance for one year cost $192. Today it is $900.

Cefalu, who owns one of the policies, is the son of a Sicilian immigrant to New Orleans. He grew up training to become a priest, but changed his mind in seminary.

He came to study psychiatry at the University of North Carolina School of Medicine and finished training at Dorothea Dix.

"I never did go into medicine for money," Cefalu says "The only thing I wanted, that unlike my mother, if anything happened to the washing machine and it broke, I wouldn't have to wait six months to get it fixed."

It is Cefalu's week to give treatments. At 5:30 this morning, he silenced the alarm, dressed in a greenish-blue sweater and corduroy pants, read the newspaper, bagged a banana and a big slab of bread and nudged into the crosstown traffic.

"I like to give myself plenty of time," he says.

His brown eyes give away the sensitivity his colleagues have spoken about. He seems relaxed in a careful way.

He opens the little black box, puts it on a table next to the stretcher and plugs it into an outlet.

Anthony's temples have been globbed with a gel that makes it easier to conduct the current and keeps the electrodes from burning his skin.

"You feel all right, Tony?" a nurse anesthetist asks.

He nods.

She covers his mouth and nose with the round end of a long, transparent tube that sends reserve oxygen into Anthony's lungs.

At 8:17, the other anesthetist injects a drug into the IV tube in his arm. Anthony is asleep. She starts the atropine, then the Anectine.

He begins breathing in hard gasps. His body starts to jerk as the medicine conquers it, first taking the toes, then moving up to take the torso.

"When he stops jumping," Cefalu says, "we'll apply the stimulant."

The electrodes are placed on Anthony's temples.

Cefalu: "OK. One. Two. Three." He touches a button on the little black box. It makes a whirring sound. A thick needle passes across some numbers.

Anthony doesn't move.

Mazzaglia: "I don't think he got it. Put it up to 150."

Cefalu hesitates, "One. Two. Three." The box whirrs again.

Mazzaglia: "He's paralyzed. He got the initial response to his feet. I don't notice any big change on the machine. What have you got the timing set at?"

He tells Cefalu to reset it and try again.

Cefalu isn't sure. He waits a moment, then makes the decision. "One. Two. Three."

"He's getting it. He's bound to be getting it. He's so paralyzed we can't see the muscles move."

He points to Anthony's lips, which are twitching as if mosquitoes are swarming and he's trying to flick them off. Otherwise he is still.

"The shock usually causes a jolt or spasm," Cefalu says. "Without the muscle relaxant it would cause a grand mal seizure."

Anthony is beginning to breathe by himself. The nurse checks his blood pressure. One-twenty over 84. His heartbeat and pulse are up. Cefalu says it's the medication.

"Tomorrow is Tony's birthday, and he doesn't want anybody to know it," Cefalu says.

He says Anthony may have a headache or muscle aches for part of the day.

The patient opens his eyes. It is 8:29. The anesthetist takes the tube from his mouth.

"Tony, your treatment is over," she says. "You're waking up."

The nurse takes his blood pressure. One twenty-eight over 92. His mouth is twitching.

"Open your eyes," she says. "There you go."

His head jerks.

The nurses head for the door.

"We'll see you guys."

"Well, what do you think?" says the technician named Baker. "He wakes up, he never knows what happens. People say it's so terrible."

He and his younger partner wheel Anthony away.

Cefalu says he decided against going from 130 to 150 volts. He shot Anthony with 140 instead.

If the ECT is working, he says, Anthony should be confused. His memory for recent and remote events should be gone. That's part of the therapy.

"They can get down to the baby level," he says. "You don't want that to happen."

Complete memory loss is the biggest risk of ECT.

"When you stay confused 24, 48 hours, it means you have had a significant alteration in the brain," Cefalu says. "When you reach that point you stop and wait for nature to bring you back to your natural base level and hope he stays there."

If in two weeks Anthony isn't sleeping or eating, that will be bad news. It will mean the treatment has worn off.

At 4 o'clock, Dr. Cefalu leaves his busy office two floors below the medical/surgery wing. He takes the elevator to the fourth floor, unlocks the door to admissions ward 401 and walks into the dark day room.

A young man and woman are talking in one end of the room. A game show is on the television.

Anthony sits on a sofa at the other end of the room, alone.

He seems happy to have company. He speaks in fits and starts, as Dr. Cefalu had said he would. He tells about the woman he had been living with before he became sick.

She won't see him anymore, he says. It seems to be causing him pain.

He says he was having problems and went to the county mental health center.

He was given a medication called Haldol, he says, which made him dizzy and unable to think straight. It made him so nervous he botched assignments in welding class.

"Haldol's one of the best drugs we have to treat mental illness today," Cefalu says. "But if it's used for the wrong thing, it's like a chemical straitjacket."

Anthony speaks and listens earnestly. He keeps his arms folded close to his body. The game show host overpowers him. He clears his throat, and begins again.

He lived with his girlfriend four years, he says.

"She's 6 feet tall. That's one reason I wanted her. I wanted a tall son. To play basketball. Football."

Cefalu asks him his plans.

The main thing he wants to do is move in with his parents, he says, and go to technical school.

"She was 6 feet tall. My mother didn't want me to date her, and I wish...I should've listened since it turned out that way. I had a very good life until...."

"That's all right," Cefalu says. "We don't want you to talk about it. We want you to forget."

"Thank you," Anthony says.

"It's been gnawing at you a long time," Cefalu says. "That's why we gave you the treatment. So you won't remember it anymore."

"I took her to Florida," Anthony says. "Bought her two cars...When my son was born he weighed 7½ pounds. He'll be 1 in March. I haven't seen him in a year."

He talks about something that happened at work. He told "the man" something, he says, but it didn't turn out as he had expected. He can't remember what it was.

"I think I left a note," Anthony says, "for my son. I don't remember."

"Good," Cefalu says, "We want you to forget."

"Thank you," Anthony says.

"See, it's like this. I think a father should be with his children. That's what I think. Just to be with him 'til he's 18 or 20 years old. Even if

I can't be with him, just to give him everything I can."

Cefalu nods.

"She wanted to party all the time. I liked to stay home. We drove to Fayetteville to buy groceries and a stereo. It was $200 cheaper."

A technician comes in and tells Anthony dinner is ready. He thanks him, but doesn't get up.

"I enjoyed living with her," he says. "I learned a lot. And I know a lot of things I won't do again."

"A chance you take," Cefalu says, "is that as time goes on and his memory comes back, it'll start gnawing him again."

He turns to Anthony and asks if his birthday is tomorrow.

Anthony nods yes.

"How old will you be?" Cefalu says.

"Twenty-three."

Cefalu asks Anthony if he plans to celebrate.

He says no.

Cefalu stands. "You'd better get on over to dinner."

"I'm not hungry," Anthony says.

Cefalu nods, and takes Anthony's arm, and ushers him out the door.

Observations and questions

1) How does the writer work the history of shock therapy into her narrative? Does this history seem a coherent part of the narrative, or does it detract from the human dimension?

2) What does the patient's letter contribute to your understanding of mental health? Speculate on the writer's motives for including it.

3) How does Tilley's description of shock therapy compare to ones you may have seen in movies such as *One Flew Over the Cuckoo's Nest*?

4) Tilley describes Dr. Cefalu's morning routine before he gets to the hospital. Does that seem like essential or beneficial description? What does it contribute to the story?

5) This story is constructed around two major scenes: the doctors administering shock therapy to Anthony, and a conversation between Anthony and his doctor. Study the structure and composition of these scenes. Consider elements of observation, description, detail, and dialogue.

On Dix Hill life moves with the mood

MAY 1, 1984

RALEIGH—The lobby of Hoey Building smells of institutional cleaner and early lunch.

People still able to do some things for themselves live here in the largest of the three geriatric units at Dorothea Dix Hospital.

A technician in white pants and jacket waits at the first-floor elevator, and turns a key to start it toward the second floor. Locks clicking open and closed make some of the hospital's less haunting music. Uniforms are optional on Dix Hill. Staff members are the people carrying the keys.

Sarah Stevens is a friendly woman who has been drawing a paycheck at the hospital for 28 years. Right now, she says, it's time to take the patients to eat.

Curses invade the elevator before it stops.

The doors open on a tall, reedy man in a state-issued green shirt and pants and a long white beard a shade paler than his skin. He is waving long arms in all directions and stomping black shoes against the floor. He looks as if he will hit anyone in his way.

"Damn it, I ain't gonna do it, I told you. You'll have to knock me across the floor. He already took all my blood. They're trying to kill me."

People wearing an assortment of garments and expressions are standing around the man someone calls John. Some stare at him. Some shout back. Some don't seem to see him at all.

Stevens moves toward them. She takes the arm of a woman jerking and crying hoarsely, leads her to the elevator and tells her it's almost time for lunch.

The woman's pink dress hangs unevenly around her knees. Her hair is white with streaks the color of nicotine. Whiskers grow from her chin. Blood is clotted on a small piece of adhesive tape above one eye.

Before the scene jells, two men in white uniforms have calmly and without force convinced John to move down the hall.

Stevens says he will be locked in a seclusion room until he can compose himself. Someone will look in on him every 15 minutes.

All patients know about seclusion. When they become abusive and can't control themselves, they are isolated in a room stripped bare of temptation.

The only furnishing is a thin mattress on the floor. The single overhead lightbulb has been wrapped in metal braces. The high window is protected by an inverted screen thick with wire. Electrical sockets have been sealed.

Disturbed people can still find targets. In one seclusion room, the black baseboards have been ripped from the wall.

If patients become too violent or try to turn on themselves, their hands and feet are buckled to a stretcher. Some of the leather restraints are scarred by teeth marks.

Stevens says the staff can tell when John starts losing his grip. He paces the floor, plays the radio too loud and dances.

Everyone was frightened of John when he came to Dix from Central Prison, she says. He was charged with killing three people and had a long record of assaults. He couldn't seem to stay out of seclusion in the months after he arrived. Slowly, he is adjusting.

Stevens hasn't stopped moving. She is directing patients on to the elevator for a ride to the cafeteria downstairs.

They walk with small, jerky, shuffle steps. They talk with tongues that roll lazily around their mouths as if they are going to swallow or bite them. Their clothes may or may not match, their skin is thin and mottled. They seem to be looking someplace far away.

Ramie, the woman in the pink housedress, has become hysterical.

"I ain't hungry," she cries. "I'm not going to lunch."

She runs from the elevator, sits on the floor and pulls up her dress. She has on white socks and no shoes.

"Nurse, nurse, don't make me eat, nurse. I don't want to eat."

In the dining room, some of the 52 people who belong to Ward B get their own trays, others have them carried. Patients push friends in wheelchairs and give away food they don't want. A technician rescues a man choking on phlegm.

Food is eaten by fork, spoon and fingers. Some meals disappear quickly. Some are only tasted. One woman chews the same bite of chicken over and over without closing her mouth.

"Hey, you work in a department store," yells a slender man with gray state clothes and more gums than teeth, "or in the cotton mill?"

Ramie sits down, eats a few bites and walks to the door still chewing. "You ready to go? Come on, Sarah, let's go."

She sits on the floor, gets up, races over to a woman drooping over her food, and pats her on the back.

"Don't touch me," the woman says.

A patient with short silver and black hair walks up. She's wearing a blue sweater, blue jogging shoes and white athletic socks with orange stripes.

"What's your name," she asks.

"I ain't got no name," she says.

"Where are you from?"

"I'm from nowhere," she says.

"That's where I'm from. Nowhere."

Ramie and the man in gray, now rocking on his haunches by the door, exchange hard slaps.

"You're gonna have to go back to your room," he says.

"Ready to go, doctor?" Ramie asks a male technician. "What ya'll waitin' on?"

She takes a coffee cup from the tray of a man quietly eating in a wheelchair and carries it off. He says nothing.

"Hey, put that man's cup back where it belongs," yells a man in a blue flannel shirt and brogans.

Ramie obeys. Her hand convulses against her stomach, a tradeoff for years of medication. Without the medicine she wouldn't be as calm.

"You ready to go? Ready to go, nurse? Ready to go, sir? Ready to go?"

She takes a cup of coffee from the hand of the woman from nowhere. The woman lets her drink.

"Nurse, I want to spit," says the man sitting in the wheelchair with a tray attached. These are the first words he has spoken. He doesn't seem as restless as the other patients.

Stevens explains that Bennett's wheelchair is a geri-chair, used as a restraint. Without it, she says, he would be violent.

"Hey, how about moving Ramie from upstairs," the woman from nowhere asks Stevens. "I can't stand this fuss. How about giving her extra medicine like they gave me."

Stevens doesn't answer. Ramie is pulling her to the door.

"You have your ups and downs," Stevens says. "You can see good changes and you can see bad changes. It's not like going to the same job every day. I can have a week off and I'm ready to come back."

The patients have been escorted back upstairs to the day room. They are watching television, sleeping, bickering, wandering, talking to themselves, and rocking in chairs. A woman sings "Jesus Loves Me."

Stevens has ducked into a tiny storage room so she won't be interrupted. She reaches into her smock pocket for a cigarette. Cigarette manufacturers would be delighted to see the amount of tobacco burned on Dix Hill.

"Right now our ward is louder than normal," she says. "Our manic-depressives are up. We seem to have about three or four to cycle at a time. It's good because if we had them all at once...The other patients that aren't manic-depressives, it gets on their nerves and they get very nervous and upset."

Stevens was hired before doctors found that drugs can ease a troubled mind. The wards were full of anxious patients in the 1940s. Training didn't come with the job.

"You were just slapped on the floor to learn the best you could," she says. "There's a difference in working with a schizophrenic and manic-depressive. It helps to know how to deal with them."

Stevens has made the rounds of jobs in the hospital. She was moved up to supervisor, but missed the patients and asked to be a technician again. In the last month she has been demoted from a shift leader to "Tech I" because there were too many shift leaders.

Like cards in a poker game, positions are frequently shuffled to adjust to the latest mandate from downtown. Rules are made by state, federal and hospital regulatory agencies.

Threats don't come only from outside. A patient threw a tray at Stevens' head. She had stitches and came back the next day. Another patient knocked her against a metal door. She cut her head again.

"You have to be cautious," she says, "You cannot be afraid. You have to tell yourself that they are mental patients and that you are there to help them."

Many patients come into the geriatric units with chronic brain syndrome such as Alzheimer's disease, or with organic brain syndrome, or as manic-depressives, whose moods swing from hysterically high to dangerously low, even catatonic.

"There are a lot of manic-depressives in these two buildings," says Kay Thornton, nurse in charge, "and they kind of cycle. We try to even them out between two buildings so they don't get too wild."

Fifteen manic-depressives live upstairs in Ward B.

"You can't stop a cycle," Thornton says. "Once they go from their manic to depressed state you can't stop it. Carol'll tell me, 'It's a full moon outside, I'm fixin' to blow.'

"They can't take too much medicine either. If you give more than the usual dose, their blood pressure hits rock bottom. You have to keep them comfortable and dry and let them holler.

"When they get in their hyper cycle they try to rearrange the ward for you. Drag furniture all over the room. That's where seclusion comes in."

Patients usually stay on geriatric wards about five years, until they die or move somewhere else. One has lived at Dix 62 years; two others for 20. There aren't many places for them to go. Nursing homes, already crowded, don't want them because they can be too aggressive or wander off.

"In Wilson, a TB sanitorium was turned into a state nursing home," Thornton says. "The Dobbin Building used to have room for 160 patients here. Well, Dobbin closed and sent all those people to Wilson. So as Wilson has one to die we send one from here over there."

Thornton has worked with older patients 20 years. It's hard.

"They don't tell you about themselves. You have to be able to tell about them by the look on their face or the way they walk. Constipation is a big problem. If they are constipated they walk leaning to one side.

"They steal from one another. Borrow each other's clothes and swear up and down, 'It's mine.' They go to the dining room and put a slice of bread in their pocket and forget about it. It gets molded and draws roaches."

A person who doesn't like the job doesn't last long in Hoey.

Attachments form. Some patients have no one; some have relatives who don't care. Some families are uncomfortable with mental illness and visit no more than one or two times a year.

So the staff becomes family. Dependency intensifies the hold. Thornton doesn't believe she would be happy anyplace else.

At lunch two weeks later, Ramie is upset again in the dining room. Somebody hit her in the eye, she says, and it's her only good eye, and she's blind and can't see, and doesn't know what to do.

She is wearing the same pink housedress with a white sweater and scuffs. A tear drops into her food, which she has been putting on John's plate.

John looks better than the day of his scene near the elevator, when his rage put him into seclusion. Jake Lane, the campus barber, has trimmed his white beard and shortened the hair around his ears. He's again wearing a lime green shirt and pants, courtesy of the state.

"Maybe I'll look pretty nice when I'm laid away," he says after a compliment on his appearance. "What I'm worried about is whether I'll be pretty in a box."

John tries to console Ramie during the meal. He asks her to eat. She doesn't.

He takes her hand, holds it, and softly tells her everything will be all right.

She can't be comforted.

"I'm blind, John, I'm blind," she says. "I'm blind," she shouts across the table. "It's my good eye, and I'll never be able to see."

John empties their trays, puts his arm around Ramie and leads her to the elevator.

Upstairs in the day room, she sits down on the floor and screams.

John stoops and talks to her in a low voice. She lets him lift her up and take her to a chair in the corner. He sits next to her and pats her on the shoulder while she talks and cries.

"Hush, Ramie, hush," William yells from across the room.

"I will, William," Ramie calls back, sobbing.

"You will, Ramie, or I'll knock the hell out of you," Martha says.

Garland Guion, a young technician with soft brown eyes, unlocks a door and comes back with a box filled with packs of labeled cigarettes. The schedule says it's time to smoke. Guion disappears behind a rush of patients pressing around the box.

Thornton nods toward a wizened little woman wearing a plain cotton dress. She is slumped in a chair. Her mouth is open.

"When she cycles," Thornton says, "she puts on all of her makeup and every strand of jewelry she owns and a purple dress. The other day, we caught her and Mr. Edwards in the bushes next to the canteen."

She points down the row of seats to a man in a red flannel shirt and glasses. He's asleep.

"We had to put their pass cards on different times," she says. "It's kind of hard to explain to him why he was wrong. She's so embarrassed when she realizes what she does. She says, 'Oh, why did you let me do it?'

"That's the way it is around here. Sad and funny at the same time. That's the way you have to look at it, anyway. You can see why."

John and Ramie haven't moved from the chairs pulled side by side. Ramie's crossed leg is swinging back and forth. John's yellowed fingers hold a cigarette.

Observations and questions

1) Good reporters use all their senses to create a sense of place for readers. In the first paragraph, Tilley helps us smell "the institutional cleaner and early lunch." Two paragraphs later we hear the "music" of "locks clicking open and closed." Find the places throughout the series where the writer uses such details to stimulate the senses of readers.

2) Tilley writes: "Some of the leather restraints are scarred by teeth marks." Such information comes from careful reporting and close observation. Discuss how such details enhance the authority of the writer in the eyes of readers.

3) Tilley writes: "...the staff becomes family" and that "dependency intensifies the hold." What evidence from this and other stories convinces the reader that this statement is true? Tilley *tells* us that it is so, but does she *show* us?

4) A worker says, "That's the way it is around here. Sad and funny at the same time." Tilley sees this hospital in terms of a complex mix of emotions. The place is sad and funny, depressing and uplifting, repulsive and appealing. What narrative strategies does Tilley employ to reflect such complexity and paradox?

Mary sings a lonely melody of hope

MAY 2, 1984

RALEIGH—The last song has ended in the Rose Room.

The dance is over.

Mary walks past the elevator with a Diet Coke in her hand. Her cheeks are still pink from rouge, but her lipstick has worn off.

Desperation haunts her voice. She says she's depressed.

She wanders into the lobby to talk to a man delivering pizza. A technician comes after her. Mary is often being tracked down by technicians.

"I got emotional at the dance tonight," she says, "I miss Jimbo. You think I should give him up, don't you?"

The technician takes Mary's arm and tells her it's time to go.

"You're always the last one."

"I know. It's my destiny," Mary says, and laughs as if her heart will break.

Night life on Dix Hill isn't better or worse than life in the daytime.

The core of the adult population, including 20-year-old Mary, lives in the renovated McBryde Building on wards divided by ability to function.

The decor is tight budget. Furniture is covered in vinyl and burns from cigarettes that missed the plastic ashtrays. Draperies sometimes sag as if they have seen too much.

Corridors and day rooms are dim and smell of smoke. TVs keep on playing. Darkness can slip in without notice.

Patients prowl the halls and sit in chairs and on floors that have been mopped to shining. They curl in a fetal position on chairs and couches.

They are dressed for bed or for that morning's music therapy class or for nothing in particular.

Selections suit mood and comfort rather than convention.

The state dresses patients who can't afford a wardrobe. Whether for clothes or for furniture, these selections are predictable. What's practical and economical is in. That includes accommodations.

Nights are hard on the restless. Bingo games, or dances such as the one in the Rose Room, help a few hours pass a little easier. But there are more hours to fill after they end.

In the day room of Ward 303 for higher functioning patients is a bookcase with a few old books and three games: Bingo, Tri-Ominos and Chinese Checkers.

A woman with silky gray hair fluffed about her face sits on a chair in the center of the room. She is wearing an ivory slip with no rips and could have just returned from a night of bridge with friends.

She talks to herself, maybe about the cards she would have played, until something distracts her and she stalks off.

Down the hall a cough rattles, someone moans, a hair dryer comes on. A woman in a green bathrobe walks in and laughs a shrill laugh. No one seems to wonder what's funny.

People on Dix Hill exist together in one world while living alone in another.

Their clock is a mimeographed schedule that tells the time of the next activity, whether it is walking downstairs to buy a snack from the vending machine, taking the next dose of Thorazine, going to horticulture class, eating lunch.

Few refer to the schedule; they know it by heart.

Their external world is focused on obsession—for cigarettes, which they beg, borrow, steal and retrieve used from ashtrays, for coffee, candy and cold drinks.

They talk about how they can get more. They talk about what kind of medicine they are taking and how they like it. They talk about the staff and the food and each other.

Secrets are hard to keep on Dix Hill. Privacy is a forgotten commodity. Patients can have as many as four and five roommates.

The seclusion room, where they are locked for punishment, may be the only place privacy is guaranteed.

Whether shut in seclusion or dancing in the Rose Room, patients are alone. Often, they are isolated even from themselves.

It is midnight, and Mary is one of the lonely.

She sits in a chair in the corridor of Ward 303, for a few seconds remarkably still.

Her yellow hair is frizzy—Lydia in the beauty shop hasn't yet talked her into the style with the soft curls—and her Panama Wolfpack T-shirt has escaped the waist of her jeans.

"Uhhmmm," she makes a sound in her throat, and grins an impish grin. "Excuse me. I was just wondering, are you writing a book?

"I've been writing since I was 10 years old. I want to be a songwriter or a singer or a disc jockey on a radio station or a fashion model or an actress.

"What's your sign?"

Her fingernails are painted red. Manicures are tricky when your hands shake from medication. In places she has as much polish on her skin as on her nails.

"My parents are separated," she says. "My father's an alcoholic. He has his own problems so he doesn't have too much time for me, but I still love him. I sent him a drawing today."

She has written a song and some poems and wants to show them off. She leads the way to her room. She is one of the few patients on campus without a roommate.

"I'm difficult to live with," she says, and apologizes for the mess.

Clothes tumble from the open closet and from bureau drawers. The top of the bureau is a catch-all for nail polish, crumbled pages of notebook paper, an overturned box of powder, drink cans, cotton balls.

A tiny stuffed puppy with scruffy white fur has fallen face down on the floor beside the bed, on top of a pair of clogs.

A cardboard cutout of a woman's face has been taped to the wall. Mary yanks the picture off.

"I want you to have it." she says.

On the back, a poem has been written in the roving hand of a child learning cursive.

"I'm so scared and all alone.

"O Dear Lord bring peace into the heart of my home.

"I need your guidance and strength.

"I need all the love that I can take. I need all the peace I can make.

"Let your spirit come into my life.

"Evil souls will cut like a knife."

Mary has been fumbling in a drawer. She throws out a disposable razor.

"For my eyebrows. I can't pluck them. I get a rash.

"Makeup's not really in that much any more. I'm gonna buy some but not so much. I used to weigh 162 pounds. They put me on Thorazine and slowed down my metabolism, and I had to go to the bathroom every five minutes."

She sits straight up on the bed and clears her throat. Her eyes dart toward the door.

"Would you like me to sing? I sound a lot like Olivia Newton-John."

Her voice is hoarse and shaky. She stops and grins.

"It's the medicine. Makes my mouth dry."

She hands over another poem, excuses herself and disappears. She returns carrying two used Dixie cups. Her hand shakes and water spills.

"Would you care for a drink? I wish I had some tea to offer you. Some Russian tea. Polly-vous francez?"

"Ssssh," she says, and freezes.

"I'm scared for some reason," she says. "I don't know. I have this eerie feeling. I close my eyes and I'm astro-projecting. My spirit leaves my body and goes down the hall. That's what I picture when I think of something weird. It's the atmosphere here. It's eerie."

Mary jumps subjects quickly and randomly.

She says she doesn't believe in terms that categorize people, such as "senior citizens." She says she likes to play Scrabble and work puzzles. Anyone can tell she has German and French in her, she says, if they really look.

"I dated this one guy, he was so high class I didn't know what to do at the table. I offered him a piece of chewing gum and he got so upset. I don't think it's so bad."

She talks about Jimbo, the boy she has loved for five years. All her songs are written for him. She has coded him "Number 2760309" for protection.

"2760309,

"I want to understand you.

"I'm about to have tears in my eyes.

"Please help me out. I wish I could have met you today, 276. I love you each and every way.

"Why am I doing this? It is totally insane. I remember how you love the pitter-patter of the rain.

"Tell the other woman to break the chain and just have her as a date. I love you more than she my sexy play-mate."

Mary says she took too much speed and has been hospitalized four years. Jimbo abandoned her when she got sick.

"This coat, all these presents, are for him," she says, holding up a fur-lined jacket. "If he ever decides to come back. My mother's gonna be mad, but I don't care."

She pulls out the spiral notebook filled with the beginnings of an autobiography.

"This book is too depressing for me to write, anyway," she says. "I wanted it to be funny, not boring. I feel like a failure. I constantly feel like a failure.

"Have you read *How to Be Your Own Best Friend*? I recommend that to everybody. I read it over and over, and it really helped me."

Mary takes a sip of water and stands. She's going to sing again.

"Let me be there in your morning,

"Let me be there in your night,

"Let me take whatever's wrong and make it right, make it right...."

This time her voice is sweet and rangy. She does sound like Olivia Newton-John.

She bows and collapses on the bed.

"I'm just trying to be patient and waiting for the time to get better," Mary says. "If the good Lord wants me to get well.

"What do I want? A good husband, maybe a couple of kids. I'm scared of that. The pain and all." She grins. "Well, maybe one or two, not 10 or 11."

Her first goal, she says, is to get into a halfway house and go to college. She'd pick North Carolina State University.

"That's all I think about. I wish I could bust out the door and catch a bus and...but where would I live, that's the problem."

The pupils in her blue eyes expand. She looks frightened.

"Life is so short, so make it easy as possible," she says. "It may be scary but you gotta be strong to survive, even with a husband. He comes home late at night and you're home alone in a big city. Walking the streets can be scary, too, even with a flashlight."

She walks into the hall and says good night. She'll probably work on a song or draw, she says. She isn't sleepy.

Down the hall, slippers scuff against the bare floor. A woman in stringy brown hair comes toward her. Her skin is dull against a green nightgown. Tears roll down her face.

"We're putting her in seclusion," a nurse explains. "She's a self-mutilator...threatening suicide. We have to watch her like a hawk."

The woman walks into the empty room, carrying her pillow and blanket, and the nurse locks her in for the night.

Observations and questions

1) In an interview, Greta Tilley says this about the character of Mary: "She seemed to be filled with feelings that contradicted themselves. She was terrified of life, yet in her lucid periods it didn't seem she had lost hope, or an appreciation for the adventure of living so refreshing in someone her age. She was one of the few patients I saw whose eyes still sparkled, sometimes. Talking with her, you were torn between believing she might overcome her sickness and knowing that she would not." Study this story with this comment in mind. Does the writer's portrait of Mary capture the contradictions she has defined?

2) Greta Tilley is that rarest of creatures, a humble writer. While she often expresses dissatisfaction with her work, she says that this story is the best in the series. Do you agree or disagree? As a reader, what criteria would you use to make that decision?

3) Describe the mood created by Tilley in the scene that opens this story. What elements of description and dialogue help create this mood?

4) Study the quotations uttered by Mary and other patients in the story. Analyze their language, rhythms, and meaning. Do the same for quotations from the hospital workers. How does Tilley use quotations to help convey feelings of illness or wellness?

5) The environment Mary creates for herself seems symbolic of her mental state. Study Tilley's description of Mary's room and discuss what it reveals about Mary and her state of mind.

6) One night in a mental ward, Greta Tilley, a writer, meets Mary, who writes poems and songs. How does Tilley make use of these? Consider what surrounds them in the story and what they reveal to readers about Mary.

Staff tackles difficult job with realism

MAY 3, 1984

RALEIGH—Dr. Joe Mazzaglia flips a match over his shoulder toward a metal trash can near the middle of the room.

No matter that it misses. The office is a mess. Diplomas and pictures framed to hang on walls look up from boxes and the floor. Books and papers have been filed where they landed after the move two months ago.

"So how do you stay sane," he repeats the question. "You joke a lot. It's a very serious situation.

"If you know how to handle the anger, at best, you go home with a very severe headache and kick your dogs and your kids. At worst there's drug abuse, drinking. You pick some poison."

Mazzaglia looks down into his brown beard. Beards seem to be a criterion for psychiatrists on Dix Hill. Right now, there aren't enough of them.

Two years ago, 28 psychiatrists worked on Dix Hill. Today there are five vacancies. Help isn't coming until July.

Mazzaglia's days are spent running.

"You're trying to make the rounds on the charts. If someone gets agitated or psychotic, you write a seclusion order and have them put in the seclusion room.

"Then the court calls, and you have to come up and testify when one of your cases comes up.

"Or you're on screening for admissions from 8 to 4, and you're down there screening, and you have a family call you on the telephone. Or you have to teach a class of med students. Or you're covering for another doctor.

"So something goes kaplooey. Somebody throws something through a window or somebody goes berserk or somebody becomes seriously ill and you have to go down and look at it.

"Plus medical committees and administrative meetings....

"How long do you see the patients? Fifteen minutes if you're lucky. Maybe five or 10 minutes alone, or running through the hallway talking. In an average week, you ought to see a patient two or three times a week for between one-half hour to 40 minutes. That would be the ideal situation. I see patients between five and 15 minutes twice a week.

"Then you get somebody like George. He can set you back a week."

George has been diagnosed as a psychotic with a severe personality disorder. He has trouble saying no to alcohol and takes his hostilities out on his 32-year-old body in brutal ways.

He holds the record for Dix admissions—74.

He has come and gone three times in the last six weeks. He has been shadowing Mazzaglia's footsteps because they don't see eye to eye on how long he should stay.

George has called a lawyer, which means more court for Mazzaglia.

"Then there's this massive amount of paperwork. If not for that, the job would almost be easy."

Mazzaglia has been on Dix Hill seven years. The last two have levied a toll.

In 1982, the North Carolina General Assembly talked about closing the hospital and sending patients into the community or to other mental institutions.

Dix had room for 2,000 patients, and was caring for 650 with a staff twice that size. North Carolina's other three psychiatric hospitals had 526 beds waiting. The chronic patients would be sent there; the others would move to community programs.

Impassioned lobbying convinced legislators that communities weren't ready or willing to handle people as severely ill as those at Dix.

They compromised by consolidation, which brought more chaos. The hospital was ordered to do the same job with less money, staff and space.

Moving, though carefully organized, was traumatic. Nurses and aides can't forget the sight of patients wandering the grounds with suitcases. Wards are just beginning to settle.

The staff's frustration isn't born of laziness, Mazzaglia says, but of the feeling that when you are split into infinite pieces, it's hard to perform as well.

"If you're conscientious, and I believe most of us here are, it can weigh heavily," he says. "But there's only so much noble you can be before you start being stupid."

Kirby and Council buildings, home for people with problems not quickly fixed, were emptied before Christmas to cut costs. Patients were moved to a lower wing of McBryde, a roomy complex with a medical/surgery unit open to North Carolina's three other mental hospitals.

The building splits a third time into an admissions center where new patients come to be diagnosed. If there after six months, they are assigned to wards set up for longer stays. The longer the stay, the harder the fight for freedom.

McBryde begins to stagger under a capacity of 700 patients. When admissions are up, it's stuffed.

Nancy Whitehead supervises the new adult unit of patients from Kirby and Council. Meetings with psychiatrists, social workers, nurses, technicians and vocational rehabilitation therapists are hair-tearing sessions to figure out a better way.

Discussion goes this way:

Whitehead: "Last night they had to move in five beds to admissions, and I don't know where they put in five more beds. They're over capacity like we are.

"We have to be realistic. We don't have any money. We've just cut back positions. We're not gonna get the RNs and social workers we need.

"How can we keep access to weapons, and disruption, which is deadly, to a minimum, get a logical group together and still make extra room?"

The first week she came to nurse at Dix Hill, Whitehead sent up a prayer.

"Dear God, I said, please help me get one paycheck so I can leave this place."

She got that paycheck 22 years ago.

In another meeting that day, a social worker seems heartened by progress a patient has made in a year.

"He doesn't spit snuff all over things," she says, "and he's less shy about approaching people about what he wants."

Billy Tate, a night technician on the adult continued treatment ward, has been around 27 years. He's known others who didn't stay.

"They just couldn't quite fight it," he says. "A lot of people leave here and go to the prisons or to other hospitals. A lot of nurses leave and go to Rex (a Raleigh hospital). The whole thing in a nutshell is too many patients and too little staff."

One registered nurse works the late shift. She is in charge of 160 patients. Six licensed practical nurses help give medication in two wards. There's one LPN for 50 patients.

On nights when no one is out sick or taking vacation, two technicians are on staff for each 30 patients. One corridor in Ward 303 measures 131 yards long. That's one and a third football fields.

Tate says he knows patients get away with things they shouldn't. He can't be everywhere at once.

"It can get stressful when you have residents begging for attention," he says. "They're pulling at you, and you want to help them, but you have to do things from housekeeping to secluding combative patients to cleaning up behind untidy patients to assisting with baths. Some of them you have to shave, bathe, dress. You try to provide 'em with some type of recreation each day."

William Baker was 18 years old in 1947 when he came from Kenly to Raleigh looking for a job. He became a technician. He has learned not to over-react.

"Never take anything personally," he says, "even if somebody spits in your face."

Baker says a manic-depressed patient hit him on the head with his fist three years ago and almost fractured his skull. He's had two fractured ribs, and another patient punched him in the corner of the eye.

"The worst I ever knowed, we had one technician get his neck broke in the management ward. There's been some fractured ribs. One nurse got her shoulder dislocated.

"You get a lot of minor injuries, strained ankles, strained backs, vertebraes out of socket. Usually these patients are psychotic. They're very sick. They're fighting for survival."

Psychologist Bill Zieger directs a unit of 56 patients diagnosed as both mentally retarded and mentally ill.

"The real zealots who come in and want to save the world, they burn up like small stars. They can't make happen what they want to make happen. They burn out, change locations or move on to the top.

"Then there are others who don't give a damn at all. It's a job.

"Somewhere in between are the bulk of the people. They've got sincere, humanistic concerns about the people they're dealing with. But they can balance the conditions of the job. They can deal with the frustrations."

Everyone on the work force at Dix Hill has something to say about the patients' rights movement of the 1960s. Much of it is negative.

They don't dispute the theory of checks and balances for mental patients. It's the logistics of carrying out the list of rules and regulations that bothers them. Zieger and his colleagues believe patients are being hurt more than they are being helped.

The staff spends hours in cubbyholes meeting paperwork requirements instead of meeting with patients. Disturbed, homeless people are cold and hungry, staffers say, because commitment laws make it harder for them to be institutionalized.

Patients refuse to take medicine or go along with the structured treatment doctors believe they must have to learn to function again.

"There's got to be some realization on the part of the public," Zieger says, "that by the time an individual gets here, they're pretty much de facto incompetent. Yet we have to allow them to make decisions we know are bad for them because to go through the guardianship procedure takes 60 to 90 days, and by the time you do that a person's gone."

Sandra Sink looks at her files and finds 37 abuse cases that have been reported at Dorothea Dix during the year.

"That's verbal, physical and sexual," she says. "Usually, it's something like a patient wakes up every morning and curses at a staff person who has to get him out of bed. One day the technician curses back."

Nineteen of the cases were found to have some substantiation, Sink says, and were dealt with by oral warnings, written warnings or final warnings.

"A case may have gotten by us," she says, "but we've never litigated a case at Dix."

The hospital made headlines with an abuse case last year when two technicians were fired for beating up a patient. They said he pulled a knife on them and they sued in court to get back their jobs. They lost the case.

Sink and her assistant work for the Governor's Advocacy Council for Persons with Disabilities and are independent of the hospital.

Their office is in the McBryde Building where many patients live. Signs are posted in all wards telling patients of their legal rights and giving Sink's phone number and location.

She doesn't want for customers.

"A lot of the complaints are 'my doctor won't see me enough' or 'my doctor is forcing me to take medication I don't want to take,' " Sink says. "They say doctors don't spend a lot of time listening to problems. Instead they are checking charts and how they are reacting to medications.

"By this reduction, they are setting people up for more seclusion, more restraint, heavier medications."

Dr. Granville Tolley brings his lunch in a paper bag, and eats it at a long table in the conference room across from his office.

He can use the time to ponder such things as how to cut $2.1 million from the hospital's yearly $32 million budget by the end of June 1985.

Tolley didn't know a fascination with psychiatry would lead him down such a path when he read a section on schizophrenics in an old textbook he found aboard a Navy troop transfer ship during World War II.

He didn't know when he framed his University of Virginia Medical School diploma that he would be running a public mental institution instead of seeing patients in a private office.

Tolley's hospital carries a good reputation.

Dorothea Dix is one of the few psychiatric hospitals in the country with a medical/surgery division for treating physically ill patients, and it has one of the nation's top residency training programs.

Seventy-five percent of the psychiatrists on Dix Hill have passed a tough exam to be board-certified; the proportion at most mental hospitals is 25 percent.

"Living barely above the poverty level is difficult," Tolley says. "Living perpetually in sight of what's better with what's not enough and never quite being able to get free of the threshold to get into orbit is frustrating.

"The expectations of what others have of us have always stayed just an arm's length ahead of what we can do to catch up."

What makes him feel good about Dorothea Dix, he says, is that people have not stopped trying.

Observations and questions

1) In her opening scene, Tilley gives readers a sense of Dr. Joe Mazzaglia's personality and values. Describe that character in your own words. Now study and discuss the elements of characterization used by the writer.

2) The opening scene contains seven consecutive paragraphs of quotations from Dr. Mazzaglia. Tilley defends her use of extensive quotations by arguing that she cannot say it any better than the source. Study her quotations of the doctor. Does she need everything she has quoted? Are there opportunities for summary and paraphrase that the writer has missed?

3) This story confronts political and economic issues more directly than the other stories in the series. Tilley touches on issues of funding and consolidation, and refers to the patients' rights movement. In the context of the entire series, does Tilley pay enough attention and give enough space to these issues?

4) Study the ways in which Tilley introduces key characters to humanize potentially dull explanations of political or bureaucratic issues.

5) Does Tilley go far enough in reporting the 37 abuse cases reported at Dix? While Tilley denies that this was meant to be an "investigative" series, does she miss an opportunity to test her observations of responsible care against reported cases of abuse?

6) Study the writer's brief treatment of Dr. Granville Tolley that concludes the story. Discuss how the writer concisely includes elements of the doctor's training and background while discussing his role at the hospital.

Talking hands give life to deaf, blind resident

MAY 4, 1984

RALEIGH—Nadine Langsdon pays the cigarette machine for Camels and scoops them from the tray.

She stops at the drink machine to buy a can of Coca-Cola. Thirty cents more for a Snickers bar and she's on her way.

"He won't be expecting to see me today," she says, unlocking a door that leads to the men's day room.

A nurse tugs at Nadine's pocket, stuffed with the presents she has just bought.

"Bet I know where you're going," she says.

"They kid me around here," Nadine says. "He's been my project since 1967."

The word in the geriatric unit is that Clark Building was constructed back in the day of Noah's Ark for men with a passion for combat. The walls are brick. The windows have bars.

The patients aren't independent enough to live in Hoey across the street or dependent enough to live in Brown next door.

In Hoey, no one wears diapers in the daytime unless they are manic-depressives too sick to leave bed. Diapers are stocked in bulk at Brown for patients who don't know they need them. In Clark, those who wear them can tell if they need changing and sometimes do it themselves.

Nadine is a technician who once worked in Clark and now works in Hoey. She slips over to Clark when she can. She comes to see Robert.

Robert is a lanky man whose white hair is losing ground to his scalp. He's crazy about clothes and cologne and could talk the bottom off the ocean.

Integration delivered him to Dix Hill. He had been living in Goldsboro in the state institution for black mental patients. Dix was for whites only. The two hospitals had been directed to make some trades.

Robert had trouble adjusting.

"He was very agitated," Nadine says. "He didn't know where he was. The only thing people could make out when he talked was, 'I want a cigarette.' "

Robert was reared in a little community 30 miles from Greensboro. His mother had more children than she could tend to. People called her feeble-minded; they said that Robert was, too.

Sometimes the sheriff would be called to the welfare office to take Robert to jail for being too forceful in asking for money.

A neighbor let him live in a little shack behind her house until he got so he couldn't look after himself.

His chart says it was a "head trauma" that caused him to go blind and deaf.

Nadine worried about Robert from the first time she watched him struggle.

He couldn't hear or see what people were saying to him. They couldn't understand what he was telling them. The Thorazine doctors prescribed to help control his agitation caused him to lose control of his tongue.

"It really just hurt my heart that a human being couldn't communicate his needs," Nadine says. "I made up my mind that that just wasn't gonna happen."

She started seeing him every day. What they needed to reach each other, she decided, was a sure system, something simple.

People nod their heads up and down to say "yes." Why not shake Robert's hand up and down to mean the same thing? For "no," she could move his hand back and forth.

If she didn't understand what he was saying, she began pulling on his hand. Finally, as she kept pulling, he would repeat himself until she caught on.

Nadine came up with signals. For a drink of water or a soda, she forms the circle of a glass with her hand and holds it to Robert's mouth. For "cigarette," she holds her hand as if she had one between her fingers and with his hand attached, guides it to her mouth to take a puff.

She worked with people from the Commission for the Blind and the social services department. She took a course on sign language and taught Robert.

Nadine became Robert's eyes and ears, his line to the outside world.

"He doesn't even know my name," she says. "He calls me 'Bertie Mae.'"

Nadine walks down the hall. She passes Dan reading aloud the instructions on the fire extinguisher. Andy stops her and asks if she's still his girlfriend. She says yes.

She opens the doors to the large day room. The chaos of life without dignity or reason has become a part of her, and she accepts it as the routine it has become.

Robert is sitting in the chair he sits in each day, a few steps away from the door of the bathroom and close enough to walk to the water fountain without losing his way.

Nadine pushes Robert to one side of his chair to make room for herself, and lays her hands on his arms. He grabs her hands, throws his head back and opens a mouth of pink gums. He almost pulls Nadine into his lap.

She presses the Camels into the hiding place they selected so no one could slip them out, between Robert's undershirt and his skin. The neck of his shirt is stained with grape drink.

She puts the drink in one hand and lets him know the candy bar is in his lap.

Robert must be pleased. He is hollering and making gurgling noises in his throat. His rolling tongue pounds the roof and sides of his mouth and distorts everything he says.

His dark hands are locked with Nadine's light ones. They push and pull and twist in a system only they can understand. As Nadine talks to Robert with her hands, she interprets their conversation aloud.

"You're not mad at me," he wants to know.

"I've never been mad at you," she says.

"Will you give me another bottle of ale tomorrow?"

"No."

"Next week?"

"Yes."

"Tomorrow's Friday?"

"Yes."

"Did you get paid last week?"

"Yes."

"Nobody comes to see him, so my family sort of adopted him," Nadine says as Robert peels the wrapper off the candy. "We have Christmas for him each year. We bring his presents and his cakes and his goodies, cigarettes and cologne."

"You're fat," Robert tells Nadine.

She hits him.

"You got heart trouble," he says.

"No, I ain't got heart trouble," she says. "Eat with your mouth closed."

Seven years ago, Nadine told Robert she needed to go to the hospital for surgery. She said she would be gone six weeks. Robert lost touch with time and began to worry.

He asked some of the nurses and technicians on the ward if Bertie Mae had died. They couldn't understand him. They said yes.

Robert stopped eating and sleeping. The doctor said he was grieving himself to death. When Nadine returned, she raced to Clark. Robert hugged her and rediscovered life.

"Before I leave here," Nadine says, "he'll fuss about these pants he's got on. These are state pants with elastic. He likes pants with a fly and belt."

Once Robert decided he wanted some teeth. The hospital dentist said it wasn't possible.

Nadine didn't relent until he made Robert an upper set of dentures. He couldn't be fitted with lowers because of his rolling tongue.

"He has a hard time keeping them in," Nadine says, "but he loves to wear them. His county puts on a picnic for patients able to go. We put them on a bus and take them on down. Robert gets his sunglasses and his top teeth in and gets him a sport coat on and he feels really good.

"They all laugh at me. One of the employees mentioned she was gonna clean out her closet. I said, 'What day?' She knew what I wanted. Pants and shirts for him because he does love to dress up."

Robert pulls on Nadine and makes sounds louder than he has before.

"He wants to know if Loris kissed me and did I kiss him. That's the name he made up for my husband."

Robert finishes his drink in big swallows, then speaks again.

"He wants to know how much longer he's got," Nadine says. "The one thing I've never been able to tell him is that this isn't a prison, because everything is locked up. He wants to know if he gets time off for good behavior.

"Listen. Watch."

She taps her toe on his and taps the floor. She does it again. Robert shrieks and stands. He and Nadine move together away from the chairs. They dance a well-timed jitterbug.

"We had another close call once when his close friend got sick," Nadine says. "He was the only person who would sit beside him. He couldn't talk but he could see. Robert would make him dress and wear socks and shoes. He'd lead Robert around.

"I'd take Robert every day to the sick room and let him sit beside his bed. I explained what was happening, that the man was gonna die. When it happened Robert was sad, but he handled it pretty well."

Robert pulls her hands toward him and talks with his head rolled back. He's aggravated, Nadine says, because she's not giving him enough attention. She tells him she has to go.

"Will you bring me some more cigarettes?" he asks her.

She shakes his hand yes.

He holds onto her arms and wants to know when she's coming again.

"He's saying, 'the Sunday after tomorrow after tomorrow after tomorrow,' " Nadine says. "That's his way of saying Sunday week."

Robert tells her he wants to kiss her goodbye. She kisses him. He smiles.

"Tell Loris to kiss you," he says.

"A couple of years ago, I had emergency surgery, and didn't have a chance to tell him," Nadine says. "Two staff members made up their mind that they'd not see him get that sick again. They kept on telling him until he understood.

"When I'd been home three weeks, they put him in a state van and took him 30 miles to my house to see for himself."

Nadine and Robert swap final pulls and tugs.

She steps away.

Robert gropes in front of him. He finds air.

Andy pulls his pants down close to Robert's chair. He isn't wearing underwear. He puts another pair of pants on backwards.

Someone coaxes a walker toward the big trash can by the bathroom door. He is coming to deposit a dirty diaper. A man sleeps on the floor.

Robert can't see. He is smiling.

He leans toward the man sitting next to him and tells him something.

"He said, 'Now I've got me some Camels,' " says Nadine, a few feet away.

The man doesn't respond.

Robert runs his hand across his head. Seconds pass in silence.

He turns to the man again and jerks his arm.

"He said, 'She said she'll be back next week.' "

Observations and questions

1)   Al Neuharth has defined two types of journalism he sees practiced in America: the journalism of hope and the journalism of despair. Discuss this story, and the entire series, in terms of those broad categories. Would you describe Tilley's vision of mental health care as pessimistic or optimistic?

2)   The writer says that Robert "could talk the bottom off the ocean." What does that phrase contribute to the story both in terms of what it tells us about Robert's character and in terms of how it helps define the voice of the writer?

3)   Tilley begins this story with a reference to Camel cigarettes, a reference that is repeated in this story, and echoes references to cigarettes in previous stories. Consider how this recurring motif contributes to the structure of the story, both to jog the reader's memory and to represent the values and atmosphere of the hospital.

4)   Dialogue is common in fiction, but rare in newspaper stories. It differs from simple quotation in that it reflects action and reaction. Study how Tilley uses dialogue in these stories, especially in the scene in which Nadine talks with Robert with her hands and translates the conversation.

5)   Tilley describes Nadine and Robert's jitterbug in a single paragraph. That dance seems a perfect representation of the remarkable relationship that has developed between worker and patient. As a reader, would you like to have seen Tilley linger on that scene and describe it in greater detail?

6)   The ending of this story is particularly important because it must also serve as the ending for a six-part series. Study the ending carefully, considering narrative detail, character, quotations, word order, sentence length, and language. What final impression is gained from reading this ending?

A conversation with
Greta Tilley

CLARK: How did you get interested in doing a story about the hospital?

TILLEY: I worked for the afternoon paper for a while, and then I left to free-lance and stayed out maybe four years. When I came back, one editor said "Here are some things that I'd like for you to do," and he named doing a story about the life of the mentally ill. I've been back now five years, so that was a long time ago.

The editor had worked at Dorothea Dix somewhere between college and law school. He just couldn't forget what he'd seen there. He always wanted to have a reporter do a project on this. Every year we'd talk about "Well, we really need to go over there and do Dix." But we put it off and put it off.

We did it last year because there have been a whole lot of budget cuts everywhere. The areas really hurt were our mental hospitals, and especially Dorothea Dix. There have also been a lot of articles in North Carolina about the new commitment laws which made it harder for people to get into institutions. There seem to be more and more people affected by mental illness, so I told Alfred Hamilton, I think I'm ready to do it now. I guess I'd been putting it off because I'd been dreading it so much. The idea of spending the time in a mental institution, I knew, would be very emotional.

How much time did you actually spend within Dorothea Dix?

Interviews were conducted and recorded over the telephone. Tapes were transcribed and edited. Some questions have been paraphrased for clarity and brevity.

We weren't sure that I would be able to go at all. This is the opposite of any way I've ever done a story before. Alfred, my editor, made the initial contact because his father is a well-known surgeon in Raleigh who had done a lot of work at Dorothea Dix. Because it's so hard to get into a mental institution for a reporter, he thought that maybe he should make the initial contact.

While people at the hospital were always very, very polite, they were understandably hesitant about having a reporter come in there and stay and do stories when what good would it do? I didn't know this was going on, but Alfred sent clips, and they were passing them out among the staff. Finally the director decided that Alfred and I could come down there for a conference and talk about what we planned to do. Then the director said that he would have to get approval from the attorney general's office—all this was confidential.

So the attorney general approved it, and then the hospital administrator wouldn't let me come unless the staff approved it. He had to have all these meetings with the staff, and the staff did not want me to come. It was a terrible time, the budget cuts had just really hurt them, they were having a lot of moving and consolidation, they were working until they were just worn out, more than usual, and why would they want a reporter hanging around and maybe finding things they didn't want them to see, and then bugging them and making extra work?

So they weren't real keen, some of them, about me coming, but the more the director talked, and then I came down and talked with the staff, and suddenly it seemed they were all for it. They voted to let me come.

When I did go, I spent one week in January [1984]. I came back to Greensboro and I let it digest and stayed here another couple of weeks and then I went back to the hospital for a second week. So I was actually there on campus for a full two weeks.

Where did you stay?

I stayed in a motel nearby. The hospital staff was just wonderful. I could go anywhere I wanted to go, I could ask any question I wanted to ask, and I could stay as long as I wanted. The only thing they wouldn't let me do is spend a night in a patient's room. They said they couldn't guarantee my safety. But I could spend as long as I wanted to in the lounge on a ward, which I did late, late almost into the morning. But I didn't actually bring my pajamas and toothbrush and go in a bed and lie down. So very early in the morning until very late in the evening I was there all day and maybe took about a 30-40 minute break for lunch occasionally just because I had to get away sometimes.

Why was that?

I know that I'll never have an experience like that again. Nothing can prepare you for what you see. It's not just one thing at one time, it's 20 things all going on at one time, and it's a straight all-day, all-night thing. It's so emotional. The people are so tragic and they're so sick. Sometimes they're fighting and screaming and yelling, and lying on the floors and kicking and going to the bathroom on the floor, and it's just not a place you would want to go for a two- or three-week vacation, so you just need a break.

It's depressing under any circumstances?

It's depressing under any circumstances, but there were times when I enjoyed myself. It surprised me. Many of the patients were so glad to see me when I came, and I was glad to see them. We learned about each other, and I could kind of understand when they were out in right field and when they were tuned in. They helped me understand that, so I grew very close to them. And there were some rewards: The littlest bit of progress was like someone had handed you a million dollars.

Could you imagine having some kind of relationship with any of these people outside the hospital setting?

Some of these people get out for a while and a few of them make it. The story I did about the man who had the shock treatment: Oh, he was such a nice, sweet young man, and he eventually was released, and I kind of keep up with him from time to time, and he's still out and doing well. But he's one of the few, unfortunately.

I became very close to the young woman named Mary in the story. She was such an intelligent person, but she was very, very sick. I just adored her, and she would write me letters and poetry, and I would write her. But it's sad. I understand she's not doing well at all. She's had a bad setback and is just mutilating herself. But she was someone I could have really enjoyed on the outside, and there were others.

There's a tradition in both popular culture and news reporting of uncovering the horrors of mental institutions. There has been a lot of reporting lately on the abuses within institutions. I was surprised when I read your series, because it was nothing like that at all. Although it was depressing, it was also uplifting at so many different points. I'm wondering whether you went into the story with any of those popular conceptions of what it would be like?

We've all seen some of those movies, and *One Flew Over the Cuckoo's Nest,* who could forget that? I tried to prepare myself for the worst, but from what you've seen in the movies and what you've read, you can't know what to expect. I talked with the staff and the director, and they tried to give me some pointers, but you can't conceive of it until you do it. They would say, "Now someone may try to grab you around the neck if you're wearing a piece of jewelry, or if somebody pulls your hair, just go back," but nobody ever did any of that to me.

Do you think people's behavior changes because they are being observed by reporters? Were the hospital workers on their best behavior?

Oh, I'm sure they were. That's why I wanted to stay a long time. They're so short-staffed there, and there's always so much going on, that after a while they have to lose themselves in what they're doing. Things just have to happen naturally after a while because too many things are going on. If a fight breaks out, you go by instinct, the way you've always done.

You said that you spent a week and came back to Greensboro for two weeks before you went back to the hospital. Do you remember what you were doing during those two weeks in between your visits?

You wouldn't believe the amount of notes I took. I spent a lot of time just going over the notes, and thinking about what I'd seen, and letting it all digest, and thinking about what I needed to see, and just trying to unwind.

Had you found how to approach the story by that point?

I found so many stories, I was just overwhelmed and terrified. But as far as saying I wanted to write one story on this and one story on that, probably I had some ideas. In fact, I'll tell you something interesting. I know exactly what I was thinking back then.

I came back and said I wanted to do this story differently. I thought the best way to do it, to give a feel for the place, to have a true sense of what it was like, you needed to get to know some of the same patients so you could see the different ways they reacted from hour to hour and day to day.

I thought the only way to show it was to write something in a journal form. Write everything as if it were happening now. I thought that was a wonderful idea. I talked to Alfred about it, and he agreed. Like "January 31: Mary is in the beauty shop having her hair done, and Joe comes in and says so and so." I felt you needed an outsider's view, and that way I could get some of my thoughts in there too.

When I started writing, it just didn't work out at all. For one thing, I have never been very comfortable doing something close to the first person. And it just wasn't working out. It was too much. I tried two stories that way and then gave it up and said, "Just do it the way you've always done it."

Can you tell me how many notes you took?

I was using little notebooks and big notebooks. In fact, I would come back to the motel late at night, and I would make myself write before I went to bed, everything that I wanted to think about and everything I saw that I wanted to record. I would write that on hotel stationery. And I'd be writing in my car, and I'd write things on napkins from Hardee's.

So I came back not only with the history of the hospital on mimeographed sheets, but all my notebooks and napkins and hotel stationery. So I had to go through a strange assortment of things. Sometimes I would be writing a story and have to pull out a napkin.

How do you begin to gain control, to get your arms around so much material?

I love to say that I'm the most unorganized person in the world, and I am in many ways, but I don't think you can do a story like that without some sort of a system. You don't just have one notebook and it's conveniently about one topic. Included in one notebook may be 30 different topics. So I went through all the notebooks, and assigned a number to a person or a topic. I would put the Roman numeral one and then put the topic "Shock Therapy." Or if I came upon a name in my notes, I would give it a number every time I came upon that name: "A1," "A2," "A3."

In other words, you would use a numbering or mapping system in order to start bringing related material together.

And then on a piece of paper under the title "I. Shock Treatment," I would list all the things in all of my notes that I thought I might want to cover. And all the quotes. I always want to put in everything. So I would just have volumes of new notes on things that I wanted to put in the story, but at least they were in categories.

So you went from these notes that had no basic organization except chronological, and then you copied your notes and impressions into some kind of logical categories.

Right. The most interesting question is when the stories started falling into place. I'm not exactly sure. I know I wanted to have something about Mary. I know I wanted to have something about the Hoey Building, which is where the older people were. I knew I'd need an overall introduction. I knew I wanted the thing on shock treatment.
    And the thing about Nadine and Robert, the last story. You talk about uplifting. I think the care there was very good. But even with good care the conditions are just depressing. They told me that some volunteers go in there and get sick and throw up, and can't even stay.
    So you're seeing that, and you're seeing this man Robert—look at his life: He can't hear, he

can't see, but yet, the most beautiful situation has developed with this woman who cared about him. The pleasure on his face, it sunk into me that they truly were communicating. For a while being a skeptical reporter I said, "Oh, he doesn't know what she's saying. He may just be familiar with her touch, and he's happy to see her." But no, he knew.

I just never felt anything like that before, and it was the first story I can remember sitting there with tears streaming down my face as I was writing it. We always think that we're supposed to be detached and not show anything, but I couldn't help it. I knew that story had to be in there.

I have never in my whole life wanted so much to communicate something and felt so inadequate to do it, felt that no matter how I did it, I couldn't have come close to doing it the way it should have been done. After I wrote that story, I felt that I hadn't even touched it. That particular story generated a lot of letters to the editor, so I was grateful for that, but still to this day I think that I failed in being able to communicate what happened inside that place.

I want to discuss a couple of the little techniques you use to link one story to another. One is what you call "background music," what I would describe as "anti-music," the strange sounds of the mental ward.

Everything is happening with this noise in the background. It's just so much a part of the inside of an institution. I wanted the readers to be conscious of it without overdoing it, to remember and think that this is always going on, and this is how it sounds.

The second motif is the way in which cigarettes become the center of life. They are the important currency inside this place. They are tokens of love, rewards, and punishments. Smoke fills the air.

It's the pressure and intensity of the place. Almost every staff member smokes and so do the patients. You would think that the main thing on their minds at all times would be, "What's going to happen to my life? Will I always be this way?" But that's not what it is. It's "When is it going to be time for my next cigarette, and Mary got her cigarettes taken away because she scratched Judy, and I'm gonna sell three cigarettes to so and so."

I don't want to give the impression that everything was desolate at all times. After you get in there and are there for a while, this is the way the staff feels and this is the way they can stay: Your expectations change. You start looking for tiny little things, and you see that maybe one woman hasn't spoken a word for a week, and she'll come up to somebody and say, "Want a drink?" It's as if she had just recited some sort of a beautiful poem.

Things are funny. Even the crazy things are funny, and they'd laugh at themselves. They know they are mentally ill, they call it "crazy," and sometimes they can laugh at that. I developed a rapport with one woman. I said, "Look, Martha, I don't understand what you're saying." She said, "Excuse me, I'm just off here for a minute, but I can't help it, would you please wait for me to come back, I'll be back in a little while." It was interesting to me that they sometimes knew what was going on.

Could you have written an editorial based on your experience there?

At one time they asked me to write a personal piece that they wanted to run on the editorial page along with the series. I was going to do it, but then decided not to. I didn't think it was needed. This was not an investigative piece.

This is me being a pessimist, but so many journalists feel that we can change the world, and that what we write is going to make such a big difference. If we point out all these big issues, if we point out all the things that are wrong, people are going to say, "Oh, yes!" and they are going to get up in arms, and storm to the General Assembly.

I don't think that's the way life works. It might work that way for a few days, but then it goes back to the way it is again. I didn't go in there with a dream of saying, "I hope after this series comes out that people are going to send money and that the General Assembly is going to realize that they messed up and that they shouldn't cut back at Dorothea Dix, and that everybody is going to live happily ever after." I just wanted people to think about it. What is it like to be mentally ill? What is it like in a state mental hospital? You're sitting here and your life is relatively stable, but, hey, there's a world over here that we all need to be thinking about at least every now and then. And here's what it's like.

And if it so happens that you'd like to volunteer, or send them money, or talk to your congressman, well, that would be great. If the General Assembly would like to read this and think maybe they were too hard on Dorothea Dix, that would be great, which in fact I think did happen. So as far as writing an editorial, yeah, I could have, but I wanted to let the stories speak for themselves.

In a previous conversation, in the midst of your general insecurity and feelings of inadequacy as a writer, you thought one part of this series represents your best work. Which part was that?

The part about Mary.

That's the part I would have guessed. Can you express what it is about that story that offers you a little bit of confidence?

I felt that I am not talented enough, not smart enough to do it any better than that. That's all I have in me. It's one of the few stories I've written that I ever felt that way. Maybe the only one.

What were you trying to accomplish by the use of quotes in this story?

You know that I'm a big "quotes" person. All these writers I admire so much say, "You can say it better than they can. You don't need a quote unless its absolutely on the money. You say it, that's your job." I'm just the opposite. I cannot say it any better than they can say it, and I don't want to. I'm writing about them, I'm not writing about me. I'm not trying to show, "Hey, look how good I can write." Everybody thinks I use far too many quotes, but I can't help it.

Someone asked me how your stories compared with your winning stories two years ago. I said, "I think she's improved in two years."

(Laughs.) That's encouraging.

I didn't mean it that way, that's just the way it came out. What I should have said was, "It's even better than it was two years ago."

(More laughter.) I know. I know.

Does praise and recognition and winning prizes earn you the kind of freedom and time you want to work on stories you think are important?

We have a very close-knit staff at our paper. I'm close to many of the reporters, and a lot of people want to do what I'm doing, and I understand that, and it makes me feel so guilty. But then the older I get, the more ornery I get about it, and I start thinking, "Well, doggone it, I did the hotline for three years and I did write obits for two years, and the community calendar for eight years, and the religion briefs for three years. I covered county government, and I covered the police, and doggone it, isn't there ever a point where you get to go beyond that, if you're doing good work? Why can't a reporter grow?" So I don't feel as guilty about it as I used to.

Are you a procrastinator?

My husband, who is a pretty good critic, says I do my best work under the gun. And I do. Like with these stories. I may spend all this time outlining, and going over my notes, and tearing out my hair, but when it came to the actual sit-down writing time, I would put it off and put it off until my editor said, "Look if we don't have these things soon, you're in big trouble." I probably did the writing of those stories in record time. When you have too much time, you try too hard, instead of trying to say it the simplest way.

One of my impressions is that your writing is simpler in these stories than in earlier ones I've read. Does that make any sense to you?

It probably is simpler. The older you get the more you realize your job is to go out and get the story, the best way you can get it. And if you have it, all you've got to do is come back and tell it in the simplest way that you can tell it. That's probably one of the few things that I know I've learned through the years. You don't have to kill yourself to show what a great writer you are. You sit there and write it and hope that the story tells itself.

Jonathan Bor
Deadline Writing

JONATHAN BOR, 31, was born and raised in Washington, D.C. He received a degree in history from Oberlin College in Ohio and a master's degree from the Columbia Graduate School of Journalism. He first worked as editor of two weekly newspapers in the Hudson Valley region of New York. He went on to write for the daily *Poughkeepsie Journal,* covering courts and city hall. Bor has worked for *The Post-Standard* in Syracuse for two years, first on general assignment and more recently on the health and environment beat. His story on a heart transplant has been honored by ASNE, the Associated Press and United Press International.

It fluttered and became Bruce Murray's heart

MAY 12, 1984

NEW YORK—A healthy 17-year-old heart pumped the gift of life through 34-year-old Bruce Murray Friday, following a four-hour transplant operation that doctors said went without a hitch.

Early Thursday morning, three surgeons at Presbyterian Hospital lifted Murray's flabby, enlarged heart from his chest cavity and replaced it with a normal heart that had been flown from St. Louis inside an ice-filled beer cooler. The operation lasted from 3:45 a.m. to 7:30 a.m.

As Murray's diseased heart sat in a stainless steel bowl at the foot of the operating table, doctors gradually weaned Murray away from a heart-lung machine that had kept him alive throughout much of the operation. The new heart, beating slowly at first, gradually took over the task of pumping blood through Murray's body. And by 5:25 a.m., Dr. Eric Rose emerged from the 19th floor operating room and proclaimed the procedure a success.

"It went beautifully," said Rose, who wore a heart-shaped pin bearing the inscription, "surgeon." At 33, Rose is said to be the youngest transplant surgeon in the world. "It was routine, nothing unusual. I do it every day, just as you hold that pad in your hand," he told a reporter.

Late Friday night, Murray was sleeping under anesthesia in the hospital's intensive care unit; spokesmen termed his condition critical but stable.

"His prognosis is excellent, at least in the short term. In terms of at least a year's survival, his prognosis is excellent." If Murray survives the first year, Rose said, his chances of living another five years is "at least 80 percent."

Within 24 to 48 hours, Murray could be expected to breathe on his own, unassisted by a respirator, Rose said. "He'll feel like his age then," he added. Within a few days, Murray should be able to sit up in bed and, within a week, pedal a stationary bicycle. Murray is the first Syracuse resident to receive a heart transplant.

Murray, of Kensington Place, has been taking an extended leave of absence from his job as manager of the mailroom at the Onondaga County Civic Center.

In 1977, a viral infection of his heart left the organ in an enlarged, weakened condition. Since then, Murray has suffered pneumonia, Legionnaire's Disease, a stroke and congestive heart failure.

Doctors said his heart was pumping at 10 percent normal capacity. "His chances of lasting a year were zero," Rose said.

Murray originally planned to fly to New York City on April 23 for a transplant at Presbyterian, one of 18 hospitals in the country that perform the operation. But the hospital asked him to postpone the trip when another patient, whose condition had worsened, was given a higher priority.

Wednesday, Murray finally made the trip with Gladys Murray, his mother, and Lucinda Cawley, a personal friend and fellow stroke victim. She is also public relations consultant for the American Heart Association in Syracuse.

Murray had publicized his quest for a new heart through close contacts with the media to dramatize the need for organ donors. By signing organ donor cards, he said, area residents may someday provide "the gift of life" to others.

As it turned out, Murray's own wait for a donor proved remarkably short.

He met Thursday afternoon with a support group consisting of three recent transplant recipients and their wives. The patients included John Drohan, a Yonkers fireman, who received a new heart April 10 after waiting 2½ months.

"It was such a boost to see those guys," Cawley said. "One of them had his operation three weeks ago and he was up walking. He (Bruce) was buoyant, buoyant."

That same day, he met with his New York cardiologist, Dr. Ronald E. Drusin, and asked him to put his name in the national computer bank that matches transplant candidates with available organs.

Cawley remembered the meeting. "He said to Drusin, 'I'm here, put me on the computer.' Drusin smiled and said, 'I put you on the computer last night.' "

At about 5 p.m. Thursday, a donor was found: a 17-year-old boy, the victim of a car accident, who was declared brain-dead at St. Louis University Hospital.

Two hours later, a three-member transplant team from Presbyterian flew out of Teterboro Airport in New Jersey to pick up the new heart. The team traveled 850 miles to obtain the heart; the donor organ spent four hours in transit.

Both are records. "About four hours is the most I'm comfortable with, but the distance really didn't concern me," said Rose.

The team—consisting of a surgeon, a physician's assistant and a nurse—removed the donor's heart at about 1:30 p.m. They placed it inside a plastic bag filled with an iced-saline solution, and they placed that bag inside three outer bags. The package was placed inside a blue beer cooler that bore the stamp "Transplant."

By the time their jet landed at Teterboro at 3 a.m., Murray was in the operating room where he was being prepped for surgery. Anesthesia put the patient into a deep sleep. A respirator breathed air into Murray's lungs via a tube inserted in his throat. Doctors cut a slit the length of Murray's chest. As many as a dozen doctors, nurses and technical assistants hovered over the patient, passing instruments, attending to heart monitors and swabbing the patient's bleeding chest.

Meanwhile, a state police escort ensured swift passage from Teterboro, over the George Washington Bridge and to the hospital for the vehicle carrying the transplant team and beer cooler. Within 10 minutes after landing, the transplant team was rushing the beer cooler through the hospital emergency room and up an elevator 18 floors.

By the time the heart arrived in the operating room, Murray's chest was wide open. Doctors had used a power saw to cut through his sternum, and a clamp-like retractor spread his chest apart. Murray's diseased heart, about half-again larger than normal, was fluttering inside the exposed chest cavity.

Surgeons swiftly turned the task of pumping blood over to the heart-lung machine. Their hands moving with quick deliberation, surgeons inserted tubes inside the heart's major blood vessels and severed the vessels from the heart.

The tangle of tubes carried the blood to a cylinder that supplied it with oxygen. From there, the blood traveled to a large console, which performs the job of the heart. Three spinning disks pumped the blood through the clear, plastic tubes back to the patient's body.

In one careful, spectacular moment, the surgical team made the exchange.

At 4:33 a.m., doctors lifted the diseased heart—milky but slightly purple—out of Murray's chest cavity and handed it to attendants. They, in turn, placed it in the steel bowl. On a platform at the foot of the operating table, the spent heart rested for the duration.

"How many things do you know that work for 34 years," Rose quipped after the operation.

The beer cooler was opened, and the donor heart was placed inside the patient's chest. The new heart, about as large as a relaxed fist, was attached to the blood vessels.

It jerked and fluttered and became Bruce Murray's.

But for the next two hours, the heart-lung machine continued to do much of the pumping. Because the heart was cold, it could not pump vigorously. But as blood pumped by the heart-lung machine flowed through it, it contracted and expanded and gradually warmed. As it warmed, it pumped with more authority.

Probes carrying mild electric shocks were used first to speed up the new heart, and later to synchronize its beat. "His rate is slow, but that's not unexpected," a technician explained. "It takes time for the heart to come back."

At 6 a.m., most everyone on the operating room floor stood with arms folded, staring at Murray's new heart and at the monitors that recorded its activity. Murray had been weaned entirely from the heart-lung machine, and his new organ worked.

"He's on his own," the technician said.

Observations and questions

1) Jonathan Bor uses specific, concrete details to re-create the drama of a heart transplant operation: the diseased heart in the stainless steel bowl, the donor heart in the beer cooler, the young surgeon wearing the heart-shaped pin. What effect does the accumulation of such details have on readers?

2) In making decisions about order and emphasis, the writer must choose among a variety of interesting news elements:

A) Bruce Murray is the first person from Syracuse to receive a heart transplant.

B) Eric Rose may be the youngest transplant surgeon in the world.

C) A travel-distance record is set for transporting the donor heart.

D) The reporter witnesses the operation.

Study how the writer uses these elements, and discuss whether or not you agree with his decisions.

3) Based upon your discussion of the previous question, describe the single most important element of news in this story. Has the writer captured that news in his lead? In a brainstorming session, come up with other possible leads and discuss which approaches you prefer.

4) The reporter is eyewitness to most events described in the story. What elements of description and explanation reflect the perspective of an

eyewitness? Bor does not reveal to readers that he is sitting in a gallery 12-feet above Bruce Murray's open chest. Would knowing that have made the story more credible or contributed to readers' appreciation?

5) An important but minor character is transplant surgeon Dr. Eric Rose. Study the ways in which the writer communicates a sense of the doctor's character. Is this character underdeveloped, or would more information about him shift the focus of the story?

6) After going without sleep for 48 hours, Bor wrote this story in 90 minutes on a deadline for the first edition. Play the role of Bor's editor. What kind of advice would you have given him on deadline? If you and Bor had another full day to work on the story, what elements would you revise or expand?

7) We learn that the donor heart belonged to a 17-year-old victim of a car accident. What reporting techniques might have uncovered more about this person? If the writer had discovered more about this character, how could he have used such information in the story? In your discussion, consider ethical issues related to privacy and disclosure.

A conversation with
Jonathan Bor

CLARK: Are you a general assignment reporter?

BOR: I used to be. In the last four months I've become the environmental and health reporter.

What kind of writing and reporting needs to be done in that area?

I'm trying to approach these very complicated issues like toxic-waste dumping and acid rain so I can bring it home to the reader. Through the process of gaining an understanding myself, not being an expert in the field, I can relate to the fellow at home who is opening his morning paper.

How about medical stories? How do you gain the readers' attention?

It's a matter of approach and also a matter of topic. There are a lot of fascinating things going on in medicine now. Transplants is one. The artificial heart is another. The ethical questions concerning the right to die. It's not too difficult to engage the reader in a story about a heart transplant.

But it's also approach. I've tried to personalize stories about new developments in medicine. We were very lucky in having the first heart transplant patient in Syracuse be a person who is very willing to open his story to the public. So we were able to write about not only what is a heart transplant, and how does it work, but we were also able to sit in the operating room and view what was happening, and describe a wondrous event in human terms. Whenever possible, we try to bring the medical story down to human level.

I wrote a story about a four-year-old child who died of AIDS because he had hemophilia and received clotting factor, a blood product, almost every day of his life. He contracted AIDS because of his very intense exposure to many, many different donors who constitute the blood pool. After about three weeks of negotiations, I was able to interview the parents about this boy's life, how they reacted and adjusted to the news that their son, just a four-year-old boy, had AIDS and was going to die with it, and how two very normal middle-class folks learned about AIDS through the life and the death of their son.

Isn't it a universal human tendency to tell stories about health and sickness? Aren't those topics at the center of much of our ordinary conversation? Does this suggest to you a large audience for medical stories?

I think people like to read about people who overcome illness, and in certain cases about people who succumb to illness. The classic example of the latter case is the whole AIDS epidemic. For a long time, we were reading about AIDS as a sort of a distant epidemic that affected only the gay community. In short order, over the period of only a year or two, it has become a disease that has affected everybody. So when you write a story about a four-year-old boy who dies of AIDS, it's something that anybody can relate to.

This year, next to the Bruce Murray story, the most widely read story I wrote was about the death of a six-year-old girl who was the area's cystic fibrosis poster child. She was a mature-before-her-time child who made many friends in the hospital and in school and accomplished in six short years what most people take 12 years to accomplish. In her life and appreciation and coming to terms with her death, I think people learned a lot about the human spirit and what a human being, even at a very young age, can accomplish. So these aren't just stories about illness, and about cures, and treatments and science, they're also stories about people.

In the case of Bruce Murray, he wasn't just somebody who almost died and received a new heart and lived. It's also the story of the manager of a mailroom in a county office building who opened a very intimate part of his life to the public and went on to be a leading spokesman for organ donations.

How's Bruce Murray doing now?

He was in the office about a week ago. He's doing very well. He's a very affable, engaging figure.

Did you tell him about your award?

Oh, yes, (laughs). He's followed my career since I wrote the article. I've had an interesting relationship with Bruce. The only time I saw him before the operation was about two or three weeks prior when he held a press conference to announce to the community before TV cameras and print reporters that he was going to have a transplant. He was going to let the public know about it because he was going to raise their consciousness about organ donations. I chatted with him and chatted with his mother, but didn't really develop any personal relationship with him.

But then very quickly I found myself sitting in a gallery looking down at the inside of Bruce Murray's chest. I got to know him in a rather intimate but strange way. Afterwards, he read the article, and he got to know my byline, and later I interviewed him several times and got to know him very well. And I chat with him from time to time, not only on the occasion of doing stories. I always give him a lot of credit for my success.

Did the idea for the story begin with the press conference?

We found out about Bruce a day or so before the press conference, and that's how the story began. He had a friend who's in the story named Lucinda Cawley. She was a public-relations consultant for the local chapter of the American Heart Association, but also she was a personal friend of Bruce's. They got to know each other through a stroke-victim support group. Both had had strokes and got to know each other through their own recoveries and their attempts to help each other. Lucinda was very instrumental in bringing Bruce to the public's attention and helping organize coverage of Bruce. She helped me gain access to the gallery in the operating room in Presbyterian Hospital.

At what point did you know that you would cover this in a more intensive way than other kinds of stories?

The evening before the morning Bruce Murray was operated on, all the pieces came together. The press conference was held a month or two before the operation. After the conference I talked on a fairly regular basis with some of the officials down at Presbyterian. I made known my desire to view the operation and would appreciate anything they could do to give me access to the operating room. They were receptive but really didn't commit themselves. It was not until the evening before the morning of his operation that I found out a) that the operation was going to take place, and b) that we coordinated with the officials at Presbyterian access to the operating room. I made plane reservations and probably within four hours of learning about the operation, I was on the plane headed to New York.

What then?

I arrived at the hospital, sat in the lobby of Presbyterian for about an hour just waiting for Bruce to be wheeled into the operating room, and to wait for public-relations officials to escort us up to the operating room. Within an hour or two we were sitting about 12 feet above Bruce Murray looking inside his chest. It all happened very quickly. The hospital was very cooperative.

Are you taking lots of notes at this point?

Another reporter and I managed to commandeer a technical nurse, who had been involved in several previous heart transplant operations. She was in charge of monitoring the heart-lung machine, which is probably the central piece of technology in this whole operation. So she was intimately familiar with the blow-by-blow unfolding of this and other operations. We got her to sit with us for two or three hours. She was our tour guide through the operation. Of course that's very important when you're not a doctor and you're sitting 12 feet above somebody's open chest, watching the beating heart and the expanding and contracting lungs, watching a flurry of activity around these organs, but not really understanding what's going on. Through her we got a rather specific and detailed description of what the physicians were doing.

Did she explain things in clear English or in technical language?

Somewhere in between. She made an effort to talk in everyday language, but fairly often would slip into medicalese. So part of what we were doing was asking her to repeat and explain things. "What do you mean by that term?"

Were you there for the whole operation?

With the exception of about 20 minutes. We sat in the gallery and watched the doctors cut open Bruce's chest, spread the chest apart....

Was that gruesome?

Surprisingly not. There was a matter-of-factness about the whole operation. By nature I'm not very squeamish. The sight of beating organs didn't bother me.

But the operation was done in such a routine manner, with a minimum of fanfare, that as a reporter I felt myself drawn into that perspective.

About a half-hour into the operation, at the point where they had his chest open and Bruce was ready for the transplant, we found out through contacts we had made in advance that the donor heart was on its way across the George Washington Bridge, which is just a few minutes from the hospital. At that point I tore out of the operating room, down several flights of stairs, and was waiting in the lobby right around the time that the motorcade arrived at the hospital and a few technicians came bounding into the hospital carrying the beer cooler.

Did you know it would be arriving in a beer cooler?

No, I didn't. I knew it was going to arrive on ice, but I was really surprised by the rather humdrum appearance of all this. It was an old beaten-up beer cooler that you could have imagined being used for years and years in softball games, with a lot of dents and nicks and writing on it. I guess what set it apart was the word TRANSPLANT stamped across the top in red lettering, and the people who were carrying it happened to be wearing scrub suits. These were the doctors and technicians involved in flying out to St. Louis and removing the donor heart from the brain dead, 17-year-old accident victim. So I spent about 20 minutes just watching that happen, to get a sense of the convergence of two events: the opening of the recipient's chest, and the arrival of the donor heart.

So now you're back up in the gallery.

Nothing was going to happen until the heart did arrive. In rather swift fashion we watched the doctors sever the arteries to Bruce Murray's old, diseased heart, lift it out of his chest, put it in a stainless steel bowl and leave it like a pair of old shoes at the foot of the operating table.

You described it as one swift, dramatic moment.

We had a real sense of wonder. When I describe it as matter-of-fact, I'm talking about the manner in which the physicians went about doing this; it was done in a mechanical way with no hesitation or fanfare. You're used to seeing these things on TV documentaries with a lot of tight editing and drama built into the narration. In this case there was no narration except the comments of the nurse sitting next to me.

But the drama of what was happening really struck me. Here is the heart that has served a person for 34 years lifted out of his chest and put in a bowl, set aside and forgotten.

That must have been a vivid image to you, because you mention it twice in your story.

Here was the old, diseased, enlarged, flabby, yellowed heart which was not doing the job anymore and which was obviously the bane of his existence. It had caused congestive heart failure and other terrible consequences.

At what point did you have a chance to do the reporting about the journey of the medical team to St. Louis to pick up the heart?

Weeks before the operation took place, we had done stories about the mechanics of obtaining a heart. This process was described to me by the heart transplant coordinator at Presbyterian Hospital. I had also talked to some organ procurement agencies around upstate New York. I was familiar with the process of how a recipient is hooked up to a donor through computer contact, and then how a transplant team goes to the site of the donor's death and obtains the heart to bring it back to the waiting patient.

Now we didn't know that night where the donor was, where the transplant team was picking the heart up, and as a matter of course the hospital likes to keep that a secret to protect the privacy of both the recipient and the donor. It happened that one member of the heart transplant procurement team was wearing a T-shirt that said St. Louis General Hospital. So we had a pretty good idea that they had gone out to St. Louis. Nobody that day was telling us on the record that that's where they got the heart from. The next day I called one of my editors in Syracuse and ran down some of the details with a tidbit of information that I thought they had obtained the heart from St. Louis, and we had another reporter make some calls to hospitals in St. Louis to confirm it. During the day we were able to work out consents from both ends to use the hospital's name.

Did you have to do a lot of reporting after the operation?

After the operation I stayed in New York for about eight hours to monitor the progress of the patient. I didn't want to leave New York and then find out that the patient died. That sounds rather cruel. But I wanted to make sure that when I left I had a pretty good idea of what his progress was going to be.

Another nice thing was happening that day. A patient from Connecticut who was a member of the Yonkers Fire Department and who had undergone a rather widely publicized heart transplant, was leaving the hospital that day. I found out about it and was able to write a sidebar about the exit of this now healthy heart transplant recipient, the same day that Bruce Murray went under the knife.

Were you writing in New York or up in Syracuse?

I wrote a sketchy outline of the story while I was in New York just waiting around for news about Bruce Murray. And really the outline doesn't serve any real function other than to get my mind on the task of thinking about how I'm going to write the story. I hardly ever hold to an outline; in fact I hardly ever write one. But I did have an hour or two of time on my hands when I thought I would run through the main events and categories just to get the facts organized in my mind. Beyond that I made a stab at writing the lead on the plane on the way back to Syracuse. The article took shape once I sat down at the computer terminal and started writing back in Syracuse about 7 o'clock in the evening after the morning of Bruce Murray's operation.

Had you slept at all?

No, I had been up for about 48 hours.

How long did it take you to write it?

They wanted the story for the early edition. The deadline was about 9:30. So I gave myself about an hour and a half to write the story, and then another 20 minutes or so to proofread it. And that was that. The article was edited for the first edition, I gave it another read for the final edition, and then I went home. I wrote the sidebar for the final edition.

Take me through a chronology of the story again.

I woke up one morning, put in a full day's work, went home, was in the middle of eating dinner when I found out that the operation was going to take place. So I got on a plane, went down to New York City, observed the operation into the next morning, stayed at the hospital all that next day, got on a plane in the late afternoon, arrived in Syracuse in the early evening to write the story and went to bed that night.

As I read the story, I was a little unsure as to where you were during the reporting of the story. All the perceptions were that of an eyewitness. Did you ever think of including an element in the story showing readers that you were sitting in a gallery above the operating table?

I didn't consider it at the time, although it may have been a good idea. I figured that by the way the story was written it was obvious that the writer was present. It may have been a good idea, just by way of a phrase, to indicate the precise vantage point.

It probably would have been possible for someone who was not an eyewitness to interview eyewitnesses and re-create the story in such a way as to appear to be an eyewitness.

If I had been doing it that way, it would have occurred to me much more plainly to indicate that I wasn't an eyewitness, that this was an account gained from secondary sources.

How did you decide where to begin the story?

First, I just conceptualized the overall story. I was very concerned with the idea of writing a narrative of this operation. I hadn't seen too many clean, tightly written narratives of a heart transplant operation, or any important life-saving medical procedure, in a way that really grabbed the reader.

So what I wanted to do was write the story in two parts with a bridge in between. The first part was a quick, hard-news lead, giving the reader some key images that indicate how the operation unfolded in a very compacted way. In the first few paragraphs or so I told the reader that this patient from Syracuse received a new heart, that his old heart was lifted out of his chest, a new heart had been flown in from St. Louis, that he was kept alive for some time by a heart-lung machine, and that within four hours or so this 33-year-old doctor, rumored to be the youngest transplant surgeon in the world, emerged from the operating room and said the operation went well and felt it was very routine. I wanted to hit the reader in a compacted way with a lead that both encapsulated the story and gave the reader some sense of the narrative, of the miracle of the operation.

And then after a bridge you wanted to spin the full narrative?

The bridge was the section of two or three paragraphs where I'm trying to convey what is going to happen to this patient. And after that I went about the narrative in a rather sequential way.

I have studied story forms and came across a number of examples of the form you described, one which begins with the news and then slips into narrative. I wrote an article about it and called that form "the hourglass." (See page 90.)

I read your article about that, incidentally. And it's funny because as I was reading it, I realized I had been writing many of my longer pieces that way and not really thinking about the geometrical configuration of the story. But it's a very workable way to accomplish two things: One is to give the reader the news very quickly, with some description and imagery; and later on to give the reader a much more descriptive narrative of what happened and how things unfolded.

Were you struck by the numbers in your lead, the 17-year-old heart in the 34-year-old man, that the heart was half the age of the man?

That was one thing I was trying to convey. There was something wondrous about a very sick 34-year-old getting a healthy heart from a donor who was half his age, which is not to say that he comes out of the operation rejuvenated, reborn as a 17-year-old. And also that a 17-year-old who died in a traumatic fashion and a 34-year-old halfway across the country trying to cling to life—that they came together in a rather random but dramatic way.

Did you have any means of finding out more about the 17-year-old boy? I was curious about who he was.

By saying he was a 17-year-old boy who died in a car accident and that he was from St. Louis, we went far beyond what reporters do in reporting a donor-recipient relationship. I would have very much liked to have written about the life of this 17-year-old, what happened to him and who he was, because it would have made the convergence of two lives all the more vivid. With the time very compressed, that was about the best we could do. It took a little detective work to find out where he was from, how old he was, and how he died.

One thing I admire about this story is the quality and character of detail, the little touches that bring the story to life: the stainless steel bowl, the beer cooler, the heart-shaped pin.

In a situation like that it's hard not to notice these details. At first you're struck by the complexity of the situation. You're looking down at a cluster of doctors and then there's a whole tangle of tubes and machinery. Your first impression is one of confusion and congestion, almost like a traffic jam. But it doesn't take long before you try to sift out these details and figure out what is this device, what does the doctor look like, how are they handling the organ, how are their hands moving. There's no better way to bring the story and the scene home to the reader than to pick out maybe a dozen or so vivid images.

How the heck do you write something as good as this under the gun when you've got a big job to do, and no rest and no time?

Part of it is adrenalin. When I received the phone call over dinner at home that Bruce was going under the knife, I was both excited and put off because I was already dead tired. I had put in a hard day at work. But when I arrived at the scene of the operation, there was a real rush of adrenalin. This was the first time I had seen anything like this. It was a fascinating and remarkable thing I was seeing. So the adrenalin rush stayed with me for most of the time I was working on the story.

To combat some of the weariness, I did a careful job of note-taking. I didn't want to run any risk that I would get back to the office a day later confronted with a pile of notes I couldn't read and that didn't make any sense to me. I conceptualized the narrative form of the story, and took my notes in a very clear narrative way. I demarcated the sections of events that occurred during the operation by noting the time.

Kind of like on *St. Elsewhere*.

Exactly. I have notes in front of me and flipping through them I see 2:15, 2:30, 2:45. When anything significant happened I noted the time because I not only wanted to convey what was happening, but I also wanted to convey some sense of space and time and how in a matter of only four hours such a remarkable thing could take place.

Are you the kind of writer who tries to solve a lot of problems in your head before sitting down in front of the keyboard?

Beforehand, I try to conceptualize the broad framework of the story. Is it going to be a narrative? Is it going to be a hard-news pyramid? I want to mentally key in on a handful of the most salient images: the stainless steel bowl, the tangle of tubes leading to the heart-lung machine, the heart placed inside the beer cooler, the little things I can use to anchor the story in reality. Before I sit down at the typewriter, I don't really know where those images are going to go. The flow of the story begins when I sit down at the typewriter. Whatever preconception I had about how the story would unfold changes immediately as I go along.

Let's get you at your desk in front of a VDT. Are you now dealing with your notebook at all?

On the plane I read through my notes and made sure I knew where everything was. I didn't index my notes, but I read over them and highlighted some areas I thought I'd want to go back to, underlining, bracketing, making standard notations. I sat down with about half a reporter's notebook full of notes and referred back to them. I usually don't find myself too tied to my notes. I write with my notes by my side, but really supply most of the details from memory. When I want to supplant my memory with details, time references and quotations, I go back to my notes. The notes are mainly helpful as a way to start thinking about the story.

What kind of a writer are you on a VDT? Are you inclined on deadline to bang it out as quickly as you can?

I tend to move very slowly for the first four or five paragraphs. In most cases that's the most difficult part of the writing. You have to deal with how you're going to bring the reader into the story. The lead also dictates what's going to happen from that point on. I recall spending a half-hour writing the first four or five paragraphs. Fatigue started to creep up on me and I got a bit frustrated with the getting off the ground process. Sooner or later the first few paragraphs did take form, and everything else just flowed after that.

A new shape for the news*

By ROY PETER CLARK

For more than a century, a single story form has been the workhorse of American newspaper writing. Born with the telegraph and the Civil War, adopted and perfected by the wire services, the inverted pyramid has served the needs of readers in a hurry, reporters on deadline and editors who love to hack from the bottom.

In the pyramid, reporters organize information in descending levels of importance. The readers absorb the most important news first and continue down the page until their interest flags:

> A 43-year-old Seffner man was killed Thursday evening when his car collided head-on with a semitrailer truck, according to a Florida Highway patrol spokesman.
> Robert Hayers of (address) was headed west on State Road 574...when his 1972 Buick inexplicably crossed the median line and hit the truck, the spokesman said.
> The truck's driver, Aubrey Gresham, 26, of (address) was not hurt, the spokesman said.

Such writing is as straightforward and undecorated as John Riggins running over left tackle. Some journalists learn no other style.

Despite its preeminence, the inverted pyramid has important weaknesses as a form of communication. Some reporters think it is an unnatural way to tell a story. "The inverted pyramid is at war with the narrative tradition," says columnist Charles McDowell of the *Rich-*

---

* This article originally appeared in the March 1984 issue of the *Washington Journalism Review*. It is reprinted here by permission of the editor.

mond *Times-Dispatch.* "We write upside-down and tell stories backwards."

"Look at the image you journalists use," says Donald Fry, professor of English at the State University of New York, Stony Brook. "You take the strongest, most durable man-made structure, and you turn it upside down."

Melvin Mencher, professor at the Columbia Graduate School of Journalism, also dislikes the image. He writes: "The term is somewhat misleading. An inverted pyramid story is an unbalanced monolith, a huge top teetering on a pinpoint base. It is a monstrous image for journalists, for the top of a story should be deft and pointed."

When badly written, the inverted pyramid peters out into insignificance, offering the reader no reason to continue. "No reader reads more than three paragraphs into a story," a reporter once told me. For him it was a self-fulfilling prophecy.

Some reporters let the pyramid control the content so that the news comes out homogenized. Traffic fatalities, three-alarm fires and new city ordinances all begin to look alike. In extreme cases, reporters have been known to keep files of story forms. Fill in the blanks. Stick it in the paper.

Reporters have always tested the conventions of news writing. In the last two decades, some have experimented with styles of writing born more of television than the telegraph. Readers discover newspaper stories written in chronological order, stories that have beginnings, middles and endings, stories that attempt to capture each event in a unique structure.

Such experiments in style can be exciting, but when badly written, these stories leave the reader hanging. The news is buried in the 11th paragraph, after the jump, the prose is thick with needless detail, and the writer's unchained melody goes on forever.

There is a third alternative for the news writer, a story form that respects traditional news values, considers the needs of the reader, takes advantage of narrative, and spurs the writer to new levels of reporting. This form has no name that I know of, so I am calling it the "hourglass."

The hourglass has three parts: 1) the *top*, which tells the news quickly to the reader, usually in three or four paragraphs; 2) the *turn*, a nimble transition; and 3) the *narrative*, a chronological retelling of events. Examples of this story form go back many years, but it is becoming increasingly popular, especially for dramatic stories that beg to be told in chronological order.

The top of the hourglass looks something like the pyramid. The lead contains the most important information in descending order:

> Bleeding from bullet wounds received earlier in a gun battle with police, a St. Petersburg man held a 5-year-old boy hostage in the child's own home for three hours Thursday evening before surrendering to police.
>
> Glenn Spradley, 24, of (address) was taken to Bayfront Medical Center and admitted with bullet wounds in both thighs. He was listed in fair condition early this morning. Police said he has been charged with attempted murder.
>
> Donny Schenck, a dark-haired moppet wearing a red-and-yellow Amazing Spiderman T-shirt, seemed calm after his ordeal. Answering a few reporter's questions from the safety of his father's arms, he said his captor told him, "I had to have a place to hide."
>
> Spradley allegedly shot St. Petersburg police officer Edward G. Placzek Jr. at the start of the incident. Placzek was hit in the arm and chest. He was listed in fair condition in the intensive-care unit of Bayfront

this morning. The officer reportedly had a collapsed lung.

If Janice Martin's story for the *St. Petersburg Times* had been picked up by an out-of-town newspaper, it could have been cut at the last paragraph. Readers would be able to discern the heart of the story.

Local readers demand more when the story is a violent incident involving the kidnapping of a child and the shooting of a policeman. Martin turns the story into narrative with "Police and neighbors gave this account of what happened." What follows is the bottom of the hourglass, 30 short paragraphs written in chronological order and filled with dramatic details:

> The intruder startled Mrs. Schenck, who was at the dinner table with Donny and her 3-year-old daughter Vanessa. Mrs. Schenck grabbed Vanessa and ran screaming out the back door, thinking Donny would follow. Instead, it was the armed man who followed.

Such a structure works beautifully for certain police stories, courtroom dramas and other incidents that lend themselves to chronological narration. I have seen it used in stories about a high-speed chase, the rescue of a man who was pinned under a car, the murder of an infant by two other children, a Miami man who saved a woman from a mob of attackers, and many others.

The key to the structure of the hourglass is the turn, which moves the story from news to narration. This transition can be subtle or obvious. Here are examples from four stories:

1) The incident occurred after Ms. Vivier left her job as a clerk at a shopping center and headed home.
2) This account of what happened is provided by the mother of the victim.

3) Graham was walking home after working in his grandmother's yard when he heard the yells of 55-year-old Robert Gasper.

4) But Dave Ohlmeyer...said Monday night that Bonvillian gave him the following account of what happened.

Unlike the pyramid, the hourglass seems a natural way to tell a story. In normal conversation people tend to blurt out the most important information, "I saw John Travolta at the airport today," and follow with a chronology: "I bought my ticket and was walking to the gate when...."

The hourglass cannot be used on many stories, but for the right story it offers these advantages:

- Readers get the important news high in the story.
- The writer can take advantage of narrative.
- The story repeats the most important information in the top and in the narrative so readers have a chance to absorb it.
- Unlike the top-heavy pyramid, the hourglass has a balanced structure.
- It keeps readers in the story and leads up to a real ending.
- It encourages editors to refrain from slashing from the bottom. The VDT permits the editor to make quick deletions within the body of the story if they are necessary.

Stories written in the hourglass structure are richer in detail than stories written in the traditional pyramid. The form seems to inspire reporters to work a little harder to gather those details that bring the narrative to life for the reader. For example, Janice Martin used this detail in describing the tense hostage episode:

> Through it all, a lawn sprinkler ticking from side to side on the Schencks' front yard kept time like an annoying metronome.

The hourglass is more versatile than one might expect. A long story in the *Los Angeles Times* on the tenth anniversary of OPEC made effective use of the structure. The top of the story summarized the impact of the OPEC cartel on the politics and economy of the world. Then, after a transition, it returned to October 1973 and, with commentary, helped take us through the tumultuous OPEC decade.

My affection for the hourglass leaves me open to criticism that I favor "formula writing," which carries a pejorative connotation for journalists. Truth be told, the sonnet is a formula and so is the villanelle. "There's a formula for a triple backflip off the high board," says Steve Lovelady, associate executive editor of the *Philadelphia Inquirer,* "but that doesn't mean it's easy to perform."

Poets have learned that a formula can be a liberating device, a lens through which they can discover what they want to say. They do not cram reality into a formula, or square words into round forms. Instead, writers discover the best story form during the process of writing. That is why journalists should master many story forms: the inverted pyramid, the hourglass and a hundred others.

Murray Kempton
Commentary

MURRAY KEMPTON, 67, was born in Baltimore and was graduated from Johns Hopkins University in 1939. He served in the Air Force in New Guinea and the Philippines during World War II. He has been a columnist for the *New York Post*, the *New York Review of Books*, the *New York World-Telegram*, and a commentator on the CBS program, *Spectrum*. He joined *Newsday* in 1981. He has taught journalism at Hunter College and Rutgers University and has lectured at the University of Notre Dame. He has won numerous awards for his writing including this year's Pulitzer Prize for commentary.

Mayor Koch refuses to take Hart

MARCH 20, 1984

When it comes to sniffing the appropriate moment for coming down from the hills and shooting the wounded, there are very few public personages with a keener nose than Edward Koch's.

The mayor is indeed so shrewd, if unchivalrous, a connoisseur of such opportunities that the major significance of his endorsement of Walter Mondale for president yesterday may well have been the support it lent the suspicion that, whatever the results in Illinois tonight, Gary Hart's star is declining from its zenith.

Two weeks ago, when Mondale seemed to lie gasping on the strand, Gov. Mario Cuomo reaffirmed an unshaken faith in him. Koch preferred silence. A stubborn gallantry in any apparently lost cause except his own is not one of those special charms he shares with the governor. But yesterday Mondale was back in the water and even flipping his tail, and the mayor could safely certify him as seaworthy.

Koch used to be one of the most engaging of politicians, but some unidentifiable worm seems to have been cankering his good humor lately. Whether the occasion calls for expressing good will or ill, the tone runs more unvaryingly toward the emanations of a grouch.

Show the mayor a surface painted gray from side to side and top to bottom and he can be trusted at once to announce that he is looking upon the difference between black and white. This unique eye had seldom been freer with its play than yesterday when he explained the distinction between Mondale and Hart.

After a scrutiny whose diligence might better have been directed at our potholes, he had detected seven Mondale opinions he found preferable to Hart's. Three involved rather esoteric subjects—minority hiring quotas, the exclusionary rule for defective police searches in criminal cases and measures to combat acid rain—and, to the extent that their blither is subject to measured analysis, Mondale and Hart appeared flatly to disagree on only one of them.

The other four issues on which the mayor found Mondale's views the more compatible all revolved around the single question of Israel's settlements on the West Bank of the Jordan. Mondale seems to have better satisfied Koch because he sounded more sympathetic than Hart to the settlement policy, an odd criterion for a mayor who has himself now and then spoken of it rather frigidly.

Before the mayor spoke, his assistants passed out copies of the correspondence with all the candidates, present and departed, on which he had based his decision. Hart's replies to Koch's inquiries seemed hardly less manful than Mondale's in the heroism of their resistance to temptations to court the Arab vote. In disposing of the mystery of his choice between Hart and Mondale, the mayor had raised the new mystery of how anyone, even with an eye as sharp as his, could draw the line between two positions with this minuscule a difference in their solicitude for Prime Minister Yitzhak Shamir's real-estate portfolio.

But that does not really matter. The difference between Hart's opinions and Mondale's is so slight that the mayor can be excused for having had to scour to find it. Mondale is a thing of shreds and patches, and the best that can be said for Hart is that he picked out a superb bolt of cloth for his suit and then skimped on the tailor. Neither comes up to John Glenn as a man or to George McGovern for moral fiber or to Ernest Hollings as an observer of the real world. The main function of the primary process seems to be to refute Charles Darwin and produce enough triumphs of the less fit to convert us all into creationists.

But such dark thoughts are not the point. The mayor thinks he has smelled the winner, and that is just as sound an explanation and as fair an excuse for his performance yesterday as it was for all those whose nostrils flared at the scent of Gary Hart two weeks ago.

Observations and questions

1) The lead uses the metaphor of "coming down from the hills and shooting the wounded." What happens when Kempton uses a figure traditionally applied to journalists to describe the subject of his column, a politician?

2) Paragraph two consists of one nine-line sentence. Later in this volume, Kempton tells us in his interview that "my sentences are so long that I can't even find the first word when I get to the last." Analyze the sentence in paragraph two and the sentence quoted above to discover how Kempton keeps long sentences clear.

3) Paragraph five ("Show the mayor...") metaphorically describes how Mayor Koch makes distinctions no one else can see, and the rest of the column tells us some of the differences Koch proposes. What would happen if Kempton moved this metaphor of the gray surface to the end of the piece? Or up to the lead?

4) Kempton uses colorful language throughout his piece, e.g., "cankering," "blither," "shreds and patches." Discuss the effects of such arch language on the authority of the writer.

5) The column closes with two metaphors of smelling, picking up the image of a nose sniffing in the lead. Does this unity enhance Kempton's argument, or does it merely lend grace to his style?

'If I leave you, baby, count the days I'm gone'

APRIL 29, 1984

Mourning is probably the only weakness that cannot be indulged to excess, and WKCR, the Columbia University radio station, did a considerable kindness to those of us to whom his memory is imperishable when it spent 36 hours of this weekend on no one's discography except Bill Basie's.

I do not suppose it possible to explain to anyone of fewer years than my own what it was like to be young when the Basie band first came east close to 50 years ago. It had started in Kansas City, a faraway place in those days. His records with Benny Moten had made us moderately familiar with Basie, and the small collection that Vocalion had issued as the Jones-Smith Seven had brought us closer still, but all the same we could not have conceived the impact of the actuality.

It must have been 1937 or so when Basie, whose eastward foray was not yet the triumph it would become, brought his full orchestra to the Albert Auditorium, Baltimore's black dance hall.

The first shock was their size. We had grown reverently accustomed to the members of the Duke Ellington Orchestra, who had a smallness of bone consonant with their elegance. But these Southwesterners looked like a waterfront shapeup. No one who came upon Lester Young, the saxophonist, after life was well along in its withering could imagine how big he seemed when he first came east.

And these roustabouts worked in the appropriately rough key. Better ears than my own recognized at once that they played out of tune, and I am grateful for having been tone-deaf and quicker to appreciate than a more acute sensibility could have been.

Even then, Bill Basie had his intervals of delicacy. Most of them came when the bulk of the band was resting. The Albert had a keener sense of duty to its customers than to its workmen; anyone booked there was obligated never to stop the music except for the briefest pause to catch the breath.

But now and then, the band's melody components would be granted a few minutes of freedom from their joyous toils, and the rhythm section would remain to work by itself. I should not be suprised to be told that it was on these occasions of demi-intermission that Basie refined that style so economical that he only played half the notes and left the others to be suggested in his silences. He too was taking as much ease as he could permit himself.

It was at one such interval during that first sight that Bill Basie forever disposed of any further temptation of mine for dope. Someone handed me and I lit the first reefer that had ever touched my lips. The rhythm section was working by itself on "Oh, Red" as I recall. At one point, Basie took his hands off the keys he had been barely touching and Jo Jones, his drummer, very quietly commenced weaving his sticks in with the bass.

The Albert was already a very old precinct, and by some device of his own, Jo Jones set the whole creaking structure to rock from side to side, east to west, and south to north just with those two thin pieces of wood, and there was the sense that if he were incautious enough to indulge a single crash of the cymbals, the whole structure would come tumbling down around us.

It was at just that moment that I took my first puff of the reefer and knew at once that the alteration that Jo Jones and Walter Paige were performing on my interior had nothing to do with the substance I would later hear spoken of as the Good Brother. Here, strangely gentled, was the force of nature and no man-contrived substitute could ever be more than a distraction from it.

And so I laid aside the gage, the muggle, the Mary Jane then and there, because, in the half-consciousness of adolescence, I had learned that nothing must stand between me and the real thing ever again. As long as I live, Jo Jones and Bill Basie will be for me quite enough of all ye know and all ye ever need to know.

The Basie band smoothed over and even shaped itself most affectingly to the ballad. But for me, its great hours would always be those when it roughened itself again and played the blues. The blues, when all is said and done, are what you finally settle for. There is no language like its: "She's yours, she's mine/ she's somebody else's too"; "If I leave you, baby,/ count the days I'm gone." In the best of languages you feel the tune from the meter of the words, and there has never been a language like the blues.

I think of them still: When Jimmy Rushing sang the blues, and Bill Basie lingered quietly and sparsely and then the whole band came home like some great locomotive, you could never afterwards forget what men can do if they are only together. Bill Basie gave us just that great a celebration of life. Death is never enough to erase a ceremony of that high order.

Observations and questions

1) Kempton's intricate and interminable lead saves the name of the subject until the end of the sentence. Discuss the effects and hazards of this deliberate suspension of the reader.

2) The second paragraph begins with the supposition that this column will fail in its attempt to capture "what it was like to be young when the Basie band first came east close to 50 years ago." Is such apparent modesty a pose? If so, what purpose does it serve?

3) Kempton plays imagery of work and ease, elegance and roughness against each other in this piece. Discuss this choice in terms of describing musical effects in mere words.

4) Why does Kempton introduce his first experience with marijuana into this eulogy to Count Basie? Would the piece improve if we edited those references out? Why does Kempton use such old-fashioned terms, e.g., "reefer," "the gage," "the muggle," "the Mary Jane?"

5) Analyze paragraph eight ("The Albert...") in terms of graphic sensations induced by simple words.

6) Kempton tells us that he learned that "nothing must stand between me and the real thing ever again." With your finger, cover up the word "ever," then "again," and then the whole phrase "ever again." Why don't any of these deletions improve the clause?

7) Having read this piece (or any of his others), do you really believe Murray Kempton is "tone-deaf?"

The discreet charm of the GOP

AUGUST 21, 1984

DALLAS—The charms of the Republicans commend themselves to tastes that are concededly special and may in some quarters be accounted depraved.

But it takes, thank God, moral fiber sterner than my own not to have surrendered to the sight of them Sunday, herded into the welcoming pen for George Bush, abiding the interval greeting various honored guests with the politeness that bespeaks entire unfamiliarity with its object and then breaking forth at last into glad and affectionate cries of recognition when the chairman introduced White House Counselor Edwin Meese and Secretary of Labor Raymond Donovan.

Both Meese and Donovan are, depending on your point of view, either steeped in infamy or bedaubed with smear. But then, we have no reason to believe that these delegates would ever have heard of either if he had not been made notorious by the jackal packs of journalism.

The Republicans are unique for the beauty of spirit that has been lost everywhere else: They are ready to stand by any scoundrel who is their own, whether or not it has been proved to a certainty that he really is a scoundrel.

Two days before he was transformed from a contender into a *nolo contenderer,* Spiro Agnew bawled his defiance of all his traducers before an audience of Republican ladies, and they rose to a woman to bathe him in their love. Let Agnew dare show his face here tomorrow and the assemblage would collapse into yelps and moans of exultation at getting him back in its arms.

The strains of "Solidarity Forever" are heard no more in union halls, but its chords throb in every Republican bosom. The impulses that bring these people together are those not of politicians but of devotees.

Yesterday morning, the secretary of labor was honored at a breakfast tendered by Jackie Presser, president of the Teamsters union. It was an occasion pregnant with amiability, the only one so far where no one in attendance had to pass through a metal detector, a discourtesy that the Teamsters may or may not have awhile ago decided was inappropriate, not to say impolitic, for any guest list as gamey as theirs usually is.

Every uncountable inch of Jackie Presser's corpus bubbled with goodwill for every stranger; nothing equals his enthusiasm for clasping any hand as soon as he knows that it is unencumbered by a subpoena. He is however a bird of a most gaudy hue to be found flocking among all these jenny wrens.

Two of his three predecessors in office had their tenures interrupted by criminal convictions, and one of them seems to have had the misfortune to fall within the jurdisdiction of the only law enforcement agency within our continental limits privileged to apply the remedy of capital punishment without waiting for permission from the appellate courts.

The moral traditions Presser has inherited make an odd fit into the litany being chanted around him; all the same he chose wisely when he chose the Republicans, because he did not so much join a party as embrace a civil religion that needs only to see the convert to extend the absolution.

To look down upon them from the press gallery is to gaze upon a meadow where sheep know they can safely graze. It has often been noted that they are overmasteringly passive, white and Protestant. But the true point about them is not that they are so much alike but that they so much want to be. A Republican delegate may now and then appear on the floor wearing a funny hat, but neither he nor she would ever indulge any such bizarrie unless every other member of his or her state delegation came there wearing a funny hat, too.

After awhile this passion to conform enforces its touch on the heart. At noon yesterday Rep. James Leach of Iowa, a lonely moderate, invited delegates to a debate on those proposals for a nuclear freeze that had been summarily dismissed by the convention's platform committee. There are 4,000 delegates here and two of them turned up. One refused to identify himself; he could not have been more embarrassed if he had been a family man encountered in a gay bar.

And both these entertainers of heresy wanted it understood that there could be no imaginable circumstance under which they would support the nuclear freeze. To be a Republican and to show up on an occasion of dissent is not to question the accepted truth but to affirm and protect it. We may or may not all be blown up in the name of their faith, but, when it happens, they will only be sweetly dreaming.

I ought to be ashamed of loving them, but I cannot resist them. As I write, Madame Jeane Kirkpatrick is at the podium, and for the first time since this herd began its soft bleating chorus, of the sheep, there clangs stridently upon my ears the preachments of a maiden aunt.

But, of course: Kirkpatrick is not a Republican; she says indeed that she intends to remain a Democrat. It is prayerfully to be hoped she will; as it is, the tireless if transient carping of her presence is an offensive intrusion upon the peace and quiet where the Republicans and I lie clasped in our mutual slumber. Wake us never, mother dear; we are already queens of May.

Observations and questions

1) The author strikes the pose of an observer who views the Republican convention with active distaste and mock sympathy. How does he maintain this pose, and how does he play with it?

2) Kempton uses the underlying metaphor of the Republicans as sheep, e.g., "herded into the welcoming pen," "soft bleating chorus," etc. How does this continuing metaphor enhance his argument beyond mere characterization?

3) Kempton uses ecclesiastical imagery, e.g., "devotees," "litany," "heresy," etc. to convey his idea of the Republican Party as "a civil religion." How does he avoid blasphemy and offending the reader when he touches a rather sensitive realm of American experience?

4) In paragraph 10, Kempton says: "To look down upon them from the press gallery is to gaze upon a meadow where sheep know they can safely graze." This near-quotation from the Bible and Bach combines the sheep and religion motifs at the middle of the piece. Discuss the effects of moving this sentence to the lead or the end.

5) Kempton assumes audience familiarity with the problems of Meese, Donovan, Agnew, and Presser. How much can a columnist assume about readers' background reading and knowledge?

6) Kempton devotes four of his 15 paragraphs to Jackie Presser, who hosted a breakfast for Secretary Donovan. How would you justify this

much space for a bit player in a larger drama? Would you be more tempted to give Secretary Donovan that space?

7) In the penultimate paragraph, why does he call Jeane Kirkpatrick "Madame?" What does the last line of the column mean?

How do these touches help Kempton make his points?

A woman burned while police had their danish

NOVEMBER 9, 1984

It is six years since the morning Nathan Giles Jr. accosted the car that Bonnie Anne Bush was driving to her Mount Sinai Hospital nursing post, forced her out with a gun, dragged her screaming into an abandoned West Side building, shot her and set her body afire.

Bonnie Bush's death did just about as much damage to the good name of the New York City Police Department as Kitty Genovese's did to Queens's reputation for conscientious citizenship. Kitty Genovese also screamed in the street through a protracted struggle with her murderer, and nobody who heard her called 911.

Kitty Genovese has been dead more than 20 years, and her ghost is still evoked whenever some moralist feels moved to arraign the callousness of this city's residents.

In Bonnie Bush's case, several citizens did their duty and the police botched theirs. The difference may be why Kitty Genovese's name has lasted so much longer than hers as a symbol of reproach to New Yorkers. Government is distinctly more efficient than the average citizen when it comes to erasing occasions for shame from the public memory.

Nathan Giles had a long struggle with Bonnie Bush before he got her to the killing floor. The first 911 call came at 8:03; there were four others, the last at 8:11. Antonio Reyes later swore that he ran up to a patrol car not many yards from the building into which the murderer had just dragged his victim. The two officers heard his story and went on eating their breakfast.

Meanwhile, back at 911, the headquarters operator had taken a succession of calls from witnesses to Bonnie Bush's peril and made such a hash of the information that the police details were scouring Manhattan Avenue for a criminal who had been identified as working his will at 15 West 102nd.

Bonnie Bush had been dead an hour when the Fire Department came to put out the blaze Giles had set, and reported a possible homicide to the police. It would be only speculation to suggest that she would still be alive if the police had done their job, but then, after all, Kitty Genovese might still be just as dead if any of her neighbors in Queens had dialed 911. The point is that each of these women deserved even a small chance of rescue and survival, and Kitty Genovese was cheated of her chance by private citizens and Bonnie Bush by official servants.

The two policemen who had tarried over breakfast were put to a departmental trial and found guilty of having failed to "take fundamental police action." The punishment in each case was suspension for 30 days of vacation time, with the option to make up the loss with extra work. Thus does the department define its sensitivity to the standards of police conduct: Two patrolmen who refuse to bother with a call of mortal distress lose their vacations and Cybella Borges loses her job because she posed in the buff before she was even a patrolman.

Bonnie Bush's parents sued the city for the neglect they claimed had caused her wrongful death. Kenneth Besterman, plaintiff's counsel with Richard Winer, said yesterday that he had entered the case with minimal hope, because "the law is 103 percent against us." And the law is indeed clear-cut—a citizen cannot expect the police to protect him from felonious assault unless he gives them advance notice of its threat. If the police do not learn of the crime until after it starts, no subsequent negligence on their part adds up to a legal tort.

Yesterday it was announced that the City of New York had agreed to settle the claim by paying $150,000 to Bonnie Bush's estate. Assistant Corporation Counsel John Ryan credited this unheard-of generosity to "the prejudicial nature of the facts," even though they were "irrelevant." He spoke in the cold tones of a government whose gelid habits make understandable its alarm that, whatever the law says, a jury might hear such a story and run wild in its outrage.

Observations and questions

1) Kempton structures this column chronologically, with interspersed comments and reminders of the Kitty Genovese parallel. Do you find this structure confusing or illuminating? Could you rearrange the paragraphs to produce different effects?

2) In his interview later in this volume, Kempton describes his writing technique: "You begin the story with some effort to make it interesting in the beginning, and then you get to a narrative line as fast as you can, and then you go through that narrative line. And then the best part of the piece ought to be in the last three paragraphs." Discuss this column in terms of that sequence.

3) The author describes the murder and subsequent events with graphic economy. Pretend that this narrative is a news story and analyze it in terms of what Kempton left out. Discuss the different demands of narrative in news and columns.

4) Kempton uses police jargon throughout the second half of this piece, but editors usually caution writers to translate and transcend such of-

ficialese. Why does the columnist use this language, and what risks does he run in doing so?

5) The author achieves a measured tone throughout what could have become a rather lurid account. Analyze his word choice sentence by sentence to discover how he produced and controlled this tone.

6) The last paragraph begins with the news peg of this column. Should the author have put this event in the lead? What reasons could you give for saving it until the end?

7) The column ends with the word "outrage." How does Kempton keep this word from falling out of his fingers too early?

A general silent on his medals

NOVEMBER 18, 1984

In May of 1967, when the world mistook Gen. William C. Westmoreland for the great captain with the highest responsibility for the conduct of our war in Vietnam, he himself was noting in his diary that he could not take a weekend's rest at Clark Field without getting permission from Ellsworth Bunker, U.S. ambassador to South Vietnam, and Admiral U.S. Grant Sharp, commander-in-chief for the Pacific.

Friday was the second day of Westmoreland's testimony in the trial of his suit against the Columbia Broadcasting System for painting him as first among all the tricksters who deceived our government and ourselves about Vietnam.

And nothing in his witness was as persuasive as its suggestion that, in his circumstance, even a dishonorable general would have been all but helpless to commit the enormities imputed to this one.

Those of us unpersuaded that an American victory would have been a just solution in Vietnam ought to concede that some day there might be a war worth winning. And once we do, we should recognize that the one important lesson of the Westmoreland case is that we have constructed a military establishment incapable of conquering any enemy of minimal resource and patience.

At the outset of his testimony, Daniel Burt, his counsel, led Westmoreland through his career from World War II—Africa, Sicily, Omaha Beach, the Bulge, the bridge at Remagen—to Korea and the 101st Airborne and at last to Vietnam.

There, at least, you would think that an ordinary man would have learned to stay close to the office; even though his last war was comparatively safe, all the same "My airplane was hit on a number of occasions and I was ambushed—well, that's what you expect on a battlefield."

Burt asked no questions about Westmoreland's combat medals, and we can only assume that the witness had forbidden reference to the subject.

It has to be said, to be sure, that in the '50s the Army imperiled his reason by enrolling him in the Harvard Business School. Still, ruined though the American industrial system has been by MBAs, eight months in their company could not totally have disabled a soldier of Westmoreland's kidney.

We may take it for granted, then, that he was a shrewd and experienced general officer when the orders came for him to take up the sword in Vietnam. And he could not take it from the scabbard at any point without checking with "my military boss," Adm. Sharp, and "my civilian boss," Ambassador Bunker. Bunker was then 73 and a shrewd old hand seasoned in all arts of persuasion except war.

We may suppose that Westmoreland was luckier than a general dispatched by President Nixon to defend England from the aggressions of the Picts and the Scots under orders to report daily to Ambassador Walter Annenberg, but even so it must have seemed odd to Westmoreland to be told how to run a war by an ambassador.

But that was the least of what was odd. Every Monday morning, Westmoreland had dutifully to take his place at the embassy's Mission Council for refreshment of his campaign plans by the CIA station chief, the Agency for International Development man, the ambassador's public-relations officer and the economic counselor.

He was, in addition, continually beset by itinerant congressmen until he had to beg Washington to "please try to control people coming here (because) they take up an inordinate amount of time." He had the help or hindrance of at least four separate and mutually quarrelsome intelligence establishments, and he was provided with an historian and a scientific adviser that he could find nothing better to do with than take them to the Weekly Intelligence Estimate Update.

CBS' main charge against Westmoreland is that he fiddled with the enemy "order of battle" reports in a deliberate effort to underplay the size of the forces against him. Whenever Westmoreland referred to the O of Bs last week, he made it easier to believe that he regarded them as one of the host of irrelevant encumbrances of his assignment. "That was really historical data," he said, "and of little use to me."

He remembers little about the conferences that settled on an increase of 183,000 in the estimates of Viet Cong irregular strength beyond being impressed because the staff work was detailed and the charts elaborate. He then took the new order of battle over to the embassy and gave it to Barry Zorthian, "who interfaced with the press." There is no underestimating the crucial nature of any document whose first addressee is a public-relations officer.

We can understand why the Vietnam veterans cheered Westmoreland in Washington last week; he had been trashed just like them. His last war had been spent as a prisoner of war, and here he had been isolated as the prime reason why it was lost. I don't think he needs a dollar from CBS but it owes him the most abject of apologies.

Observations and questions

1) The key word in the lead is "mistook". How does that word set the tone for this column?

2) This piece bristles with charges, against the military, CBS, General Westmoreland, Ambassador Bunker, etc. Can such a short column present so many issues fairly? How does the author disarm potential reactions of unfairness?

3) Paragraph eight ("It has to be said...") ridicules the Army's educational program, the Harvard Business School, American business, and MBAs, all in 51 words. One reader might call these cheap shots, while another might praise Kempton's economy. What do you think?

4) Kempton presents his most disturbing idea in paragraph four, that the U.S. military can no longer win wars. Can the Westmoreland case, then still in progress, support this huge generalization? Does Kempton present the reader with sufficient information and analysis to support it? Can you think of reasons why he might not want to include such information?

5) Paragraph 10 ("We may suppose...") seems rather obscure in its reference to the Picts and the Scots. Can we expect readers to catch such an allusion? Does Kempton play the allusion in such a way that the reader does not have to understand it fully?

6) General Westmoreland appears in this column as a fool and a victim. Discuss how Kempton presents the general sympathetically, but not too sympathetically.

7) Explicate the ideas in the last paragraph. Why does CBS owe the general an abject apology but no money?

8) Any one of Kempton's paragraphs might expand into a full column by another writer. Speculate on how he thinks and writes so tightly.

A conversation with
Murray Kempton

FRY: How do you find ideas for your columns?

KEMPTON: I'm very much a datebook journalist. I'll look at the Associated Press schedule for the next day, and whatever seems to me the most promising (and very little ever does), I'll go to. I also cover a lot of trials. So I'll wander around for the day. If I don't get anything, I have to take refuge in some abstraction, Gorbachev or Jeane Kirkpatrick or the president of the United States, someone else who's not part of the reality of my life. Sometimes I get an idea in conversation, and then execute it. But I don't like abstract pieces. I'd much rather work the way a drama critic does: Go find a play and watch it.

What do you do if you haven't found anything?

Sometimes you come in, and you sit down, and you haven't got a damned thing. Maybe you had some conceit about how a piece would work. You can go to a conference, but those things are always incredibly fatuous. Or you read something. I've always worked on the premise that there is no 50-page document from which something can't be extracted. But sometimes you go out and bring nothing back. Then you've got to work it out in your own mind, because you don't want your editors to know you totally wasted your day. So you look at your notes, and then you work at some general thesis. From this dreary material, I try to make some kind of general proposition, then state it, and then make the argument. The fun is making the argument; I enjoy that. But sometimes it's a terrible day; I had a bad idea. I followed it through to its logical conclusion, and there was nothing there, and then I've got to contrive something to get me through the day.

You also do interviews and cover news stories, don't you?

I'm very much in favor of covering stories. I've always had a sneaking feeling that I never wrote a good piece that didn't have a quote from somebody else in it, though that somebody else could be Marcel Proust. But I happen to be an atrocious interviewer because my interviews consist entirely of long statements by me, and then the guy says, "Well, you may be right." And that's the interview. So, generally speaking, in order to get my quotes, I usually sit and listen to something somebody says, a press conference or something of that sort.

Do you avoid abstraction by seeking local angles and characters?

My first instinct is very local; that is a basic prejudice. Try reading Mike Royko in New York sometime, and you'll see that local is local. Royko is just not Royko in New York, whereas in Chicago, you pick him up, and you're there. I think Breslin is the best New York local columnist; he *is* New York. And you do get more localized as you get older.

Can you explain this prejudice for the local?

There are two reasons for it: First, I like to write overnight. I like to write today for tomorrow's paper, which is getting increasingly difficult as technology improves. In the old days, when I was happiest, I used to love to sit down at 11 o'clock at night and write the piece. In his later years, Westbrook Pegler and I got rather close, and he went quite loony in the end. We were having lunch one day, and he said to me, "You know, everybody thinks I went crazy because of Eleanor Roosevelt, but it wasn't that at all. I went crazy writing on Monday to be printed on Friday." And I took that very much to heart, so I like to work overnight. That's why I like local material, because you can write overnight.

That's your first reason; what's the second one?

Second, I believe in the tangible. I don't feel that I have much inside my head. I know some writers who have remarkable heads, such as Russell Baker and Art Buchwald, and their packages are wonderful. But I think it's never a good idea to compete with guys who are better than you are. That's not false modesty; I just generally stay away from that sort of competition. I hope I'm not arrogant in saying this, but I feel that I know the city, that I've been around for a long time. I have by American standards a staggering historical memory, and it's possible for me to know more about most stories than most people I'm covering them with. That doesn't mean I'm superior. Take Jimmy Breslin, whom I admire strenuously, although we don't compete that much anymore. I remember covering things that are long ago and forgotten, that Breslin had come to brand-new, where I knew the parties very well. On the first day, I would kill him. On the second day, he would hold me even. On the third day, we'd do other things. I'd shrink back from what was about to happen. And on the fourth day, he would kill me, get my blood. So I've always felt that I have the edge of age. I wouldn't say experience; I don't think experience is that valuable. You tend to get a little better all the time anyway. You have your package, and to a certain extent, it comes easier to you.

Do you find the writing easy?

When it comes to writing, you have to remember that a column is the easiest thing in a newspaper to write. You don't have the problem of writing a lead; you don't have to get everything up front. You've also got somebody around you writing the basic story, but you have to work on the assumption that this is all people are reading. You're safer than a daily newspaper reporter who has to clutter up his sentences with expressions like "Senator Jesse Helms (Rep.-N.C.)," as though anybody in the world doesn't know that Jesse Helms is a right-wing redneck. You have to add all these identifications, but you don't if you're writing a column.

So the apparatus gets in the way?

Yes. A newspaper story is a story. But the conventions of the form make writing a story in the conventional way the most difficult thing in a newspaper, conventions which are very sound, and very good, and very necessary to complete communications. But those conventions take up story room. You write a 12-paragraph piece, and some editor blights it at the top. I have a set piece of real estate; it runs about 610 or 611 words. As long as I fit in that, I know I don't have a cut problem. A guy working for a daily newspaper comes in, and he's trying to tell a story. The desk tells him to write a thousand words, and those thousand become five hundred in the editing process.

Is the reporting easier on a column?

Yes. I preferred being a columnist because I didn't have to sit on the phone and call some policeman's wife and tell her that her husband had been shot in the back and was dead. I just haven't got the stomach to do that. When I was young, I did things that were outrageous, totally outrageous. Lady Emily Peel once asked Disraeli why he had been so vicious to her father, Robert Peel, so many years before; and Disraeli replied, "I was a young man making my way." Well, I was a young man making *my way*.

Tell me about your writing techniques.

I've never found out whether anybody ever finishes my pieces or not, but I try to keep the person reading to the end. It's a story. You begin the story with some effort to make it interesting in the beginning, and then you get to a narrative line as fast as you can, and then you go through that narrative line. And then the best part of the piece ought to be in the last three paragraphs.

How do you keep the reader interested in the middle of the piece, where interest tends to sag?

Roger Simon says the middle is very crucial. It sounds like a selfish thing to say, but I'm more interested in bringing *myself* along, more interested in keeping myself interested. But in all cases, it becomes tremendously important to me to keep my concentration, and the only way I can do that is to spin this web, with all its themes upon it, to get to the middle. It can be a web of words or ideas or whatever. But it can be very boring unless you yourself are interested, and keeping the process from getting boring is terribly important to me. If I can go through this process, I may be able to think of a few last paragraphs, a couple of good last lines. I'll feel better about the whole thing than I would otherwise.

Do you write quickly?

I've always had to write fast. But now that I've got to a point in my life where my laundry list takes 20 minutes for four shirts, I can no longer call myself fast. I used to say a long time ago that there are two reasons why I'm incapable of teaching writing and why I'm possibly not capable of writing: I seldom know what the last word of a sentence is going to be when I type the first, and I almost never know what the end of a piece will be until I get to it.

You don't think of your ending before you start to write?

No, I try to get to my ending. I never know what my ending is. I start out to tell a story as truthfully as I can, and I keep going. Somehow or other, I can get an ending out of it, an ending which seems to make a point. Now whether the point is there or not, I don't know. I don't mean that I do dishonest work, but sometimes you get a little desperate.

But your endings seem neatly unified with your beginnings; surely that's a conscious technique?

I work on a Tandy word processor. On these damn machines, you can't see the lead by the time you get to the end. My sentences are so long that I can't find the first word when I get to the last. But it's in your head; you are conscious in some mysterious way of every word you've ever written in a piece.

Tell me about your relations with editors.

I happen to like editors. Except for being out for 12 years wallowing in writing books, I've been working for papers ever since the War, even before the War. I've been a free spirit as a columnist, picking my own stories, for roughly 35 years. Every time an editor gives me an idea to go cover something, an idea that sounds to me perfectly terrible, I go do it. If it turns out badly, I can say I did what they told me to do. Yet that idea is an idea I would not have had, because all of us are lazy. You get to a certain age, and every contemporary of yours is now an editor, or a publisher. You're blundering around with kids 25-30 years younger than you are. Campaigns are getting awfully exhausting, and the glamour of spending hours and hours in Howard Johnson motels begins to wear off. But I go, and I find I do better work than I would at home. Whether editors are smarter than me or dumber than me, more often than not, their dumb ideas turn out to be very good for me, so I almost never turn one down.

Do you get edited much?

I've got to be edited because of the kind of stories I cover. New York is full of people with names with nothing but vowels in them, and I don't mean that critically. If I type out a man's name correctly the first time, say "Andrew," I'm bound to call him "Alfred" in the third paragraph. I get so close to deadline that I can't check my copy, and there are a hundred infelicities in my sentences. But sometimes it seems to me the corrections are a little heavy-handed. You can always say to some guy, "Well, to me that doesn't sound right. I don't think it can be read aloud, and it's just not the human voice."

Do you read your pieces aloud?

No, but they ought to be read aloud. To some extent, my rhythms aren't that good anymore, if they ever were that good. They're in my head. They sound like my conversation, though my conversations are unlike anybody else's. When I was doing books, and editors would make suggestions, I would say, "Try reading that aloud." And sometimes when I've had fights with editors, and they've suggested some word, once or twice I've said to them, "Try my word and try your word, both aloud, and then we'll think of a third word which *can* be read aloud." And they would read it and say, "That's not right." Your ear does say something to you when you're singing off key. Whether rhythms are instinct or habit, I think it's very good to try reading everything aloud, though I haven't done it very often.

I did radio for a while. I had to read my stuff aloud, and I was shocked at how much of my copy could not be read aloud without amending it. So if there is a crisis about a sentence, and it bothers you, you try reading it aloud; and whatever gaucherie there is in that sentence will leap out at you. I write like those horses who used to pull the milk wagon. I just walk at the same pace, arrive, unfortunately, at the same word, and just go on. At least it's an even pace. But when you're young and finding your way, it's a very good idea to read your pieces aloud.

You have a distinctive writing voice; are you conscious of it when you're revising? Is the test whether it sounds like you?

No, it doesn't sound like what I like to hear. Russell Baker doesn't sound like me; he sounds a lot better. I don't aim at sounding like me. You just go with all the equipment you have. John Crosby wrote this sentence about Bill Stern, the radio announcer (I knew exactly what he meant, but I don't know exactly how to define what he meant): "Bill Stern is a master of all trades, and a jack of none." And I think, to some extent, I'm that way.

Are you an avid newspaper reader?

As I get older, I read the front part of the paper less and less. I just read the local news and the sports pages. You could send me to cover a St. John's game, although some editor would have to spell the names for me, and I could do jazz. Older reporters have found their way by now. The only thing I have against older reporters is that they read too much political science and not enough novels.

Do you think the special requirements of reporting and newswriting get in the way of understanding people?

The problems in this business don't have to do with writing but with attitudes. I learned that when I was covering the Deep South during the Fifties. First, guys would say to some sheriff, "I'm down here to tell your side of the story; that's all I want to do." Of course, then they cut him up the back, which was fine except that you might have to see the guy again. I didn't want that sheriff saying, "You lied to me." I'd say to him, "Look, don't trust me one little bit. I'll look at you with an open mind, but I'm very prejudiced. My mind will close, and I'm not going to be fair to you." And I discovered that they were fine that way. And I'd say to them, "Don't say anything to me you wouldn't want quoted, because you'll do something perfectly terrible in about two months, and I'll have to come down here and cover you again, and I'm not going to have you say I lied to you." I have a second rule: If I ever got to hate a guy too much, if I began to feel from my own definition that I bore him malice, I would simply stop writing about him. Now you can't do that if you're a reporter and they assign you to do it, but if you're a columnist, you can lay off a guy.

You're a nice fellow.

Everybody says I've mellowed, and most people find me much too pleasant in terms of being an effective writer. I write four times a week, and I'll go on writing four times a week until I'm fired or die.

I don't find you too pleasant in some of the prize pieces, particularly the one about the woman who burned to death while the cops ate breakfast.

If you're going to get mad, feel mad and then write; don't sit down and work yourself up into a lather. You really have to care. I used to manufacture rage a lot, but now there's enough to make you mad. You don't whip yourself up into a "fancy prancy," because then you're an actor, and you won't be on the stage very long.

In the Red Smith Lecture in Journalism at Notre Dame, you warned against letting an idea get in the way of the real; is that notion analogous to keeping manufactured emotions from getting in the way of real ones?

Remember T.S. Eliot's line about Henry James' having a mind that was never violated by an idea? I agree with that very much. When I first read that sentence, I thought he meant something entirely different; he doesn't mean that at all.

Can you give me an example, a journalist perhaps?

I'm fond of Bill Buckley. I thought he wrote a perfectly wonderful column, and I used to put it down to something that made him different from most conservative columnists and different from most ideological columnists. He had his television show, and that meant he knew the people he was talking about. He had seen the faces of these people, and he was off that "treadmill of abstraction" Henry James used to speak of. In *The Awkward Age,* James says, "I am very fond of the character of Mrs. Brook because it is one I think I could stand cross-examination on." As he paraded felons, ranging from Eldridge Cleaver to Howard Hunt on that TV program, Buckley was able to stand cross-examination. So he would not say that all Black Panthers are alike, or talk about these faceless people, for example, "the Republican Party in Mississippi" or "Democrats on the west side of Manhattan." You end up talking about individuals.

Can you apply that principle to newspapers as well as to columnists?

The New York Times is a blanket of abstraction, with its gospel of public service. *The Washington Post* is much livelier; Ben Bradlee makes it a wonderful paper.

Let's return to what you said about anger. How do you control anger in your writing?

When you're young and middle-aged, you have adolescent children, which is a difficult enough burden to bear; and you have various other things. You tend sometimes to take it out on the typewriter. Now that I'm 63 years old and suitably bankrupt and have very few aspirations, I don't have much of that rage left to displace. If you keep your interests up, you get pleasure, and you get affronted. The thing I admired so much about Red Smith's last years was the extraordinary power he had both to enjoy himself and to take offense, when it was proper to take offense. It's not a question of whipping people up. Sometimes you can improve people's behavior, and sometimes you can do pieces which will actually help somebody who is in trouble. And when you have the chance to do those, you should do them. I think there should be two Pulitzer Prizes, one for someone who put a scoundrel in jail, and another equal one for someone who got another scoundrel out of jail.

If rage cools with age, how do you keep your edge honed?

I think you keep your edge by staying interested. This is a delightful life, you know. One night a long time ago, Bob Alden and I were sitting up outside Rockefeller's house in Albany, waiting for some ridiculously forgotten fiscal crisis to be resolved. It was cold, and we had a drink or two to keep warm. It was pretty miserable, and Bob said, "You know, this is no craft at all, but it's a wonderful job." It *is* a wonderful job, and there is no reason why you should ever get bored, providing you get decent assignments.

Let's talk about what Roy Peter Clark and I call "Climate Control," about what makes a newsroom a rewarding place to work. What's the best newsroom you every worked in?

The one I work in now is great. As Lord Chesterfield said to his son, "You take your tone from your company." I never worked in a bad one, though the old *New York Post* was the worst.

How was the best atmosphere created? What made it work?

Collegiality in any job is tremendously important, but I have few complaints about newspaper collegiality. Most guys were nice and pleasant people. I loved the old *World-Telegram* city room; the guys who worked there were just absolutely wonderful guys. I never worked on a newspaper where I felt I was being told what to write.

How about Rupert Murdoch?

I would have worked with Rupert Murdoch until the day I died, except there were two problems. First, running into politicians who thought Murdoch had treated them unfairly, and being embarrassed for not being able to say how often I agreed with them. Second, he was paying me an awful lot by his standards, and I suddenly realized that he could get ten Emmett Tyrrells from a syndicate for what he was paying me, and that someday he would drop me. But I enjoyed that city room. There was an awfulness about it, a kind of irresponsibility, an amazing craziness. Murdoch was such a crazy and such a throwback. He does prowl the city room as if he were looking for someone to fire. But if you get a big story, and Murdoch comes in to run the paper that night, the man is a journalist. I used to write late, and he came in with some idea for a front page editorial that was really hysterically funny, and

I said to him, "You know, when you became a tycoon, the world lost a great assistant managing editor." He smiled. But many who own newspapers are not journalists.

What makes a good editor?

A good editor is "with the paper." The important thing is that people will work for the rottenest bastard on earth if they feel he really is with the paper, and they really will like him. I don't want to work for an intimate managing editor. People should not be friends with their publishers. There are two types of people in the world, those who own property and those who work for a living. And they have nothing in common except the necessity to display good manners; otherwise they cannot be friends. The idea that you can be intimate with someone who is telling you what to do is a very big mistake. I used the word "sir" until I was forty, but now we have this fake democracy. All this first name basis is disgraceful. If you returned any institution in America to old-fashioned manners, it would be more pleasant.

Don't good manners get in the way of effective interviewing? How can you keep a proper distance and still get in close?

I'm not very good at intimacy. Sometimes a guy will give you something that way, but I'm sort of stuck with keeping that distance. As I said earlier, I'm the world's worst interviewer because I tend to make speeches. But I always observed certain rules. I always wore a tie and a jacket. If you're covering a Teamsters convention, it would be a little embarrassing for someone to take you for one of those hoodlums. I always try to look a little different from the people I'm covering. It's very self-conscious. I think the locals and the common man have a very good sense of what constitutes good manners. I always try to be a little bit formal. I do think our profession is an invasion of privacy, and I don't like to do it, but if you say, "I'm invading your privacy," people sometimes respond.

In general, do you think the press can be accurate and fair?

You read something in the newspaper about someone you know, and it seems all awry. And eventually you tell your friends, "If you get a call from a reporter, don't talk to him." The last few times I've talked to reporters, I've had what I said ripped out of context. But you can't blame the guy. You'll say something slightly complicated, and he has to do you in 200 words. Norman Mailer used to say, "Never say anything to a reporter that takes more than 30 words." He's right. Or the desk will do something. If an Associated Press man writes a story, he has to get everything into the first paragraph, because even though he might write 50 paragraphs, some editor in Fort Wayne is going to cut it off in the second paragraph anyway.

Do you have a reader in mind when you write?

No, I've never known who reads me, and it's not a good idea to get the imaginary notion that too many people do. I don't think I do have a reader in mind.

Perhaps you make one up?

Perhaps some lovely girl. I don't know who I write for; I have no particular reader in mind. Well, I do have one reader in mind, and that's a reader who may know something about what I'm writing about. I'm very careful about him. I don't want somebody to say, "That son of a bitch doesn't know what to think, doesn't know what he's writing about." He may think I'm unfair, and he may think I'm a million things, but I don't want him to know I'm faking it.

Any other imaginary readers?

I can think of another reader, one I don't suppose I'll ever reach, a rare creature, maybe beyond me. I remember when I was a kid, reading a piece Westbrook Pegler wrote about a fight between Jack Sharkey and Tommy Loughran. I'll remember that piece until I die, and I think there is somebody young that you're talking to.

You've got to remember that this is a very transient business. At my lowest point during the day, I think I could be run over by a truck, and this would be my last piece that was ever printed, and I really wouldn't want it to look too bad under those circumstances. A newspaper lies around, and it may be left on the subway. Who knows whether some Theodore Dreiser of the future might not pick it up, and you wouldn't want him to judge you harshly. I think you write for the future. I would like someone to read it and say, "This is someone who knows." Or if he can't say that, at least he won't say, "This is someone who is a damned fool."

Perhaps your ideal reader is yourself when you were reading that Pegler piece a long time ago.

Yes, I think probably it is. But unfortunately I don't think I come up to Peg on Sharkey, but I would not like to fall too far below him.

Do you come up to that young reader?

Yes, I think you're writing for him. I don't think you're writing for your contemporaries. You write for your juniors. Everybody likes to think that he is writing for the future, and the future is the young. So you just do the best you can. I think that is the ideal reader: a lovely young woman who is torn between being a mother or a nun, or a novelist, but hasn't quite made up her mind. And that's what I'm writing for.

Thank you, sir.

Thank you.

Richard Aregood
Editorial Writing

RICHARD AREGOOD, 42, joined the *Philadelphia Daily News* as a reporter in 1966. He was features editor, deputy sports editor, news editor and day city editor before joining the editorial page staff 11 years ago. He has been editor of the editorial pages for six years. A graduate of Rutgers University, Aregood worked at the *Burlington County* (N.J.) *Times* and the *Mount Holly* (N.J.) *Herald*. Aregood's clear and punchy style have earned him numerous awards, including the 1985 Pulitzer Prize for editorial writing.

Just in time

MARCH 2, 1984

Just in time for the election campaign and, not coincidentally, just in time to conceal the many mistakes made by the Reagan administration under a veil of public piety, the drums are starting to beat again for a school prayer amendment.

This time they're really serious. The witnesses before a group of congressmen this week were the true religious and cultural leaders of our nation.

Football coaches.

The congressmen were not likely to differ with the idea of forced prayer in the public schools either. All were House members who have already announced their support of a prayer amendment to the Constitution. And the whole exercise was choreographed by the House Republican Study Committee.

As usual, the argument is with things that don't exist. The Supreme Court never banned prayer from the schools. It banned officially-sanctioned group prayer.

And predictably, the witnesses at the congressional pep rally took on the same old villains.

Washington Redskin coach Joe Gibbs said, "Marxist doctrine and pornographic presentation are allowed in our society as freedom of speech, yet we deny to our youth in schools the freedom to make any statement to and on behalf of God."

That all sounds very convincing—at least until you think about what the court actually said. The court banned government-organized school prayer, not prayer itself. It only said the government had no business promoting anyone's religious beliefs.

To anyone's knowledge, the government isn't sponsoring or organizing pro-Marxist rallies or pornographic film festivals in the schools either. As a matter of fact, Coach Gibbs is not barred from asking the Almighty to help him smite the Seattle Seahawks or anything else he wants to ask.

Nor have they particularly hampered Tom Landry, coach of the Dallas Cowboys, who said "The Supreme Court, in my opinion, took God out of every part of our life except church." That's simply not true. Coach Landry, a religious man, no doubt carries his beliefs with him everywhere. No one can take them away and no one has tried.

The only thing that has been taken away is the right of any group to force children to be indoctrinated in a religious faith in the classroom. There are churches for that; there are parents for that. It is not un-Christian or un-American or un-anything to render religion unto parents and churches.

Today, the Senate begins debate on the school prayer amendment. It will be full of the same kind of rhetoric, including the accusations that anyone who opposes forced public prayer in the school is some kind of communist pornographer who probably believes in evolution.

It's no such thing. It's a question of people's right to be left alone. It's a question of the guarantees in the United States Constitution. It's more important than a re-election campaign or any religious sect's desire to force its beliefs on other people's children.

In fact, there is one very convincing witness on the question of public prayer, even of the unforced variety. Even the school prayer advocates might want to hear the words of Jesus Christ on the question of whether a believer's dialogue with God is better if it's ritualistically public. In the words of the King James Bible (Matthew 6:6):

But thou, when thou prayest, enter into thy closet, and when thou hast shut thy door, pray to the Father which is in secret; and thy Father which seeth in secret shall reward thee openly.

That about closes the argument, doesn't it?

Observations and questions

1) Richard Aregood saves this editorial's major players, "Football coaches," until the third paragraph, which consists of one incomplete sentence of two words. What effects does he achieve by this delay and emphasis?

2) Aregood tells us the relevant point of law in paragraph five ("As usual..."), repeats it in another form in paragraph eight ("That all sounds..."), and restates it in the first sentence of paragraph 11 ("The only thing..."). What does he gain and lose from this repetition with variation? Would putting all the constitutional points in one paragraph improve his argument?

3) The structure of this piece alternates short quotations from coaches with longer refutations from the author. Is the reader likely to perceive this imbalance as unfair? Must editorials observe fairness standards?

4) The author ironically describes football coaches as "the true religious and cultural leaders of our nation." Does such irony run the risk of confusing or offending the reader? How does Aregood control his reader's response to ironic statements?

5) In the 12th paragraph ("Today..."), Aregood's irony turns to sarcasm: "It will be full of the same kind of rhetoric, including the accusations that anyone who opposes forced public prayer in the school is some kind of communist pornographer who probably believes in evolution." Is sarcasm even riskier than irony, and how can writers control its effects?

6) Aregood responds to Coach Gibbs's charge by stating what the reader might have just thought: "That all sounds very convincing." Does the writer gain authority by apparently reading the reader's mind?

7) The 13th paragraph ("It's no such thing.") begins each of its sentences with the contraction "It's." Why does the author use this weak construction instead of powerful graphic verbs? What effect does he gain from the parallel repetition?

8) Aregood quotes Jesus Christ as an authority on prayer and concludes: "That about closes the argument, doesn't it?" Does the biblical quotation really settle the intellectual issue or does it merely provide a satisfactory rhetorical ending? Does the kicker have to form part of the logical argument?

The Reverend Moon

MAY 17, 1984

The law is simple: Church funds used for church purposes are tax exempt; funds that belong to individuals or which are generated by non-church business are not.

A jury decided that the Rev. Sun Myung Moon's personal fortune belonged in the latter category and sentenced him to 18 months for tax fraud.

Some American churchmen took his side in an appeal to the U.S. Supreme Court, asserting that making the reverend gentleman pay taxes on $162,000 in personal income and tossing him in the clink for fraudulent non-payment amounted to an infringement of his religious freedom. His followers, after saying the prosecution was based on religious and racial prejudice, claimed that because Moon claims to be the Messiah, his personal funds and those of the church are indistinguishable.

Humbug. Moon got off easy.

Nowhere does the law say that folks who claim to be the Son of God are exempt from taxation, even if they have heavy bills for therapy. Nowhere does it say that claiming to be a church means that secular income is exempt.

Moon's enterprises include grocery stores, newspapers, munitions manufacturing, importing, fishing fleets and the now-routine "Moonies" peddling flowers on street corners. It is hard to understand how a legitimate connection can be made between religion and any of them.

Moon's businesses compete with those of people who don't claim to be deities and therefore pay their taxes. Moon's businesses compete with others who actually have to pay their workers instead of frequently setting glazed-eyed children to work for nearly nothing. Moon's businesses are worth an estimated $100 million.

The courts dealt with none of that, though. After all, some pretty screwy things have been part of theologies through history. They dealt only with the issue of large chunks of income that Moon didn't report on his tax return. A jury found that Moon had the unreported, taxable funds in his name, controlled them and used them for personal expenses.

That was that. And it should be. Whatever else is involved, the basic question is still a simple one. Moon violated criminal law by failing to render unto Caesar. He'll be paying the price, just like anyone else would.

Observations and questions

1) Richard Aregood reassures readers throughout this piece that things are simple, and he simplifies complex issues for them. Yet readers know the inherent complexity of any issue of Church and State. Is the author educating the reader by highlighting basic issues? Or does he write this way to invite debate? Or both?

2) The author gives no background on the Reverend Moon, not even naming the organization he heads. Does every editorial need some explanatory material or even a background paragraph somewhere close to the beginning? Or can the writer assume that the reader knows enough about famous public figures already?

3) Aregood opens his editorial with a clear statement of the relevant distinction in the law, and restates it in a biblical allusion in his final paragraph. Discuss how this framing unifies his argument and how it helps the reader.

4) The third paragraph ("Some American...") sets forth complex arguments by Moon's defenders, expressed in long and complex sentences. Aregood answers: "Humbug. Moon got off easy." Discuss the rhetorical effect of this contrast. Think about simplicity versus complexity, tone achieved by slang, typographic emphasis, and rhythm.

5) Aregood begins paragraph five like this: "Nowhere does the law say that folks who claim to be the Son of God are exempt from taxation, even if they have heavy bills for therapy." What idea does that last clause induce in the readers' minds?

6) Paragraphs six and seven list Reverend Moon's enterprises, concluding with the sentence: "Moon's businesses are worth an estimated $100 million." What effects would result from moving that sentence to the top of the list? Should this list appear higher in the editorial?

7) In the eighth paragraph ("The courts..."), Aregood quips that "some pretty screwy things have been part of theologies through history." Why doesn't he give the reader some examples?

8) Aregood closes his editorial with a pun: "He'll be paying the price, just like anyone else would." What is the point of this editorial, and how does that pun advance that point?

Justifications

JUNE 26, 1984

Every once in a while, the Justice Department's Office of Special Investigations pounces on somebody who's accused of taking part in the Nazi slaughter of civilians in World War II. Invariably, they are people who lied about their backgrounds in order to enter this country.

Just as invariably, defenders appear, citing excuses.

The excuses are almost as frightening as what the former Nazis are accused of doing.

He was only following orders.

This doozy was disposed of at the Nuremberg trials of the highest-ranking Nazis. If you follow it logically, only Adolf Hitler would have been liable for any of the hundreds of thousands of atrocities committed in his name. He was, after all, the man at the top.

Accepting this argument means accepting that no one has responsibility for his own actions—even murder—as long as someone told him to do it. That's absurd and oddly childish. Children don't get away with the "Johnny told me to do it" defense; why should murderous adults?

He's an old man. Why don't they just leave him alone?

That one's even crazier. People who evade justice for a generation should be allowed to get away with murder because they manage to keep from getting caught? If those same people had not slithered out of Europe at the end of the war, they would have been punished then. Their reward for hiding out is that justice has been deferred. They cannot be allowed to get away with crimes altogether merely because they've cheated justice for this long.

The Soviet Union has fixed the evidence.

Has anyone ever figured any kind of reason why the Russians or their KGB would bother to chase down innocent old immigrants to the United States? No matter what one thinks of the Soviets, they generally have a reason for what they do. Their documentation generally agrees with that of the Germans anyway.

He did it because he was anti-Russian.

Just how does being anti-Russian require a person to murder his neighbors? Just how does slaughtering Jews help to fight Russia, which has a history of anti-Jewish violence itself? Does being anti-Russian require doing the most horrible things the Nazis wanted done, merely because they were fighting the Russians at the time?

The fact is that there is no excuse for crimes against humanity, for the slaughter of innocents at the behest of a gang of evil thugs. These old men that the OSI has found and proven to have lied about their wartime activities to enter this country deserve no sympathy.

They're killers, and they don't belong here. Deportation is too good for them, but it's the best the United States can do now.

Observations and questions

1) In an interview later in this volume, Aregood tells us that the objections quoted in this editorial generally come from the large Ukrainian community in Philadelphia. Why does he not mention this specific part of his audience in the piece? Are the issues too universal to single out a particular group of readers?

2) Most of Aregood's editorials focus on specific actions and persons. Why does this editorial give no examples of accused Nazis or describe a few atrocities? Would it become more effective with a specific case in the lead?

3) The structure of this piece turns on simple excuses simply stated, alternating with complex rebuttals from the author. Does this technique give the other side its intellectual due? Why are the excuses so conversational in tone? How does Aregood avoid abstraction in his answers?

4) Paragraph 10 ("Has anyone...") seems rather vague in comparison with the other refutations. Does the editorial sag in the middle? How can writers keep reader interest up during slower points in a series of arguments?

5) Paragraph 12 ("Just how does...") offers three complicated questions in rebuttal. Are these rhetorical questions effective? Does using three such questions in one paragraph magnify or diminish their effect?

6) Aregood tries to answer sympathetic objections to the arrest and deportation of discovered war criminals. In his penultimate paragraph, he

says that such "old men...deserve no sympathy." Would he have improved the emotional climate of his piece by admitting a little bit of sympathy? Would he have undercut its power?

7) What action, if any, does the final sentence of the editorial call for? Does the final word "now" suggest the need for new legislation, perhaps harsh penalties and treatment for ex-Nazis?

We must be crazy

JULY 23, 1984

We must indeed be crazy.

We Americans have sat by for years taking casualties because some people like to fire off guns and don't want to put up with any hassle when they buy them.

We're not alone in the world for lunacy—the Germans get downright surly whenever anyone threatens their sacred right to drive at 130 miles per hour on the autobahn. But we stand pretty much alone in pretending that our country is still some kind of frontier where a citizen needs a few pieces in his home in case of surprise attack.

James Oliver Huberty is not unique. But he is an excellent example of why gun laws must be tightened. He was a surly, resentful man who hated almost everyone. Both he and his wife had a history of waving firearms at people with whom they had had minor squabbles.

Why Huberty—or anyone—should have a legitimate need for an Uzi assault rifle is something nobody can justify, although the gun nuts will try. Why Huberty—or anyone—should have armor-piercing ammunition is equally unjustifiable.

But he did. And he also had the 12-gauge shotgun and 9mm pistol with which he walked into a California McDonald's restaurant last week. With them, he killed 20 people and wounded 19 before a policeman put a well-deserved rifle bullet through his chest. Pity he didn't suffer.

How many surly sociopaths are there out there thumbing through *Soldier of Fortune* magazine and fondling their Uzis? How many kids can buy a handgun on the street about as easily as they can buy a hot dog? Doesn't that frighten you?

In their own defense, the gun lovers will tell you that the Constitution allows them their deadly pleasures, although they customarily leave out the part about a "well-regulated militia." That means organizations like the National Guard, although the gun lovers will tell you all of them automatically qualify.

They will say that cars also kill people, forgetting that you need a driver's license and auto registration to buy and operate a car. They will say that kitchen knives can also kill, although they choose not to talk about how one could go about slaughtering an entire McDonald's with a kitchen knife.

They will also say that they like to collect weapons, as if that were some kind of constitutionally protected pleasure. It doesn't matter to them that burglars just love to rob gun collectors and peddle their swag to any criminal who will buy them. Would the country be as understanding of some nut who liked to collect various strains of anthrax?

The defenses are so much bull----.

What legitimate purpose is served for hunters or target shooters by assault rifles, machine guns and heavy handguns that aren't accurate enough to shoot at target distances? Those weapons are good only for killing people or playing soldier. And what legitimate purposes are served by permitting anyone, even a whacked-out head case like Huberty, to walk in and buy any kind of deadly weapon he pleases?

Sixty Americans die every day—*every day*—in this country from handguns. Is it worth it?

There is no good reason why this country cannot ban the sale of military weapons to civilians. There is no good reason why handgun sales cannot be severely limited to target shooters and those with other good reasons to own them and their resale tightly regulated. There is no good reason why the majority of people in this country who favor controls have to be cowed by the minority that likes to play with guns.

There is only one reason, in fact, that makes any sense.

We must be nuts.

Observations and questions

1) Aregood labels virtually everyone as insane: Germans, gun collectors, James Oliver Huberty, "we." Discuss the virtues and hazards of this kind of overstatement.

2) James Oliver Huberty first appears at the beginning of the fourth paragraph, and we learn about his connection with the McDonald's killings two paragraphs later. Would you be tempted to remind the reader of the news peg in some greater detail a little earlier in the piece?

3) Paragraph six ends: "...a policeman put a well-deserved rifle bullet through his chest. Pity he didn't suffer." Although Aregood seems to touch the limits of editorial toughness here, notice the restraint of the paragraph, especially the verbs.

4) Aregood uses highly-charged phrases: "gun nuts," "peddle their swag," "whacked-out head case," "surly sociopaths." Would you call such phrases colorful or overwritten?

5) Explicate the punctuation of this sentence: "The defenses are so much bull----."

6) Beginning with paragraph eight ("In their own defense..."), Aregood quotes the counter-arguments of the gun lobby. Discuss the language and sentence structures of this section in terms of fair presentation of opposing views.

7) Discuss the parallel structures of the sentences in the last three paragraphs. Why is this rhetorical device effective?

Standing tall

SEPTEMBER 28, 1984

As soon as the smoke cleared and the dead and wounded were taken away after the tragic explosion at the U.S. Embassy in Beirut, the president explained what we should do about it.

We should stand tall, he said.

He did not say how it helped to merely stand tall and do nothing else, especially since the blast was the third of its kind to victimize Americans in Lebanon.

Then the president explained why security forces at the embassy were unable to stop the truck that carried the explosives and why work was not complete on tighter security.

He compared it with the delays people often experience in kitchen renovation projects.

He did not point out that, as president of the United States, he bears the responsibility for not pushing to get the embassy job done. He does, after all, have a lot more control over federal employees than the average homeowner has over a contractor who's putting in a new sink.

Yesterday, the president explained how all this could happen.

He blamed it on the "near-destruction" of the Central Intelligence Agency he claims happened in recent years—before he took over. The strong implication was that the disaster was yet another thing that Ronald Reagan could blame on Jimmy Carter.

Today he blamed the reporters who heard his speech for having gotten that impression. He said they distorted what he said, although there are tapes that show otherwise.

He did not say what spies had to do with the explosion, especially since the problem seems to be one of inability even to keep pickup trucks away from our buildings, not one of inability to infiltrate groups of homicidal lunatics. Besides, hasn't Reagan been president for the past 3½ years and had enough time to fix things, if he had been so inclined?

In the meantime, the secretary of defense seemed to shrug off the whole truck-bomb problem, saying that if the mad bombers didn't use pickup trucks, they'd use helicopters. The secretary did not remark on how much easier it is to find and buy pickup trucks and train crazy Iranians to drive them.

It's a waste of time to expect this president to develop a cogent strategy for Lebanon—or a reason to be there, for that matter. And it's a bigger waste of time to expect him to break the habit of blaming Jimmy Carter for everything. Even loyal Republicans can't hold out much hope that they can stop Reagan from saying dumb things in public. Besides, the public seems to like the dumb things he says.

But there are things that can be done to protect our diplomats and soldiers, and Reagan has run out of excuses for not doing them. Visitors to embassies in dangerous places can bloody well walk a few hundred yards to get to them. Put up some solid walls and keep all vehicles out. That won't take long and it will solve at least the truck-bomb problem. The president could have that done today if he has the will and the guts to order it done.

Otherwise, he'll still be standing tall while helpless Americans abroad are too busy keeping their heads down to stand at all.

Observations and questions

1)   At what point does the lead in this editorial end? Does the reader benefit from clearly demarcated sections in an editorial?

2)   The first half of this editorial reports a series of statements about the Lebanon bombing. Study the verbs used to attribute and introduce the statements ("said," "explained," etc.) How does Aregood capture the repetitious nature of the actions without sounding monotonous?

3)   Paragraph seven ("Yesterday...") contains the news peg of this editorial. Should the author give us more detail about the context of Reagan's explanation?

4)   In paragraph eight, the author says, "He blamed it on the 'near-destruction' of the Central Intelligence Agency he claims happened in recent years—before he took over." Why does Aregood use a dash instead of a comma in that sentence? Do dashes call for a longer pause than commas? Does the phrasing cast doubt on Reagan's assertion?

5)   In paragraph 12 ("It's a waste of time..."), Aregood observes that the president keeps "saying dumb things in public" and that "the public seems to like the dumb things he says." Discuss how Aregood uses a light tone and simple wording for this serious pair of charges.

6)   The penultimate paragraph lists actions the president should take. Does the author expect any of these things to happen? Why suggest actions that will not take place?

7) Despite the simple wording, the ending creates a graphic picture based on two metaphors. Does the reader really picture the two stances described? Should the author embroider the descriptions to make the metaphors more graphic?

8) Make a photocopy of this editorial and mark out every word you think could be deleted without diluting the power of the writing.

We reprint here two of Richard Aregood's earlier editorials: "Yes, the Chair" (November 21, 1975) and "The British" (May 7, 1981), both from the Philadelphia Daily News. These pieces, frequently referred to in the interview and the observations and questions, illustrate the author's least compromising work. Aregood says they exemplify his paper's continuing stances for the death penalty and the Irish Republic. Neither the paper nor Aregood duck what they see as a basic issue for public discussion: Real people die because of their own and other people's decisions.

Yes, the chair

NOVEMBER 21, 1975

It's about time for Leonard Edwards to take the Hot Squat.

Edwards, for those who haven't been following his worthless career, has been convicted of two murders. He's awaiting trial on another murder and the rape of a 14-year-old girl.

He's 29 years old. Hope of rehabilitating this piece of human crud is doubtful. It's even wildly optimistic to use the word doubtful.

The last time Edwards was freed, it was on bail pending appeal of an overly generous third-degree murder conviction. He had just stabbed somebody to death and justice, in all its majesty, had found him guilty.

Edwards then went out and killed somebody else.

His second murder jury was right. He's not worth the upkeep.

Fry him.

The British

MAY 7, 1981

In the 12th century, the British first moved into Ireland with troops, so that they might protect themselves militarily.

The British, after all, are a strategic people.

By the 14th century, a batch of laws had been passed by the British that clearly showed that they thought the Irish were an inferior people with whom they should not mingle.

The British are a proud people.

And then there came to be Protestants, once Henry VIII decided he wanted his own church. That gave an excuse to actually slaughter Irishmen and women because England had to protect herself against the Catholic powers.

The British are a practical people.

The call came for the most rigid of Calvinists to go forth into Northern Ireland so as to take land away from the native Irish and give it to the recently arrived Protestants. It rewarded the Brits who had helped put down the Irish by turning over their country as spoils of war.

The British are appreciative of services rendered.

Oliver Cromwell then presided over what one might call "the final solution of the Irish problem," slaughtering thousands of people, persuaded that "this is a righteous judgment of God upon these barbarous wretches."

The British are always righteous.

After King William of Orange crushed the last Irish military resistance in 1689, the real work began. England passed tough "penal laws" for the Irish alone. Even though they owned little of their own land and were no threat to Mother England, it was thought necessary to make it clear to the Irish that they were second-class citizens.

The British go first class.

George III, who might be remembered from our own American revolution, referred to the Irish people as "human cockroaches."

The British have a way with words, even if their politeness is overrated.

Rebellion followed rebellion. England put them down brutally. In the 1798 rebellion, led by Protestant Irish nationalist Wolfe Tone, the British are estimated to have taken the lives of 30,000 rebels.

The British are not squeamish.

All along, England was not averse to using the Irish for the things they'd rather not do. By the time of World War I, it was high art. Some 60,000 Irish soldiers died in that war.

The British value human life. They merely put a discounted value on Irish life.

Came the 1916 Easter Rising, and Ireland declared a republic. The British shot everyone they could, including James Connolly, who had been wounded and could not stand. The British shot him to death in his chair. Not until 1936, after a long and nasty struggle, would Ireland's southern part become a republic. The British kept their implanted Protestants, who by now had a vested interest in keeping things the way they were, in power in the North.

The British keep a commitment, no matter how stupid.

And the troubles continue. Bobby Sands, like Terence McSwiney had in 1921, starved himself to make his point about freedom. Margaret Thatcher, the prime minister, said she couldn't give in to any of the demands of Irish political prisoners. So Sands died. And Maggie hadn't yielded.

The British are a principled people.

They are also a remarkable people, the only ones on earth to have consistently conducted themselves as brutal fools for eight centuries. The blood of generations is on their hands. And they show not a sign of having learned a damn thing.

A conversation with
Richard Aregood

FRY: How did you get to where you are now?

AREGOOD: I started with the Mount Holly *Herald,* worked for the Fort Dix-McGuire *Mirror* and the *Burlington County Times,* and came to the *Philadelphia Daily News* in 1966 as a police reporter. I feel really fortunate to have been a police reporter in the middle and late Sixties during Frank Rizzo's reign; I've seen all this outrageous stuff. Then I came inside as a rewrite man, assistant city editor, day city editor, features editor, and rock critic. Then I did films, but sitting down at ten o'clock with some bad coffee and watching a grainy Swedish sex film is not my idea of a good time. Then the copy desk and the editorial page, and a stint as deputy sports editor; but I've never been a photographer. And in 1977 I returned to the editorial page as editor.

How would you characterize your paper?

The *Daily News* is a rather strange creature, about to become 60 years old. It started off as a bad carbon of the *New York News.* For a while, readers correctly perceived us as the "Dirty News." We were always expected to be the next newspaper to go out of business, but the others did it instead of us. It's a better newspaper now. In the old days we tried to make up with flash and filigree, and the rewrite man was king. Now we've got a pretty complete newspaper, which tries to maintain the attitude of a highly intelligent street urchin, snapping at the heels of the mighty. (Laughs.)

How did that past shape the paper and your writing?

Our past was shaped by a lack of resources, and all my predecessors were essentially rewrite men. That plus tabloid journalists writing short meant that we developed a short, crisp style. I loved Reuben Maury's work, so I kept writing that way, the way a smart-ass rewrite man would have written.

Who are your readers?

I try to avoid the bias that a lot of younger reporters come here with, better educated with theories about who the readers are. They think of our readers as ghetto blacks and rowhouse whites, each of whom hates the other. Not only is that not particularly accurate; it's also patronizing as hell, because as soon as you start thinking that way, you start writing that way.

Did your attitudes toward the readers come from the paper?

I was born in Camden, right across the river. We may be the only newspaper in the country that still takes the working class seriously. Our readers are a surprising mixture. We get terribly intelligent comebacks, really expert responses, from people you might not have assumed were that sophisticated. For example, we got a letter from a printer who supports the PLO. He's not an Arab; he just studied the issues and came to his own conclusions. We have a large number of elderly history teachers who read the paper, who will correct any misstatement involving their particular interests.

So you can write seriously for serious readers?

If I'm writing on a serious complicated subject, I will attempt to write a serious complicated editorial, without much thought as to who the readers are, beyond the fact that I always try to write simply, just because I think that's good writing.

Do different editorials have different audiences? Do some have more than one audience?

You have to decide to whom you are addressing an editorial. Some editorials have an audience of one, the mayor, for example. And some editorials aim for an elite audience, and there are some editorials for everybody.

Sometimes your audience is the target of your criticism. Do you see any problems there?

I think there is an effect, almost erosive and corrosive in some cases, where you have an obligation to be continually there, what the British call "the loyal opposition." But at the same time, you have to pace it, so you don't become a kind of Cassandra. It's the most difficult thing that I try to do.

Do you imagine a reader?

Not unless I'm envisioning a dialogue with one person, no one in particular, just a person.

Bill Blundell of *The Wall Street Journal* says he writes for an imaginary intelligent friend, who is not himself, but someone very like him.

That's not a bad guy to talk to. We're pretty well read in the bars, the union halls, and the police stations; normal people read the *Daily News*.

How do you get good ideas for editorials?

Generally I read something and get this visceral reaction to it, and assemble whatever is necessary to learn more about it. I wander around and drink coffee and talk to reporters and all that sort of thing until it takes shape, and then I sit down and write it. It's really useful to talk it out with a reporter, particularly one with expertise in the area.

Do you do worry about crossing the line between editorials and news?

No, I'm asking them what they know, not taking their opinions. If we have an editorial about the gas works, I'll ask the guy who covers the gas works; he can save me from falling into some pits I don't even know are there.

Do you do some reporting of your own?

Sometimes I do research, make a few calls, get out once in a while, but until just recently, I was the only one here.

Do most of your editorials start with visceral reactions?

A lot of them do. A good *Daily News* editorial writer needs both passion and subtlety, which may be the key to it. You're not really the guy on the barstool raging about this or that, but you're taking something that guy might see, and you're framing it the way he might like to say it if he were somewhere other than in the bar, where it doesn't much matter.

Your editorials certainly have passion!

A big thing missing in lots of editorial pages is passion; I have this feeling that many people writing about stuff don't really care about it. Some don't have the passion. The way most journalists think about the editorial page now, it's kind of a bloodless thing, even a committee thing. We assign editorials at the *Daily News,* but we try not to write by committee, because that does seem to take all the blood out of it. Although I agree with it only every other solstice, I really enjoy *The Wall Street Journal's* editorial page because it's got some passion. There's real fire in there.

Does your editorial page have a slant?

We don't consider ourselves ideologues. On some issues, we're conservatives, and on others we might be seen as raving radicals. We have done things like proposing the legalization of heroin. We're big on gay rights and feminism, but at the same time we're fiscally very responsible. On education, we're real conservatives.

How do you keep your editorial page fair?

We report for an editorial just as anybody else does. We talk to people we might be pummeling at any given time, and we maintain a basic fairness for anybody we pummel. We print a full page of guest opinion, five to six hundred words apiece. But if you think somebody's explanation is just tendentious horsecrap, I don't see any reason to include it on an opinion page. Just this week, one of our columnists took issue with our newspaper; it's that kind of newspaper.

But you point your editorials very sharply.

Why have an editorial page at all if you're not intending to say something? We try in each editorial to focus on a single point and to make our position as clear as we can. If you think some public official is a horse's ass, why say that you have certain difficulties with his performance record? You say he's a horse's ass. (Laughs.)

Talk about the "Hot Squat" piece.

If someone has done loathsome things, and you believe the death penalty is appropriate, then come right the hell out and say it. Don't say: "I think the death penalty should be imposed in this case." Just say: "Fry him." It upsets people, but these issues of life and death should make people uncomfortable, because there is really no right conclusion. And if people don't recognize how loaded these issues are, I don't think they can consider them.

But how do you keep the passion under control?

Take the piece on the British, for example. I tried to make that a very restrained kind of fury at all those hundreds of years of colonialism, mistreatment, and religious pogroms. I think you cheapen something like that if you're raging and tearing your hair. Sometimes I'll try to use rage for a comic effect, for instance, really be outraged that the world does not appreciate Ray Charles. The heavier the subject is, the more important the subject is, the more you try to harness the rage so you don't bring up irrelevant issues. If you're angry, rather than say, "I think all those mothers should hang," you go in and establish it piece by piece. Of course, with some real villains, for example, Idi Amin, you can let it all hang out.

What prompted the Reagan piece, on "Standing Tall?"

I just thought the man was so cosmically full of - - - -.

How do you control tone? Do you read your pieces aloud?

No, but I worry a lot about tone and timing. My son is the world's youngest Henny Youngman fan, and once I took him backstage to meet the comedian. My son asked him the secret of being so funny, and Youngman said: "The whole secret of this is timing, son. 'Take my wife please.' That's not funny. But 'Take my wife —2—3—4— please.' That's funny." It's as if you're writing comedy, because your timing has to snap. In some editorials, you try to build, try to roundhouse at the end. And there are others where you try to maintain the heat all the way through. Tone and timing are the secrets in any kind of writing.

Your editorials have lots of information mixed in with the passion.

I try to space the information so I don't screw up my timing and my tone of voice. I might write it all the way through and then sprinkle the data in afterwards, which is an old rewrite man trick. But I try to avoid lumping the data just to get past it.

Some writers put all the numbers in one paragraph and let the uninterested reader skip it.

The reader can skip it, and he can also run into this brick wall and not read anything else.

How do you organize your thoughts, especially when you're dealing with large amounts of information?

I have no real secrets. People tell me I practice management by walking around, but I'm just walking around. (Laughs.) The brain is a wonderful thing; it sorts things for you, particularly if you're not maintaining a hard focus on something. Lately I've been working up to an editorial on the MX missile. I've just been feeding information into my head for weeks, and I realize that just this morning, a piece is starting to take shape. Julius Erving trusts his body to do things, and I think a writer ought to trust his mind to do something. You feed it what it needs, and you let it know what you want at the other end, and it'll do a lot of the work for you. There is no point in forcing it, because it'll come out stiff. I may get to the idea that way, but it won't feel right. It's the difference between hitting a Texas Leaguer and hitting a line drive right through the box. You feel it.

That's thought. How about instinct?

Being instinctive is important. All of us have made walloping errors of judgment by using just our heads, and all of us have kicked ourselves for not listening to our bellies. If you can find issues that you really feel in your innards, then you've got something, something you can really run with. I think that really is a key.

How can you tell when feelings are real, not just cooked up because you've got a deadline roaring down on you?

You just get better at sorting it out, because you start to know when it's your head and when it's your belly. You read something in which someone has intellectualized feelings about something, and it comes off oddly masturbatory, just doesn't have a real jolt to it.

Do your ideas jell as you write, or do you have it all worked out before you write anything down?

It's all jelled when I write it down. When I start to write, I mostly just write it through, and then I go back over it a couple of times. One of my kids watched me work, and the next day a schoolmate asked, "What does your daddy do?" And she said, "He types." (Laughs.) When I get a story together, that's really what it feels like: I type.

Do you revise much?

Only when it's not pretty well formed to start with, generally on my bad days.

Do you think up the lead or the ending first? Your pieces seem neatly knitted.

I'm not aware of which comes first, but I do try to keep it as seamless as possible. In typical rewrite-man style, if the lead doesn't come to me, I hack out the rest of it and come back to it. The thing I admired most about Jimmy Cannon was the economy with which he could express something. He could absolutely devastate a topic in eight words, and the fewer words you use, the more impact you have. As things cook in my head, little things keep falling out of my fingers. I ran an editorial this Monday on the MX missile. This little riddle kept running through my mind: Do we need the MX because of the Russians, or do we need the Russians so we can have an MX? I don't know where it came from; it's just part of the process. And it's not a total editorial, but it's better at that length than it would be if I elaborated on it.

Do you write long and cut back, or write to length first?

I'm an old rewrite man, so I write to length; it's almost instinctive now. Longer pieces are very difficult for me, and I have to force myself beyond my habit patterns. I've been at a tabloid for 19 years now, and I've been writing editorials for much of that time. Generally, even the full-length editorials we do, like "The British," are not that long, not like a *Philadelphia Inquirer* mega-editorial. And I guess I've just accepted that discipline, and I write to that length.

Your editorials have a wonderful sense of authority, which I attribute mostly to clari-

ty of thought and wording. These pieces seem carefully polished to eliminate complication, and your key sentences tend to be very simple.**

The more complicated you make a sentence, the more likely you are to confuse not only the reader, but also yourself. When I find myself raging forward, with commas and various other connectors and that sort of thing, I generally know that at the end I'm going to have a real crap sentence. And I'm going to have trouble understanding it when I reread it, and I'll have to go back to Kathleen Shea, who edits my copy, and say, "Please, Kathleen, fix it for me." (Laughs.) It baffles me as much as it would a reader.

I like your technique of giving the opposing position in a complex sentence and then smashing it with something simple, like "Hogwash!"

(Laughs.) I do try to give the poor bastard his due, but I also try to kick him while I'm at it.

In the piece on war criminals, you invert the technique, giving the simple statements to the opposition and the longer refutations to yourself.

Philadelphia has a great number of Ukrainians, and every time the Justice Department digs out some doddering old Nazi, the Ukrainians bring up all these general objections, and they are very simple ones. It would be really unfair to them to distort their objections through technique, because their objections are basically something like this: "These are poor old men, and we were fighting Communists," etc. Even though I might consider them dead wrong, they certainly are clear; and if I complicate them just for the sake of making myself look good, I'm really doing something awful to those people.

Do you mix long and short sentences for rhythmic effect?

Every once in a while, if I think a concept is hogwash, I just bring it up real short, in such a way as to say, "Well, you've heard from him, and now here's what we think: Hogwash."

You use a lot of irony and some sarcasm; don't you run the risk of being misunderstood?

I feel very comfortable with irony, and I think most people understand it better than one might imagine. There are people out there who will misunderstand a simple declarative sentence; you can't do anything about that. Then there are some things that have to be expressed in an ironic tone, and I don't know how you would pick out which ones ahead of time. The *Columbia Journalism Review* gave me a dart on the "Hot Squat" piece, and I was very proud of that. (Laughs.) Another magazine did an editorial on that piece and said I was a bit arch; they were probably right. I try to space it now, but then I was kind of a smart-ass kid.

But you still run the risk of being misunderstood. For example, some people might think you added the last paragraph to "The British" just to make sure no one missed the irony.

No, I didn't. That's part of not patronizing. I'm assuming that the people who read the *Daily News* can read, although legend has it that we have this totally unsophisticated audience with little pinheads. It's really not true. These are intelligent people, and they care about an issue. I got a lot of response to that British editorial from Irish saloons, from normal people. They got the point. I don't see the need to underline anything, because when you start doing that, you're leading people by the nose. You're telling them that you think they're fools, and they know it. A lot of writers make the mistake of assuming they're a lot smarter than the people they're writing for.

How about sarcasm, the nasty side of irony?

Sarcasm should be used in a very limited way, because sometimes the bitterness of it can become the issue rather than the issue you're talking about. If you use George Carlin's seven words in the newspaper, 20 percent of the readers see those words and don't see anything else. Sarcasm really screws up your tone; if you're going to use it, it had better be at the end, because it's hard to get your pace back. Sarcasm turns people off almost as much as being patronized.

Understatement, which is a form of irony, seems to be one of your favorite techniques. Why do you think we find so little of it on other people's editorial pages?

That's part of the great editorial writer's disease, assuming that readers have to have everything explained to them, to the point that you create this kind of turgid stew that even the most determined advocate of a position has to chop through with an axe just to find out where you're standing. It's not just patronizing; it's also ineffective.

Your prose is very spare; you follow Hemingway's advice not to tell the reader too much.

When I teach a journalism course at Rutgers, I bring in pieces by Donald Barthelme because he writes a spare, sometimes elliptical, but clear kind of prose.

Do you think readers take offense at the sharpness of your editorials?

I think editorials should say something, but most newspapers don't seem to grasp that simple statement: that they should really say something, that it almost doesn't matter what your position is. I can see the craft in *Wall Street Journal* editorials, though I don't agree with any of it. We have a lot of readers, loyal readers, who violently disagree with a lot of our positions, but they don't hate us as a result. We're like crazy Uncle Max. (Laughs.) He comes to your house, and he starts saying some outrageous things, but you don't hate him as a result. A lot of newspapers get chicken; they don't want to rock the boat. But if you think the Republican or Democratic candidate is a bagman and a boodler, you don't say "bagman" and "boodler" because he'll sue you, but you come as close as you possibly can. There's no point in saying, "We don't believe that he has the accomplishments and so on of his opponent," when you really think we don't like this guy because we suspect he might make off with the state treasury. There's a kind of deadliness.

Do your editors just let you say what you think?

I feel fortunate to work here, because editors at the *Daily News* all understand (or don't care about, I don't care which) controlling the nature of the statement as long as it's well done. A function of any page in a newspaper is entertainment, and that includes the editorial page. You shouldn't have people snoozing in their cereal over your newspaper. You're not more believable and compelling because you haven't said anything. We have something to learn from television. They speak to one person; they try to keep people diverted. This is not a paean to TV news, but they actually understand that there is a person out there. So if you're going to say it, spit it out.

Such freedom presupposes a diversity of voices on the editorial page, doesn't it?

We've got a house conservative, a columnist who likes to write editorials. I don't assign him anything until I can find something that we can present in the paper that he can get behind. I don't want him writing some wimpy-ass liberal Democratic editorial, because it'll come out that way, like a wimpy-ass liberal Democratic editorial written by a right-wing fascist who's very unhappy at the moment. (Laughs.)

Such freedom suggests a happy and productive newsroom.

I praise my editors because they turned me loose. They just let me wander around, and they don't say I should be working. You've got to stay loose with people; that makes for a yeasty kind of newsroom. Even for reporters with heavily fact-laden beats, you have to give them the opportunity to do what they have to do. Our labor reporters have to spend most of their time schmoozing, eating and drinking with union guys; that doesn't show up in anybody's productivity surveys. It's just good journalism.

As an editor, how do you reward and encourage good work?

You let people work; you let them be as good as they can be. Freedom itself is a large part of the reward. You let them know that you think they're good; you let them know that you take their professionalism seriously.

Thank you, sir.

My pleasure.

Daniel Henninger
The Wall Street Journal
Finalist, Editorial Writing

Daniel Henninger is a native of Cleveland, Ohio. He was graduated from Georgetown University in 1968 with a B.S. degree in foreign service. He then joined the staff of *New Republic* magazine until becoming a writer for the *National Observer* in 1971. Henninger joined *The Wall Street Journal* to write editorials in 1977. He has served as arts editor, editorial features editor, and is now assistant editor of the editorial page.

If Richard Aregood is master of the editorial broadsword, slicing his victims into huge hunks, Daniel Henninger's weapon of choice is the editorial rapier, a sophisticated, witty, pointed editorial that leaves its victim unbloody, but nonetheless dead. In four editorials reprinted here, the writer's commentary ranges from politics to economics to popular culture. Henninger is one of those rare editorial writers who can explain a tax bill with style. He can also offer an appreciative "Right on!" to Michael Jackson for an audience thought to be more concerned with depreciation write-offs.

Who is Michael Jackson?

MARCH 6, 1984

Needless to say, *we* aren't the ones asking, who is Michael Jackson? It is our business to know, among other things, who Michael Jackson is. But we must confess that the question is indeed heard these days among that particular sector of U.S. society that always somehow finds itself just a stroke or two behind the forward wave of American life.

These are the same people who once said, who is Rudolph Valentino? Then they said, who is Frank Sinatra? Who is Elvis Presley? What are Beatles? Oh, they know a lot about moving yield curves, inventory-to-sales ratios, the affairs of great nations and the burdens of leadership. But they can't hum "Billie Jean." While their children walk through the house singing "Beat It," they, as always, are out of it.

Now we don't want to suggest that this eternally beleaguered fraternity of lost souls draws a complete blank on the Michael Jackson question. They are men, and increasingly women, of the world, and they have read about this Michael Jackson. They have read that his hair, like that of Cleveland's former Mayor Ralph Perk, once caught on fire. They have read of his Grammy Awards triumphs, of how in one night he carried home the prize for best album, best record, best rhythm-and-blues song, best rock vocalist, best R&B vocalist, best pop vocalist, best producer and best children's recording, for narration on *E.T., the Extra Terrestrial*. (Lest we too much depress or annoy our readers in suggesting they toil beyond the mainstream, it should be noted that the four Grammys won the same evening by Sir George Solti made him the lifetime leader with 24, four more than the immortal Henry Mancini.

We believe our readers may take some comfort in answering for themselves the question: A hundred years from now, which song will they be playing in the world's cocktail lounges—"Beat It" or "Moon River"?)

We would also guess that at some recent moment in one of their 18-hour days, the captains of industry and government learned that Michael Jackson's album, *Thriller,* has sold some 30 million copies and that at a listed retail price of $7.98 it would have grossed, as they say, in the area of $240 million. Our readers also may no doubt wonder whether the Marxists are right that it is an irreparably unfair world that rewards a man with this level of gross revenue in return for an album of some 60-or-so minutes of song, and leaves him time to dance and be photographed night after night in the company of Brooke Shields.

Still, we have not yet answered the question—Who is Michael Jackson?—in the deeper sense that one would answer, do angels exist or do cats have souls? A friend of ours—a lawyer who works on Wall Street, who understands the federal tax code and who learned about unexplainable cultural phenomena in 1968 by working for Eugene McCarthy in New Hampshire—leaned his head against the window of a commuter train recently and said, "I know who Michael Jackson is." We stopped reading about George Shultz's testimony before the Senate Appropriations Subcommittee on Foreign Operations and said, "Oh? Who is he?" And the lawyer said, "Michael Jackson is the Liberace of the 1980s."

Everything is explainable.

I, Danny

JUNE 26, 1984

The nation's capital doesn't have a baseball team during the summer, but it does have a Roman circus—the House-Senate conference over the annual tax bill. About dawn this past Saturday morning, House Ways and Means Chairman Dan Rostenkowski—"Danny" to the Washington aristocracy—gaveled down the conference's final agreement. Bleary-eyed conferees, lobbyists and reporters stood uneasily or reclined all about him, besotted from days of almost nonstop tax revels. The Emperor Claudius, we suspect, would approve.

At least, in our efforts to plumb and explain the essential meaning of this remarkable piece of tax legislation, which it is claimed will raise $50 billion of revenue across four years, we found ourselves repeatedly drawn to the image of gladiatorial combat in the Roman Colosseum.

The tax on liquor will rise $2, to a whopping $12.50 a gallon. The liquor industry's well-armed lobbyists were carted from the field, bleeding if not dying. But taxes on demon cigarettes will be cut in half come October, since tobacco gladiators deftly fended off attacks menacing a previous trophy. The redoubtable Helms of North Carolina receives the roars of his people.

But this was mere prelude to the contest most eagerly awaited by aficionados of these congressional blood-lettings—that featuring Spartacus himself, Sen. Robert Dole of Kansas. Mr. Dole, reported our correspondent on the scene, "wanted to stretch out the real-estate depreciation period and pit his own influence against that of the powerful real-estate lobby."

Armed only with a short knife and his now-famous tax net, Mr. Dole eviscerated the real-estate faction's agile favorite—speedy depreciation write-offs. This was sport for only the strongest stomachs. The man from the *Times* caught the scene: "It was 4:28 a.m. and Sen. Bob Dole had just walked back into the hearing room, not looking the worse for the wear—suit jacket on, tie cinched." The mob stirred: "A few claps and then, after catching on, the rise of applause."

Losers littered the conference floor. The egregious excise tax on phone service sticks. The "windfall" profits tax on newly discovered oil stays at 22.5 percent rather than falling as scheduled (the revelers particularly enjoy this sort of perverse humor). Tax shelters, as usual, took their cuts. The committee made quick work of fancy business cars and deductible home computers. Ditto various senior management perks. Ditto income averaging. And so on and so forth, as one tax specialist put it, to the outer edges of the tax code.

Finally, a fellow named Reagan showed up with something called urban enterprise zones. He got stomped. Conservatives are screaming that Bob Dole sabotaged the enterprise zones. Evans and Novak's Tax Report says our editorial, "The Rostenkowski Ghetto Bill," caused Mr. Rostenkowski to fall on the zones in a homicidal rage. Any way you cut it, though, people who live in the ghettos aren't very good tax gladiators.

The big winners, it appears, are the securities industry and foreigners. The former got the capital-gains holding period for stocks and bonds cut from one year to six months, and the latter will get relief from a 30 percent withholding tax on their U.S. portfolio income. Now why do you suppose the mob voted thumbs up on these two? We will guess. We suspect it may have something to do with the committee's "estimate" that this tax bill is going to raise revenues $50 billion.

Like everyone else, we have seen those stories that break down the individual revenue expected from particular parts of the bill. The liquor tax will bring in this many billions, and the frozen windfall-profits tax will produce that many billions. And if you get down on your hands and knees and look at the bottom of the printout, you'll see a figure that says, "Total: $50 billion." Now we may be able to look on while Bob Dole gores the real-estate business, but we're afraid we just wouldn't have the stomach to peer into the static calculations Congress used to arrive at the revenue assumptions in this tax bill. And so (with apologies to Chairman Danny, who fought valiantly for the commodity straddle), it appears to us that Congress hedged its tax compromise by including a few supply-side tax cuts for investors, which we have seen is a good way to enhance revenue.

Speaking of tax cuts, we are reminded that President Reagan said recently that he wouldn't be snookered again the way he was on TEFRA, the bill that falsely promised to give him $3 of spending cuts for each $1 of tax increases. Well, we noticed while we were down on the floor with the conference committee's computer spew that the revenue figure says $50 billion, and the spending-cut figure says $11 billion. That's almost $5 of new taxes for every $1 of spending cuts. Perhaps the president would do well to attend to the Roman Circus on the Hill. He runs the risk of holding a throne and losing an empire.

Radical Chic returns!

OCTOBER 12, 1984

Radical Chic invariably favors radicals who seem primitive, exotic and romantic, such as the grape workers, who are not merely radical and "of the soil" but also Latin; the Panthers, with their leather pieces, Afros, shades and shootouts; and the Red Indians, who, of course, had always seemed primitive, exotic and romantic. At the outset, at least, all three groups had something else to recommend them as well: They were headquartered three thousand miles away from the East Side of Manhattan...
—Tom Wolfe, *Radical Chic*, 1970

It was a golden age for many people, the decade of radical causes. It's a lot tougher now, serving on the front lines night after night, washing down pound after pound of semi-ripened brie with lukewarm chardonnay on behalf of one more common cause. How many more causes can there be?

At least one—Nicaragua.

We got onto this last week, when we read a long story in the Style section of the *Washington Post* about Nora Astorga. Nora Astorga is the deputy foreign minister of Nicaragua. Ms. Astorga is famous. By her own account, Nora Astorga joined the revolution to overthrow Anastasio Somoza by luring one of his generals to her home with the expectation of a liaison. Ms. Astorga excused herself momentarily from her bedroom, and her colleagues emerged from hiding and slit the general's throat.

Last week she was in New York. Accompanied by Daniel Ortega, Commander of the Revolution, Nora Astorga caused the resurrection of Radical Chic at a reception given by New

York attorney Michael Kennedy for the two Sandinistas in a setting entirely appropriate to our times—the New York Athletic Club. The *Washington Post* reported:

"Across the room, a swelling crowd of women talked about Astorga beneath ceiling murals of men wrestling, boxing and running track. 'Oh, God,' said Susan Horowitz, a political activist who champions liberal causes (and the wife of MTV president David Horowitz). 'To try to get the guy to bed, and then kill him! Fantastic. It's like a western. That's my dream, to do that to Reagan, George Bush, go right down the line. I've got to meet this Mata Hari.' Ms. Horowitz said, 'She's the most exciting modern female revolutionary around. I love it.' "

Three days later, on *60 Minutes,* much of America met her. In an interview-profile conducted by Ed Bradley, Nora Astorga spoke of her life, her ideals and the revolution. More interesting, though, was the film footage of Ms. Astorga visiting a "refugee camp" inside Nicaragua. The deputy minister, Mr. Bradley intoned, was visiting "people who fled their villages following attacks by contras, or counterrevolutionaries, many of whom are former Somoza national guardsmen who get their money and their weapons from the CIA."

Hmmm. It's widely known that there are "relocation camps" in Nicaragua containing Miskito Indians moved forcibly from their homelands—with some loss of life—by Ms. Astorga's colleagues, and there are camps in Honduras of Nicaraguan refugees who fled the Sandinistas. But refugee camps in Nicaragua? It was not mentioned that the contras are led by former anti-Somoza comrades-in-arms of Ms. Astorga. One of the most famous, Eden Pastora, was shown—but inexplicably not identified by Mr. Bradley—standing beside Ms. Astorga in an old photo. The *60 Minutes* reporter probably didn't want to ask impolite questions.

On to Hollywood and Harvard.

Hollywood first. After a speech at San Francisco's prestigious Commonwealth Club, Comandante Ortega flew to Beverly Hills, where he spoke before a group of concerned Hollywood residents called the Committee of Concern for Central America. Mr. Ortega is a sure-thing candidate for president in Nicaragua's Nov. 4 elections which explains why he can do his campaigning in glitzy Hollywood rather than grim Managua.

He addressed the committee outside the home of Elizabeth Montgomery (formerly of *Bewitched*) and her husband, Robert Foxworth (of *Falcon Crest.*) "We are a small, poor nation of barely three million people that is being submitted to a policy of aggression and extermination," the comandante told the Sunday gathering, which included committee chairman Mike Farrell *(M*A*S*H)*, Charles Haid (Renko on *Hill Street Blues*), Darryl Hannah (the mermaid in *Splash*), Bonnie Franklin *(One Day at a Time)*, Orion Pictures President Mike Medavoy and Sen. Chris Dodd, normally of Connecticut. On Monday, he flew to Harvard.

Speaking at the invitation of Harvard Law School, the comandante told an audience of 1,300: "The American government has poised itself to exterminate the Nicaraguan people." To this the students shouted back, "No pasaran!" meaning, "They shall not pass." *No pasaran* is a famous revolutionary slogan from the Spanish Civil War. Possibly this means the Sandinista Directorate can soon expect to find the Harvard Law Brigade in Managua. More likely, the brigade will get no further south than Capitol Hill, which responded to the comandante's campaign this week by cutting off U.S. aid to the contras.

Tonight in Chicago, Hollywood's Committee of Concern kicks off a five-city tour titled "Town Meeting on Central America." A spokeswoman for the entertainers' committee emphasized that the group is "nonpartisan," and favors "self-determination and nonintervention in Central

America." Jackson Browne is going to sing. Haskell Wexler's going to show his new film on Central America, *Return to the Front.* Studs Terkel will talk. There will be dramatic readings. We'd like to suggest one, delivered by Commander Ortega in Managua in August to honor the Sandinist Youth Movement. Perhaps Studs Terkel could read it.

The comandante was deriding his critics and praising the youths for their work in Sandinist Defense Committees (CDSs), Cuban-style groups that spy on neighbors, parents and priests and report any grumbling to Sandinist leaders. Proclaimed Senor Ortega: "Yes, the CDS, even if the haughty gentlemen and ladies vomit curses. Even if they get headaches and their stomachs turn upside down. Swallow your vomit, curses, headaches and spleen, gentlemen, because the CDS will be here today, tomorrow and always."

Back in the glory days of Radical Chic, the owner of a Manhattan art gallery, after listening to appeals for support for a Marxist revolution long since past, asked a question that puts the American travels of Nora Astorga and Daniel Ortega in perspective: "I won't be able to stay for everything you have to say, but who do you call to give a party?"

Armageddon, at last!

OCTOBER 25, 1984

Moving right along in the 1984 campaign for the presidency of the United States, we have arrived at Armageddon. Anyone could have predicted it would come to this. We all knew deep down that neither the candidates nor the press wanted to spend two months talking about national productivity, employment levels, the growth rate in federal spending and all that other dull, boring junk. Heavens, no. Give us Armageddon.

We have to admit we were caught off guard Sunday night when Marvin Kalb, following on the president's remarks on the prime rate, said: "Mr. President, I'd like to pick up this Armageddon theme." This what?

Armageddon. And sure enough, the President of the United States—who earlier had been pulled into a colloquy with his opponent over whether nuclear missiles can be called back—thereupon offered a brief disquisition on the theory of the final days. Then, two days later, 100 "religious leaders" materialized to denounce the president for raising the Armageddon issue. "We join with religious leaders throughout the country," they said, "to denounce the ideology of Armageddon." They said the president had implied that a nuclear exchange with the Russians was foretold in Holy Scripture.

Somehow the ideology of Armageddon started to sound familiar. But of course—the "nuclear winter." Carl Sagan, an eminent astronomer, recently propounded the theory in *Parade* magazine that a nuclear exchange would blot out the sun and end life on Earth. Or as John the Evangelist said, "Then the fourth angel poured out his flask upon the sun....Everyone was burned with this blast of heat" (Revelation 16:8). John continued: "Hailstones weighing a hundred pounds fell from the sky on the people below." Hundred-pound hailstones. Anyone who's been following this campaign knows the feeling. Happily, the end—Nov. 6—is near.

Mark Patinkin
Providence Journal-Bulletin
Finalist, Deadline Writing

Mark Patinkin, 32, grew up in Chicago and was graduated from Middlebury College in Vermont in 1974. He worked two years as a general assignment reporter on the *Utica Daily Press*. He arrived at the *Providence Journal* in 1976 where he worked in regional bureaus before moving to the night staff of the city desk. He has written a column four times a week for the past six years, which is probably why he named his dog Royko.

The five stories reprinted here represent a portion of the remarkable work Patinkin turned in during a month's journey through drought-stricken Africa. Patinkin's stories represent some of the most dramatic and compelling narratives ever to appear in *Best Newspaper Writing*. The stark setting and human suffering inspire an understated passion in Patinkin's prose. But the true power of this work derives from the writer's ability to identify and chronicle the courageous among the victims of terrible famine, and the selfless who seek to ease suffering in the face of terrible obstacles.

They flee from hunger but keep their humanity

DECEMBER 12, 1984

KOREM, Ethiopia—The first thing that struck me was the sound. Except it was not sound. It was the absence of sound. People everywhere, and so little sound. Starvation does make a noise. It is silence. And it is very loud.

Then I noticed the flies. They covered the eyes of the weaker children. And the weaker men, too, and the weaker women. I once worked on a farm. The flies on the cattle were not as bad as the flies I saw now.

Thousands of people. Tens of thousands. The fortunate few live in sheds. The fortunate many live in pits of dirt covered by plastic.

The rest—more than 15,000—live on the ground, measuring wealth by that one possession most treasured here: a blanket.

There are blankets for only a few. Each serves a family of four, sometimes more. At dusk they huddle beneath them, and each morning, perhaps 20 families wake to find one of their number no longer alive. It is the paradox of drought country that here, where the sun has become such an enemy, it is the cold, at night, that does much of the killing.

Five thousand straw tepees stretch toward the mountains. Three thousand plastic tent shrouds stretch toward the town. Up to 20 people are packed beneath each.

Wandering souls cover the rest of this ground, as dense as a crowd at a stadium. It can take five minutes to move 10 yards. Most are so thin they don't even show the slightest trace of muscle. It has been consumed by the body.

Truly, I have arrived in Korem.

Before I left America, I wondered how this could go on. How long can it take to master a refugee problem? Now I understood. Even a nation of resources would find it hard to serve 55,000 suddenly destitute people—even if they had appeared near a city. But these people are not near a city, they are in mountains difficult to reach.

And Ethiopia has few resources, few planes, few trucks.

Nor are there just these 55,000. There are other camps, other refugees. Throughout the north country, and some of the south, there are hundreds of thousands more, all having clung to their mountain homes until this last failed harvest left them starving, finally leaving, streaming for hope, walking for days, arriving near death at camps unable to handle those already there. And still, every day more people arrive than supplies.

There is only one force in this place stronger than the pain. A surprising humanity.

It is a nearly impossible humanity. Shipments of wheat will come into Korem. They will be placed on the open ground. People will gather around—people quite literally starving. People so hungry they think only of their hunger. People perhaps days from death. And they will not touch the wheat.

They will sit nearby, waiting patiently, sometimes for hours, sometimes more than a day.

Several times, trucks filled with food have broken down en route to Korem. It is the same route the newest refugees travel on their journey to the camp. Never once have they touched the trucks, even those left unguarded. That would be stealing. That would be wrong. So they continue walking.

An Ethiopian named Simachew, fluent in English, is the supervisor of the camp. He tells me there are two days of food left, with supplies down to a trickle. The weaker children weigh half what they should. The day before I arrived, they ran out of dry milk. Even if it comes, it will solve little. They need wood to boil it. And there is not enough wood.

There is not enough medicine, either. Or enough plastic for more tents. Nor enough stretchers, making it difficult to transport the dead.

I walk outside, stopping at a waiting place for the sick, one of many. A child next to me is crying. He reaches up, I reach down. He encircles his fist around my finger and the crying stops. He encircles his arms around my leg. He will not let go. So, together, like that, we stand for five minutes.

I walk again, and the children gather, as they had in the Addis Ababa ghetto, only more of them, hundreds of them. All reach for me. I was told to try not to touch; there is much disease here. But I have nothing else for them, and touching seems to be a medicine, so I give them my hands.

All have the same name for me. *Ferengee.* Foreigner. From their lips, it sounds less like a greeting than a prayer. When I look at them, they each make the same gesture. They draw a line across one palm with the other hand, then pat their chests thrice. "Ferengee," they say again. In the future, whenever a child touches my hand, I think I will remember Korem.

At first, I did not use my camera. It seemed more than an intrusion. Then they began pointing to it. They wanted photographs taken. It had nothing to do with vanity, of course. They understand something even many Americans do not, that help can come through lenses.

"They know," said Mr. Simachew. "They understand the world is trying to share their problems."

He has heard people say it: Foreigners are coming to help us. Americans especially.

Nearby, I spot a child picking slivers off the ground, bringing them to his mouth. I cannot imagine what he could be eating. The earth was hard and cracked, the mosaic of a broken windshield. I bent to take the child's picture. I shot for three minutes. When I looked up, I was in shadow. Maybe two hundred people had gathered around me.

As I stood, they chanted their prayer. *Ferengee.*

That night, I found a room in the nearby town for one dollar. The floor was cement, the ceiling corrugated steel. It contained a bed and nothing else. The hallway was dirt. There was no water or electricity. A cold I did not expect settled onto the mountains. I slept in a flannel shirt, huddling beneath the covers, and still I found myself shivering. I wondered how those in the fields, without blankets, could endure this. Soon, I would see.

At dawn, a thousand roosters woke the town. By 6:30 I was heading back to the camp with three of the young French doctors who work there. Morning in Korem, the worst time.

The mist was beautiful. We stopped the truck by a section of tents. Nearby, three men were dismantling a thatch tepee.

"One of the people inside must have died," said the doctor I was with. I asked how he knew. He explained that it had become custom to use tepee poles as slings.

Nearby, in another tent, a second child had died. Weak first from hunger, then disease, the night cold finally took him. I did not want to look in. Then I decided I should. I had not come here to look away.

The child lay half-covered. He was very young. He was horribly thin. The family had begun a ritual washing.

All around me, a wail began to spread. There is certainly no wealth here, or possessions, or food, but there is community. One family's loss becomes the loss of all families, and all join in the mourning. The men cry, too.

We walked toward the morgue.

"Twenty-one so far," said the man outside it.

Nearby, 50 people sat vigil. All were wailing softly.

It was mourning, but more than mourning. It sounded like fear, too—perhaps of the pain they knew this would bring. As I left, the wail got louder. I did not look back.

We walked on, into one of the hospital units. I paused by a father and son. The son lay in the father's arms. The father called softly to the son.

I turned to the doctor. "That child looks bad," I said.

The doctor bent over for a closer look. "He died during the night," he said.

Back outside, the sun hit the mountains with a beauty that made me stop and stare. We moved toward the more hopeful side of the camp. A hundred fires were going. The day's cooking had begun, with the last of the wood. This was not a secret place. The whole camp knew this was where the limited food supply was prepared. And no one bothered it.

"I still find that hard to understand," said the doctor.

He had long since been able to pull the curtain down to the tragedies of this place. The one thing he still could not get used to was the decency.

On our way out, we passed lines for everything. Water, medical help, food, of course. The lines stretched hours long.

No one complained.

No one jostled.

The people crowded around as we climbed into the car. They smiled and reached out. "Ferengee," they said.

Other than that, there was no sound.

We drove in silence. I looked back, watching them begin their day: 55,000 of the most desperate of people, living in near-impossible conditions.

And it occurred to me that there were no police in this city of refuge. And no crime.

I had never before been to a place so inhuman. Or more civilized.

A medical heroine battles hunger and dirt

DECEMBER 13, 1984

KOREM, Ethiopia—I'd heard about her in Addis Ababa. Small legends emerge in famine country and she is one of them, the senior doctor in Ethiopia's biggest feeding camp.

I met her during my second hour here, which to me was a long time in this place. She has been here seven months. She is 32 and from France. Her name is Brigitte Vasset.

In Korem, every day, she tends over a hundred patients, only not like most patients—these are all critical. Nor are they her only concern. Always, at the door of the hospital, a thousand more wait for her. And there are more still, uncounted numbers who reach for her, pleading, wherever she walks.

The word hospital implies a building. In Korem, it is not that way. It is more a depository, a long shed with a dirt floor. The patients lie on foot-high platforms built of rock and mud. The platforms are the size of an average bed. Four people are squeezed onto each.

I follow her inside, into the isolation section, where she kneels to touch a woman's abdomen, searching for an enlarged spleen, a sign of a disease called relapsing fever. It can push your temperature to 104.

I ask her how it's transmitted.

"By lice," she says.

"Aren't you risking exposure yourself?"

"I've already had it," she says, "so I'm okay."

She explains that she gets a lot of things from her patients. It's all right, she says; in a place like this, it's unavoidable. If it's bad, you take a day off. Either way, you get over it.

Her cloak is dirty. Her hair is auburn. She is tall and thin.

I find it hard getting used to her being here. You think of doctors as humanitarians as long as they can have their comfort. There are few medical choices less comfortable than this.

Together, we walk outside, into an extraordinary sight. There are hundreds of some of the sickest people I have ever seen, but not sick enough to get into this hospital.

Many show knees that are swollen triple size, expecting her to work such magic. She tells me the knees are not swollen at all. They are normal. It is the legs that are astonishingly thin.

Vasset pauses as they gather around her.

"These old people," she says. "You leave them outside, they will die."

I ask how she chooses.

"I don't know how we choose," she says. "The oldest one, the weakest one."

"It must be hard."

"It is the hardest part," she says. "But I must."

Most hospitals have more doctors and nurses than patients. Here, it is 10 staff members to a thousand.

She mentions the shortage of blankets.

"We only have enough for the weakest patients," she says. "The worst of the children."

I expect her to ask me to stress the need for more. She doesn't. She has come to understand she must work with what she has.

A woman wraps her arms around Vasset's leg. Others reach for her, pulling at her. They are not rough, just desperate. Still, I expect her to get angry at any moment. She is so overwhelmed, so overworked, in such a hurry. And now they are pulling at her.

She does not get angry. She kneels and touches the face of the woman holding her leg.

"Mama," Vasset says softly. "Oh, mama."

She moves to another unit where three new patients await admission. They are shockingly thin. She examines all three, then turns to an aide.

"Starvation, starvation and starvation," she says. I had not known it was a medical diagnosis.

She moves down the corridor. Those too weak to reach for her draw lines on their palms and pat their chests three times, the sign of need. Flies are everywhere.

She spends an hour going from platform to platform. Soon, she learns there have been two recent deaths. It means two spaces have opened up.

We walk outside. It is the moment of selection. The people can tell by her face that she is about to choose.

I could not do this job. I could not pick one of a hundred, of a thousand, and leave the others to wail. I could not do that.

She scans the crowd, examines some, then does it quickly.

"Come, mama," she says. "And mama, yes, mama, too."

The two women move slowly inside. Vasset helps them.

"Others are so sick, too," she says. "But there is only room for these."

As she turns to go back, an elderly woman touches her forehead to Vasset's hand, holding tight.

"Mama," says Vasset, and then places her hand around the woman's upper arm. Vasset does not have big hands, but she is still able to encircle the arm, touching her right thumb against her right forefinger.

I have never seen anyone do that. How could any adult be so thin?

"It's all right, mama," Vasset says, and rejects her.

"She is not so bad," she tells me as we walk inside. She pauses to demonstrate on an in-patient, again encircling the upper arm, only this time there is much room to spare.

It is the dirtiest medical area I have ever seen. It is extraordinary that they're able to keep it this clean.

Again, she kneels on the floor. She begins to examine a very old woman who sits by a younger one. She looks into her eyes.

"The grandmother?" I ask.

"This one is not so old," she says.

I ask her to ask the patient how old she is.

"Twenty," the patient says.

Vasset looks surprised.

"I would have said 25," she says. She is used to this.

I try talking as she works.

"How do you get to them all?" I ask.

"It is better," she says. "Once, we had 200 patients each. Today, it's 100."

She explains that there are now five doctors. Five doctors, 60,000 people.

"It doesn't sound like a lot," I say.

"This is how I measure," she says. "Two months ago, 100 died each day. This morning, only 23."

Patients aren't the only ones who pull at her. Aides do, too. And nurses. And other doctors. At every moment, she is talking to three people. There is no such thing as five minutes to rest. Not even one.

"I don't know how you've kept up for seven months," I say.

She smiles, explaining that she's spent four years in places like this, most recently Afghanistan and Chad.

I ask when she plans to go home.

"Not yet."

"Why not?"

Again the smile, and for the first time she looks square at me.

"I like this place," she says. "I like these people."

I try asking about her motivation. I wait for her to tell me about commitment to the Third World. She doesn't. Her calling is medicine, not philosophy.

It's quite simple, she says. She is a doctor. There is healing to be done here.

"You have family back in France?" I ask.
"Oh yes."
"When did you last get to see them?"
"A long time ago."
"And your pay for all this?"
She says it is four hundred dollars.
Per week?
"Per month."
"What about your personal life?"
"I get off at 6," she says. "I eat. I fall asleep. It's enough."

She continues her rounds, stopping suddenly to stare at a bed.

She lifts the cover, scanning the patients underneath.

"We have a place," she says. "There are only three on this bed."

Immediately, she walks outside and selects another. For her, it is a victory.

I'd begun to feel guilty about taking her time. I told her I'd let her go.

I shook her hand, then watched her move back down the dirt floor, a very bright light in a very dark room.

Drought took his land, famine took his sons

DECEMBER 16, 1984

KOREM, Ethiopia—It had always been difficult land, but it was his land, as it had been his father's and his grandfather's. So, four harvests ago, when the rains did not come, he saw it not as an omen, just as a bad year. There had been other bad years. There was no reason to think of leaving.

This mountain was his home. He was telling me this in Korem, which is where he now lives. It is also where his son is buried. There are 55,000 people here, but really only one story. Any farmer, anywhere, broken by weather knows it. This farmer's name was Badassie. His wife, Fatuma, sat beside him. She was very beautiful, although weak from hunger.

The camp supervisor, Mr. Simachew, did the translating.

During the good years, his life took on the rhythm of the land. He would sow in April and harvest in November, always corn, wheat and sorghum. He was a good farmer, harvesting enough to market.

They ate meat in those days, big meals like Americans eat, often throwing out what was left over.

He even had oxen, four of them, and he grew to see them as a farmer often sees his animals, like sons. He named one of them Strong, one Black, one Red, and the last In-between. Sometimes he'd bring them food from his table. Those were the fat years.

Then a child came, a son. They were a family now. Soon, the boy began to talk and there was little quiet around the house.

Evenings, the family would take walks along the land. They saw it like a mother, fertile, a source of life.

That was the year the rains stopped coming. Slowly, the young crop withered. The corn turned brown, the wheat burnt. Badassie waited until late November and still harvested only a little. But he told himself a farmer is a farmer. He bends with the weather. Next year, it would turn.

A second son came and, once again, the rains did not. But the child made their place here more rooted. Now two had been born of this land. The young son became special, as youngest children often do.

Even before the child could talk, the father found himself bending over him at night, telling him what he would inherit when he was a man, the oxen, the land, these mountains.

What is mine will be yours.

By now, into the second year of drought, the land was no longer like a mother; it had turned dry and resistant. Still, Badassie sowed his crop.

Farmers, he knew, must be gamblers. True, the land was now not fertile, but the rain would soon make it so. It was his wager.

But again the rains did not come. Now, every day, he would poke through the ground, looking for shoots. None emerged. None at all. In November there was no harvest.

That year, the food began to run out. There was no more meat, no more vegetables.

But even as the land dried out, he vowed to hold on to it, as his father had, and his grandfather. They had made the land work. He would, too.

So he made the hard decision. First he sold his furniture. Then his farm implements. Then the donkeys. And eventually, when his sons grew thinner than he could bear, he sold Black. And Red. Then In-between, and finally, the most loved of them, Strong.

That was when the first tragedy occurred. It occurred suddenly. They were all weak from a fragile diet and, as happens, the children were weakest.

One day, his eldest boy caught a cold, which normally is nothing, but these times were not normal. Because hunger had taken his strength, the cold turned into pneumonia. And one night, the pneumonia took him.

The father buried the child, and that same day decided it would only harden his resolve.

His place was here. Land does not turn against you, the weather does, and this land was his. It was hard land, but striking land. Live among the mountains long enough, and they become part of you.

The land was his soul.

Now he would sit up at night, holding his youngest, telling him the time of pain was over. He would make promises.

For you, things will be different, he would say. When a family takes a stand, even weather can be beaten. And they would make a stand.

Every day he watched the sky. Occasionally clouds came, bringing hope, but they passed as quickly. And again the rains failed.

This time, even the pasture weeds died.

Cows died, too. The money for meat had long since gone, now there was no money for bread either. Or wheat. And even if there had been, there was no wheat.

Amongst themselves, the men began to talk. Perhaps we should go. But where? Anywhere; there's nothing left here.

But it's all we know. And rain is due, long due.

But children are starving. Yes, but surviving. We're still surviving.

One day, as the men agonized, word came to town about a shelter beyond the mountains. In Korem. There was food there. Food from America. It was enough to draw the most desperate.

Slowly, in a trickle, the town began to empty.

But he resisted. He had promised his boy so much. They were impoverished now, but leaving would impoverish them forever. He would not do that. He was a man, he would provide.

He began to wander the fields, scratching the ground, finding the merest bits of sorghum, bringing them to his wife, who made it into soup, though it was really more water than soup.

And then it touched him again. Illness came to the daughter of his brother. Weakened by hunger, she could not hold. His family was a close one, and a death for one was a shared loss, belonging to all.

It was as if the daughter had been his own.

And finally, he understood.

The land could go. All of it could go. But not his son. His son he had to protect.

The next day, the three of them left for Korem. Before setting out, he knelt on his land, placing his palms against it. It was still his land. His soul. He had no anger at it. Just pain.

The walk took four days. There was no food. And then it happened.

His boy began to fail. They had all grown so thin, so gradually, that he'd lost sight of what starvation looked like. Now he saw it had been happening to his son.

There was nothing but leaves, so he tried to feed him leaves.

There was no hope but in this journey, so they tried to walk faster. But the sun and the mountains were hard.

And at night, the cold settled down, and his son weakened, and weakened more. And by the time they made Korem, two weeks ago, the son had entered that difficult phase, so hungry that he could no longer eat.

He died on the third day. The father's new neighbors, living nearby in Korem's open field, mourned with him, then offered to help carry the dead boy to the morgue. The father asked if he could first have a moment.

He held the boy close, and out loud, he said goodbye.

Ethiopians are people of dignity. The father did not cry once during the telling of this story. Afterward, he and his wife willingly posed for a photograph. Then they walked back toward the field where they were to sleep.

I looked down at my camera. It was for only a moment, but when I looked up, I could not pick them out. They were lost among the thousands like them.

The desert spreads and brings famine with it

DECEMBER 25, 1984

DORI, Burkina Faso—Finally, I am about to see true desert. It is the symbol of this journey: the final wasting of the land.

I have chosen Dori carefully. It is said that slowly, desert is claiming North Africa. Every year, it moves south another three miles, another five, in some places 10. On the crest of that movement, the story of food crisis is told. Dori is on the crest.

It sits 150 miles north of the capital. There is no good road, just a four-wheel-drive path. My plane leaves at 10 a.m. I am traveling with Baba Philipe of Save the Children. For years, they have been in Dori making a stand against the weather. Lately, the weather has been overwhelming them. We are bringing up our own food and water—there is little left where we are going.

Our carrier is Air Burkina, the national airline. Its fleet consists of two planes. Actually, three, but one has been broken since January. We are lucky, we leave only two hours late.

I see it happen from the air. Mile by mile. The green fades. Soon, though, I lose view of the land. There is a heavy fog outside, only it is not fog. This is the season of the harmatan, a strange steady wind that carries Sahara dust hundreds, even thousands, of miles, filling all the air of West Africa. Many who live here wear rags over their mouths for months. I cannot even see the sun.

It makes plane travel difficult. We fly over Dori's dirt strip once, but we lose it in the harmatan when we turn for the approach.

We try again, and miss again.

It takes us five tries to get it right, and even then we only find the strip in its middle, lurching down violently with barely enough runway to stop.

We climb down to the sand of Dori. Philipe says never again, from now on, he'll travel by jeep—this was too close. Another Save the Children worker smiles and tells him to look on the bright side. In Burkina Faso, there's little chance of a mid-air collision.

Because I have just come from Kenya's good country, the starkness here hits me with a clarity. The town is a black-and-white photograph. No, in a way it is worse. There is only one shade here. The walls are sand and the streets are sand. The sky is the color of sand. Even the trees are covered with the fine film of the Sahara.

I ask Philipe why he would want to work in such a place. He answers that he himself has wondered why the people of Dori stay here. But they do, and that is the answer. You see souls who hold to hope in a hopeless place, and it makes you want to hope with them.

Until a few weeks ago, I'd never heard of this country. It used to be Upper Volta, then came a coup and a name change, and now the drought has brought it an odd kind of prominence. Go to Burkina, people in the hunger business told me, you will see how it is happening.

It is how I've come to be in one of the most obscure towns in one of the most obscure of nations. As I walk among the sandwalled huts, I at first feel as though I've left the planet. In fact, here in Dori, I have perhaps come closer to it than I have ever been before.

America, in the end, is not the world. In numbers, the true world is the Third World. And this is how it lives: not in cities, but in villages poised on the edge of conditions, people trying simply to wring bread from hard sand.

We stop in Save the Children's stark Dori compound. "This is where Jerry stays," says Philipe.

He is speaking of Jerry Pasela, the group's Burkina director. He is an American from Cleveland. He lives in the capital, but spends half his time—two weeks a month—working here in the desert, a day's jeep ride from his family. He has been in Dori almost five years.

In these past weeks, I have begun to grow hardened to the suffering of Africa. But there is something I've seen that still continues to surprise me: Walking into places that God has truly damned and finding an American there by choice.

Philipe tells me even he is confused by it. For his own commitment, there is a reason—it is his country and these are his people. But his boss, he says, is different. Why, Philipe asks, would an American come across an ocean for this?

I wonder who this Jerry Pasela is. I decide I must visit him when I get back to the capital.

Philipe and I drive into the desert. I had not realized it before, but there are two deserts in North Africa. There is the great Sahara where almost nothing can survive. And then, just beneath it, there is the Sahel. The Sahel is the crest of hunger. I am in the heart of it now.

The land is harsher than I thought. There is as much stone and rock as sand. It reminds me of some of the sun-killed mountains of Ethiopia.

And for the first time, I realize how big this drought is. It is as big as all of America, and even bigger. I have now traveled 3,000 miles and I have yet to outrun it.

It is almost as if it has been mapped out for me, east to west, in neatly packaged stages. I have gone from famine camp to refugee camp to land turned to desert. Slowly, level by level, I am moving backward through the progression of starvation. First Ethiopia six months ago, now Ethiopia a year ago.

Philipe tells me how it has happened. April came and they sowed crop, waiting for the rains to lift it. But there was no rain, and the seeds burned. So they sowed again in July, and again, the seeds burned.

A third time they tried, and a third time it happened. Finally, rains did come, but by then they were out of seed. Nor were the rains good rains. They came harsh and quick, cutting and depleting a hardened soil.

The statistical men now measure the loss of crop at 90 percent.

The old men say the last time the weather conspired this destructively was 1926—and that was a green time. The livestock men point to the hides of their animals and say it is beginning, soon the herds will start to die.

There are two other signs. From the countryside, hungry Bedouins are moving into Dori—newcomers.

And, in town, there is the Save the Children health center. A program has begun for malnourished infants. The capacity is 30. The program is full. And the outpatient load is building.

I sleep this night in a lightless room beneath a mosquito net. Before I drift off, I hear laughter and drums. Not jungle drums, but the kind you might hear in an American city—the sound of rhythm and youth. Every night, the teen-agers of Dori gather to dance in the dust, to flirt and hope for connection. As I lie here, I think of teen-agers back home, doing the same, being young in the towns they grew up in.

Certain things seem to be universal. I wonder if these children may soon find themselves in a feeding camp.

There is no plane scheduled back to the capital for four days, so we decide to do the trip by vehicle. The harmatan is throughout. The dirt road is worse—half the time, it is impassable, forcing us to wind through the desert.

We pass too many goats, which are killing the land, and too much cut wood, which is also killing the land. The drive takes seven hours.

My back is shot. It will not be easy to truck food up to Dori.

That evening, I find Jerry Pasela in his office. He tells me he heard about my plane landing, he says it is why he never flies Burkina anymore.

"Those kind of landings make you get old real fast," he says.

He has a deep voice, big forearms, and is unique among Westerners I've met here. He is 44. It makes him the old man of relief work. It is as rare to find that age in the bush of Africa as in the fields of American sport.

I get right to it, asking how he copes with it. He is not in the world's garden spot.

"My God, no," he says. "And it's getting worse."

I use the word famine. He is matter-of-fact.

"Definitely," he says. "It's coming."

I ask him about his projects, and he goes for a half-hour nonstop.

He takes out an elaborate project chart: gardens, irrigation, reforestation. I glance around the office. There are charts everywhere—it looks a bit like a war room. I think, if given a choice between this battle and a military one, I would risk facing weaponry.

Pasela's enemy seems more difficult.

He admits it. He says the scientist in him has no faith in Dori's land.

"So why are you there?" I ask.

He tells me about the other part of him. He tells me how he was once a teacher. And how a certain kind of moment made teaching worth it—those few times a student's face engaged.

"Something turned inside that human being," he said, "and at that moment, they grew. And would keep growing."

He sees the same look here.

"Suddenly," he says, "people we're working with will realize their own creativity, and it'll change their lives."

Still, I say, the land is dying.

He agrees. But that's all right. Even if you can't win, you can hold things back, and there is victory in that. He says it's all right to fail, but not to give up. I leave him, hoping that someday, if I am lucky, I will learn to have half as much faith as he.

Before I left Dori, I asked to see one of the outlying villages.

Philipe took me there. My arrival was announced. A decision was made. A journalist was here. It was important enough for a meeting with the elders.

Twenty of them came, and 20 others stood nearby—40 black African villagers, one white American. Children peeked from around trees.

The elders brought me a chair and laid out a mat for themselves in front of me. We had to triple-translate. They spoke in tribal tongue. A villager put it into French and Philipe put the French into English.

I told them I'd come from America, where crops are always bountiful, to find out how they're able to live in the desert. They all laughed. The contrast, they explained.

I asked if they'd ever talked to an American journalist. No, they said, but John Denver. He was here on a hunger tour the month before. They asked if that was as good as a journalist. I told them it was close.

The harmatan seemed to pick up. I wore chinos, an L.L. Bean shirt and Rockport shoes. They wore robes.

They asked why I came.

I told them that food problems in villages like this are now a great issue in America.

They said they have always seen Americans as human kin, they were glad we saw them as the same.

I asked how bad hunger had become here.

They laughed again. Look at us, they said. What do you think? The harvest?

They've never seen a year this bad.

Is there back-up food in storage.

Yes. But it will last only a month. Then, no one knows.

They listened intently. They laughed often. In America, poverty seems to dim the spirit. Here, there was no sign of that.

What would have happened without Save the Children's food programs?

They laughed again. They would have all had to leave by now.

And where will you go if you do have to leave?

Now there was no laughter. This was a difficult issue. This they do not know.

We talked for an hour. They asked if I had any final thoughts. I could only say I was sorry for what had happened to their land.

They each took my hand and thanked me, asking if I would tell my countrymen that they need our help and embrace it with gratitude.

Then they said they had something to show me. The walk took 10 minutes. We came upon a stand of trees. What lay on the other side made me stop. It was a vegetable garden covering more than an acre, as lush as any in America. It was the first color I'd seen in Dori.

There are five wells here, and all day dozens of villagers work them, drawing water, asking all the wells have to give.

This should not be able to work. This soil is not even as good as beach sand. I do not know how much longer they can maintain. But right now, this one corner is holding.

If there is a single image I would hope to carry home with me from Africa, it is that garden. I now understand why an American from Cleveland has given five years of his life to this piece of the desert. It is something to think about on this Christmas Day.

Life is being made to happen in this most inhuman of places, and it says much about believing in the not-quite-possible.

A simple story of loss that speaks to all

DECEMBER 30, 1984

TIMBUKTU, Mali—We are all of us homeless this night. They are nomads who have lost their land; I am a traveler, far from everything I am part of. Together, we are spending Christmas Eve in the desert.

We are the oddest of couplings. They wear Moslem robes; I wear a flannel shirt. I grew up in Chicago and live now in New England; they've known only the Sahara. I have with me enough cash to cross the ocean in a morning. If they want to visit the nearest village, 10 miles distant, they must walk.

They have nothing. And tonight, I, too, have nothing.

I am in their camp. I am their guest. I am here because I want to know their world, what they had and what they lost. For this one night, we share our lives.

The best way to get here is by Land Rover. My guide is a Western doctor. He gives introductions, then leaves for his own Christmas. It is now only I and them.

The name of this tribe is Touareg. They live in newcomers' tents on the banks of the Niger. They came in from the deep desert only a month ago, driven by hunger, refugees all.

I am taken to the tent of the chief. He gives me his hand, he tells me his name. "Hamzata," he says.

I tell him mine. We smile at each other's foreignness, and it brings us closer.

Only one thing about him speaks of wealth— his turban. It is bright blue and of fine silk. It must be the only thing of value in this camp. He has as much pride in it as I in the three things that have gotten me through this trip—my L.L. Bean shirt, my Swiss army knife and Ray Ban sunglasses. Little items, perhaps, but treasured things that have been with me for years—things necessary in this desert, and right now, my only comfort.

The chief is well educated, fluent in French, but still we share less than half a language. My French is only marginal. This night, there would be many gaps to bridge.

I watch them unfold the visitor's mat, and light a fire for tea, rituals now familiar to me. But unfamiliar, too. I am thinking only of home.

I miss some things. I miss the winter ocean. I miss music and movies and the energy of the American spirit.

I wonder if it is snowing back home. Tree lights must be everywhere now. Here, I see only sand. Nearby, a tent of newcomers are settling to sleep without food. It is hard to feel the season in famine country.

I explain that it is Christmas Eve. I explain that in America, this is the best-loved of nights. They say they know about Christmas. It is not theirs, but they know it.

The chief motions to some of the others. He has them set up a special bed for me, in his tent. I tell him it's not necessary —it's bad enough I've imposed unannounced at 5 p.m. The ground would be fine. But he insists. I am his guest. It is important to him.

Soon, it begins to get cold. A fire is lit. I tell the chief I'm here to understand how his people came to be hungry.

It is simple, he says. They lived off cattle. The drought came. The grass disappeared. The cattle died.

"There must be more of a story than that," I say.

Yes, he says, there is. There is a story of loss here that speaks to all people who have lost something dear. But he did not want to take my time with it.

More tea is poured. More men come around. We gather close to the fire.

Why the desert, I ask. Americans would consider it a banishment.

That makes him smile. It is the opposite, he says. Desert, for them, is freedom itself. All men, he says, have an ache for land. With the nomad, it is only keener. It is why they choose not a piece of land, but a world of it. This way, they can even own night.

He began to tell me of the good times, the fat times. They were wealthy then. They'd have been wealthy even in America. Hamzata's family—just he and his brothers—owned 1,000 cows. Had he been born in Texas, he'd have been a rancher.

As his ancestors had for centuries, he too followed the rhythm of the desert. From October to May, they would find a stand of grass, and this would be the time of settlement. And it was a good time. But they could not shake the love of road, the need for road. Even the cattle knew the rhythm of this movement, and were themselves restless by June.

Now they would follow the time of wandering, a week here, a month there, the stars guiding them, the camps numbering 100 souls, though they did not call them camps, they were families.

And they brought with them a culture, hiring learned men to join them during the season of teaching. Always, from the sale of cows, there was money to buy comforts in town, where their wealth was regarded with awe. Good times. Fat times.

The chief did most of the talking. The others gave him the respect of their silence. I had to struggle with the French, but slowly, the same words were coming again and again.

"*Avant.*" Before.

Before, when things were good, they had fresh steak every night, and fresh camel milk, too, which is the best of all milk. There was guitar music, and even hunts, the dogs tracking gazelles, the chiefs following on their horses.

"It sounds like the perfect life," I say.

Yes, says the chief. It was...*avant.*

Before. Before the sun became a constant thing, the nurturer of life changing to the enemy of it, the grass curling under it, the animals beginning to die, dying year after year, until, last May, the last of them was gone. And a world gone with them.

"And now?" I ask.

Now they are trying to find a new way of living. They are trying to learn cultivation of crop and a rootedness of their own. Now, there is no steak, only rice from UNICEF, and not always that. If the women sell their crafts in town, there is dinner. If not, there is none.

And around me, I could feel how it is ending. I can feel the ache of loss, the confusion of men and women who no longer have the things that make them what they are.

"*Les peuples ont faim,*" says the chief. It is another phrase I would hear throughout the night: The people are hungry.

Soon, the cold becomes too much. We go into the tent. And he takes out an album of photographs. A nomad with a Polaroid.

He brings a lantern over and begins showing me what times looked like when times were good. His camels...his cows...his soul. It is important to him that I see this. He understands I am a journalist. This is for history, he says. So people will know there was once such a life.

I had expected we would sleep without food. But as we leaf through the album, I smell cooking.

He says it is because I am a stranger who cared enough to come. Tonight, there would be dinner, a true feast. They were preparing the meat from one of the last of their desert sheep, meat they'd until now been saving for more difficult times. The women bring it to the tent. The chief begins cutting the portions with a dull sword. I see he is having trouble, and offer him my Swiss army knife. He marvels at it and cuts the rest with ease.

Sixteen of us are in the tent. There is enough for each of us to have five bites. There is a seriousness to eating here, a respect for it that only people like this can know. The chief eats only half his portion. He insists I have the rest. He says he isn't hungry.

When it is done, we go back to seek the fire's warmth.

There is no talk for a while. Then I ask how hard this has been for them.

The chief says it is the hardest thing in experience, leaving the one life you know. Even the secrets understood only in their hearts are secrets that tie them to the desert. How do you give that away, he asks. How do you start over—not after a lifetime, but after an ancestry?

We stand and talk for more than an hour. I tighten my flannel shirt. I notice he is shivering.

"Is there no clothing?"

"If there is no food...," and he lets the sentence go at that.

More phrases become familiar with repetition. *Rien a manger* —nothing to eat. Or simply, *rien,* nothing.

Whenever I bend to take a note, two of the men bring lanterns to help me. Slowly, I begin to feel an unexpected kinship. We are all far from home.

There are only two beds in the tent, the rest of the floor is sand. The chief takes one, I am given the other. At 10 p.m., we say good night. The lanterns are put out.

"*La Noel joyeux,*" I say into the dark. "*Tu comprends?*"

"*Ah, oui,*" he says. "*Je comprends.*"

Christmas Eve in the Sahara. I lie there for an hour, but cannot sleep. The cold comes into the tent, and into my bed. I wait outside for the embers of the fire. I am alone.

When this sky is clean, there is no sky like the Sahara sky. Under a full moon, you can read a newspaper. It helps me understand the draw of this place. When nature imposes a harshness, it seems to give back a beauty as great.

And now I find myself thinking about the things I've seen this month and what they mean.

What I've found here in this Touareg camp is what I've found everywhere: A man had a life he loved, the weather changed, and now he can't even feed his children.

I was where I'd begun in Ethiopia, in a tent city, hot by day and cold by night, where people of the land had gathered by force of weather, people now dependent on nations alone.

But here, as there, in the midst of this pain, I find a familiar twist of hope. There is a knowledge of spirit among famine victims here, a knowledge that says if you lose everything, you can still have civility, and there is wealth in that. I have never known the hospitality I've been given this night.

And I will always remember the hungry of Ethiopia, days from death, walking past a disabled food truck, ignoring its load of wheat, because touching it would have been theft.

I try again to sleep. I drift in and out. Finally, morning comes.

I recognize this morning. I have seen it before. It was the morning of the Korem feeding camp, at least on one level. Here, now, as happened there, the children come to me. I can walk nowhere without the children. And always, they grow quiet and content when I give them my hand.

Why is it that they, and the adults, too, are drawn to Americans so? I did not expect that. There is a warmth for our country I had not known existed. And it has nothing to do with politics or allegiances, only with what the people here see—that when there is pain, this nation reaches out.

And I realize more than ever before, that what we are, and what we stand for, rests with that compassion.

Before I leave, the chief wants me to see what I've come to see. We walk to the newcomers' tents. I notice he is squinting hard into the sun.

Soon, we pause at one tent, and there we find a true child of famine, one of the more troubled of this flock. The chief embraces him.

The child, to him, is a stranger. But to see the hurt in his face, it could be father and son. The little arms are so small. He holds him close long after I am finished with my photographs.

"*Rien a manger,*" he says. "*Rien a manger.*"

There is a kinship here Americans don't know. The greatest of this people feels truly diminished by the difficulties of the least of them.

I ask the chief about this. My French could not keep up with him, but I did not need it. I know, from a month in famine country, what he was saying. That we are one family here. Joined together by weather. And joined also by the little we have. The things we do not have are things that join us, for he who, like me, has nothing, is my family.

We hear the grind of an engine. A half mile distant, we see the doctor's Land Rover.

We walk back to the main camp. The chief tells me to wait, then disappears into his tent. Soon, he emerges. He is carrying his blue silk turban. He places it in my hands. For you, he says.

I take off my L.L. Bean shirt and hand it to him. Then I give him my Ray Ban sunglasses and Swiss army knife.

"For you," I say.

Christmas morning in the Sahara.

I climb into the Land Rover.

"Until next time," says the chief.

I say it, too. We begin to drive away.

And as we do, I turn to look back at these people who have been changed but not broken by hunger.

And as I leave this place, I am thinking one thought: One world.

(In this brief essay, reprinted in part from The Providence Journal-Bulletin, *Mark Patinkin describes how he came to write his dramatic series on Africa.)*

The man who runs the *Providence Journal* newsroom is named Chuck Hauser. We were having lunch one day when he asked if there was anything new I'd like to try with the column I write. Like any reporter, the first thing that came to mind was travel. He asked where.

"I don't know," I said. "I've been reading about Ethiopia lately. But I know that's pretty far."

I then suggested some more realistic trips. Maybe an occasional story in New York. Washington. I didn't mention Ethiopia again, and even dropped it from my own mind. Newspapers don't send columnists on foreign assignments.

That was on a Friday. On Monday, shortly after I walked into the newsroom, another editor called me over.

"Chuck wants you to go to Africa," he said.

It's what the best of editors are about. They're able to see which door a writer should walk through, even before the writer sees it. This project was Chuck Hauser's idea even more than mine, and a piece of it belongs to him.

It belongs to a few other people, too.

Getting these stories into the newspaper was almost as hard as getting the stories. Usually, when on the road, we dictate by phone. You can't do that in a continent where most phones don't work. The only choice was to telex them. Telexes are machines usually used by businessmen to send 30-second notes overseas. They limit them to 30 seconds because it's not cheap. My stories took about 40 minutes each.

The machines were bears to work. Most were in hotel offices and looked like old supermarket cash registers. After I'd compose my columns on a portable computer I'd brought along, it often took three hours more to retype each onto the telex before pushing the send button. They'd arrive in a computer bank in Missouri. There was no way the *Journal* could tell when a story got there, so throughout my trip, Linda Rasmanis and Gordon Smith, who work in our systems division, would spend their days checking the computer bank every hour or two. When they fetched out a dispatch, they'd send it over to my key editor, Joel Rawson.

If anyone gave a pint or two of blood to this project, it was him. The telexes put every letter of my stories in capitals. They often send without paragraphs. On the French side of Africa, the keyboards even had a few letters in the wrong place. I sometimes ended up typing each A as a Q, each M as a W.

Worse, the transmission often garbled entire sections. Linda would have to cable back to my hotel, sometimes on deadline, asking what I was trying to say. I'd have to resend paragraphs for Rawson to plug in. It took him up to five hours to refine each piece, and there was no way he could put it off until tomorrow. We were writing daily.

For Rawson, it was more than clerical labor. He also cut out an occasional sentence or paragraph, sometimes refining ragged prose. Writers usually hate seeing their stuff tampered with that way. Being 7,000 miles away, I was unable to protest. When I got back home and finally saw his refinements, I had a reaction reporters almost never do.

"Gee," I thought, "that reads better."

I happen to have a writer's ego. It makes it hard for me to understand how those behind the scenes, who get no glory, can invest so much of themselves into making us look good.

John Carman
Atlanta Journal/Constitution
Finalist, Commentary

John Carman, 38, was born in Des Moines, Iowa, and raised in Detroit, the son of a newspaperman. He was graduated from Kenyon College in Ohio and earned a master's degree in journalism from Northwestern University. In 1970 he worked as a general assignment reporter for the *Milwaukee Journal.* He then spent 10 years at the *Minneapolis Star,* the last five as a television critic. He went to the *Atlanta Constitution* in 1982 as the television columnist.

Carman's reviews and columns reveal an interesting blend of reporting, media criticism, political analysis, and cultural commentary. Carman understands the links between what we watch on TV and what is happening in our lives. His critical tools include clear explanation, sarcasm, irony, word play, and a sharp point of view. He likes to go beyond individual television shows to teach us larger lessons about our culture, reminding us of "television's capacity to glorify mediocrity."

Is erotic pay TV a social disease?

JANUARY 1, 1984

American popular culture is a tireless provider. You can now sit in front of your TV set, munch a bunch of Fritos, and watch people have sex.

Or at least watch people pretend to have sex. Sometimes it's hard to tell.

In the years ahead, video sex will be refined. You'll be able to catch the acts on wall-size screens, hear the moans in stereo, and maybe grapple with arms, legs and assorted other appendages in 3-D.

But will you respect yourself in the morning?

Cable television, with its relative freedom from the legal entanglements of over-the-air broadcasting, made video orgies possible. The profit motive made them likely. Public taste made them inevitable.

Home Box Office, the nation's biggest and richest pay cable channel, learned quickly that R-rated movies were popular favorites. That may mean scenes of actresses being hacked to bits in dark houses. It may mean profane language. It certainly means sex and nudity.

The best of all possible worlds, I suppose, is to find a movie in which a naked actress is hacked to death while her killer talks dirty to her.

HBO supplemented that with special productions of burlesque shows and, until recently, Allen Funt's *Candid Camera* excursions into nudity. On Cinemax, another pay cable channel owned by HBO, it sprinkled such film masterpieces as *Sex Machine* and *Goodbye Emmanuelle* onto the late-night schedule. A Cinemax magazine show, *Eros America*, is billed as "a discriminating look at sex in the '80s."

Showtime, HBO's principal rival, wouldn't be outdone. To HBO's garden of earthly delights, it added naked soap operas and other erotic goodies. Showtime strives to be a little bit saucier than HBO.

But cable television's real sex channel is The Playboy Channel. Autoerotic television came of age when The Playboy Channel signed on a year ago last month. The Playboy Channel currently has nearly 600,000 subscribers on more than 300 cable systems in the United States. That includes about 28,000 subscribers in the Atlanta area.

The Playboy Channel is a world unto itself, a shake-and-bake paradise presided over by Hugh Hefner.

Playmates aboard yachts fling their bare breasts to the winds while they talk about longing to make people happy. A studio audience hoots and hollers while contestants undress each other on an unabashedly tacky game show called *Everything Goes*. On a show called *America Uncovered,* female models tell an interviewer that they get turned on wrestling in front of a camera.

Nudity is the specialty of The Playboy Channel's original programming. But The Playboy Channel cablecasts movies, too, and simulated sex is the draw there. Courtship and romance are not major elements in the movies. Men and women, or sometimes women and women, see each other and reach for their zippers. Just like that. There is some muss, but no fuss.

Playboy Channel officials say they show no X-rated material. Their films that have been reviewed by the Motion Picture Association of America have been rated R, or have been trimmed back from their X ratings to reflect R standards. But some of the films are rating mysteries; they never were submitted to the MPAA review board.

It's no revelation that sex sells. But The Playboy Channel and the sexual niches on other cable channels are surprises for anyone who recalls, not so long ago, a time when the NBC censors declared Barbara Eden's navel off limits on *I Dream of Jeannie.* Video sex has come far, and very fast.

The Playboy Channel has done one thing, and only as television can. Into it went *Playboy* magazine and all of its myths. *Playboy* was a "lifestyle" magazine, a forum for fashion, humor, advice on food and drink. Famous writers contributed to its pages. Some men said they bought it for the articles.

But television, cable or broadcast, is a distillate. It has neither time nor use for extraneous nonsense. For The Playboy Channel, it took *Playboy* magazine and distilled it into its essence: sex.

Sex is the lowest common denominator. Television is the cultural epitome of the lowest common denominator. The history of the medium is one of steady movement toward identifying public taste in its broadest sense, and catering to it. The irony is that cable, which was to satisfy the viewing needs of diverse groups, now is headed in the same direction.

In the 1950s, sponsors directly controlled network programming and tooled it to enhance their corporate images. It was the Golden Age of Television, a time of live drama on *The U.S. Steel Hour, Armstrong Circle Theatre,* and other prestigious shows. People watched the shows and often talked about them afterward.

By the 1960s, TV ownership had spread across all lines of affluence. The networks wrested control of programming from the advertisers. They began to churn out whole slates of situation comedies and action-adventure shows.

The idea was to hook a mass audience at the start of the evening and hold it until prime time ended. Don't touch that dial. Program executives such as Fred Silverman and Paul Klein (now the president of The Playboy Channel) developed theories about audience flow and least-objectionable programming.

Intellectuals grew disenchanted with television. But there weren't many of them, so they weren't much of a market for ceiling tiles and cat food. The networks hit their groove with physical comedy, action-adventure and sentimental melodrama.

Contrary to the theories of only a few years ago, cable networks are finding that they need something approaching a mass audience to survive and prosper. The evidence is that there may be sufficient audience support for news, sports, rock music, children's entertainment, movie and sex channels.

The Playboy Channel is a hot seller where it's available. Despite the reluctance of many cable systems to carry it, the sex channel concluded its first year of operation with a profit of about $200,000, and with good prospects for the future.

Meanwhile, the fine arts are duds on cable. CBS Cable sustained huge losses before it capitulated last year. The Entertainment Channel, which sought to include the best of British television in its schedule, flopped this year. ABC's ARTS channel is starved for viewers and advertisers. Bravo, a premium cable service distributed by the same company as The Playboy Channel, has about one-third as many subscribers and isn't even offered in the Atlanta area.

Clearly, the message is that there is a preference for watching a *menage a trois* to seeing a skillfully executed *pas de deux.*

I can make no moral judgments about nudity and sex on cable TV, beyond what I think for myself. One man's pornography—meaning simply material that is sexually stimulating and including, perhaps, the works of some classical composers—is another's obscenity—meaning something that is morally revulsive. For some Americans, there is no distinction between pornography and obscenity. In my opinion, I've seen both on cable TV.

I can say that I believe most of the material I've seen on The Playboy Channel was badly produced; that a small portion of the nudity struck me as artful; that much of the sexual material seemed demeaning; and that American sex films appeared cruder and consequently less erotic than their European counterparts.

Watching a big amount of it in a short time, I felt cast into a universe that is as far removed from reality as the *Love Boat* and *Fantasy Island* tandem Saturday nights on ABC, and potentially more damaging. It's a mythical place where flesh is oxygen, where the sex act is the sole sustenance, where the identifying marks on the landscape were gadgets sold in sex shops, where every woman is primed for sexual pleasure anytime, anywhere, with anybody.

The line of reasoning at The Playboy Channel is that mature people will want to use the channel as an occasional diversion or turn-on, as one viewing choice among many. There is, I'm told, evidence that subscribers choose The Playboy Channel as a novelty, and that subscribers tend to watch less of it after their initial curiosity is satisfied.

What bothers me isn't that there is nudity and sex on HBO, Showtime, Cinemax, The Playboy Channel and the rest, but what their growing prevalence says about us.

The late Vladimir Zworykin, an electronics genius who was largely responsible for the invention of television, hoped it would be a beneficial means to advance communications, to enhance cross-cultural understanding, and to make the best of civilization accessible to all people.

Too many of us use it to relieve boredom and to retreat into false worlds.

Lynda Carter: Body but not soul

MARCH 16, 1984

All body, no soul. Lynda Carter's career, especially after *Wonder Woman,* is testament to television's capacity to glorify mediocrity.

She strikes me as a pleasant but uninteresting woman with a transparently single-minded devotion to convincing the public she's a multi-faceted star.

Miss Carter certainly seems to have bamboozled CBS. The network never tires of giving her oodles of prime time for these self-indulgent musical specials.

Given time, she does it all:

She sings! Her voice would charitably be called passable. But why be charitable? She is to a song what Long John Silver's is to lobster thermidor. What she can do is get her sizable jaw behind a tune. When she hits full throttle, you could back a cement mixer into her open mouth. Come to think of it, I say go for it.

She dances! Her style of movement falls somewhere between a drugged heifer and a beached whale. Big and awkward. Just wait till you see her flop around to "Gimme Some Loving." When the choreography heats up, Miss Carter wisely moves into the wings and leaves most of the tough stuff to the professionals.

She acts! Yes, even here. You get the idea that in some dull way, she actually *feels* every superficial emotion that her songs express. So, of course, she acts out her feelings with all of the range she brought to *Wonder Woman.* One of her ballads, late in the show, is so wrenching that it very nearly moves her to tears. But the ensuing wave of applause pulls her back from the precipice and leaves her beaming.

She raps! Miss Carter evidently believes that no personal revelation is too trite to withhold from an audience. You get it all here, folks. She pays freshly videotaped homage to her home state, Arizona, which she describes as "serious hide-and-seek country." She reads her own fan mail. She shows us scrapbook photos of her own glorious girlhood.

When Miss Carter runs out of snapshots, she turns to Super-8 home movies. I liked them better. Here's little Lynda jumping up and down. Here's Lynda trying unsuccessfully to manipulate a yo-yo. And my personal favorite, a pubescent Lynda opening her trap and wiggling her tongue. It may revolutionize TV.

But the personal showcase doesn't end with that. The old snapshots lead to a stab at a 1940s medley. Later there's chitchat about her childhood doll, somehow a cue for a "Blues in the Night" venture that's as soulful as margarine—someone seems to have doused her torch. Still later, decked out in feathers, she swoops around the stage on a crane and trills, "Heaven, I'm in Heaven...."

Two guests are wedged into the special. Eddie Rabbitt does a western saloon bit, followed by an inevitable duet with Miss Carter. The song is "Just You and I," and it's a magical moment in bad television. Ben Vereen is on hand, too. Even he is in bad voice, though he's still a flash afoot.

Alas, there is more Lynda Carter in our futures. NBC is likely to pick up a new fall series starring Miss Carter and Loni Anderson as private eyes. Lynda and Loni. Body and...well, body.

The future of PBS: Masterpiece commercial?

JUNE 8, 1984

PHOENIX, Ariz.—You're watching a Shakespeare play on PBS a few years from now. The curtain falls on act one, the screen fades to black and the voice of Falstaff booms from the speaker.

"Don't go away," he'll say. "We'll be right back with *Henry IV* after these messages from our sponsors."

And then it will be over. The fragile reality of an American public broadcasting system that broadcasts ideas and entertainment uncontaminated by commercialism will have ended.

The new president of PBS stood before a gathering of TV critics here this week and said, without a trace of discomfort, that commercials are "a certainty for public broadcasting if we can't find the money we need."

It was a startling way for Bruce Christensen to observe his third week on the job. But there it was. He described advertising as "an issue that will be with us until we settle once and for all if we have enough money in this system to make it work."

There's always the possibility that the 41-year-old Christensen, who resembles a fleshier Ed Herrmann and exhibits the solid blandness of his native Utah, was merely blowing smoke in the general direction of Washington, D.C.

After all, PBS at this moment is awaiting congressional approval of an appropriations package that gradually would raise its federal funding from $145 million in 1984 to $253 million in 1988. And beyond Congress lies President Reagan, who regards public TV as an annoying leak in the federal budget.

"He believes public television is important and ought to be continued," Christensen diplomatically explained, "but that it should be funded by the people who watch it....He's a foe of federal funding for public broadcasting, but not a foe of public broadcasting."

With friends like that, PBS needs no enemies.

Whatever its intent, Christensen's message was chilling. Granted, he presented commercials as something of a worst-case scenario—a final resort if membership contributions to PBS stations decline and federal financing is denied. Presumably, too, if the Mobils and the Exxons of the world go elsewhere to scatter their spare dollars.

But Christensen, who used to work in commercial broadcasting in Utah and Illinois, sounded surprisingly unoffended by the idea of commercials on PBS. Asked for a personal opinion, he said it would "depend on how they would be used." It would be "tragic," he said, only if advertising became the dominant reason for the existence of public broadcasting, as it is for ABC, CBS and NBC. He said too that commercials probably would be sold and inserted on a local option basis by the member stations.

The fact is that PBS has been inching toward an uneasy accommodation with the mercantile world. An advertising experiment involving a handful of PBS stations ended inconclusively a year ago.

More obvious to PBS viewers nationally is the higher profile of corporate programming underwriters. On-air corporate logos are now kosher, along with a few discreet words about wondrous achievements of these companies. PBS ingeniously calls it "enhanced underwriting." Mobil and the rest would probably call it thoughtfulness.

Public television has done a stalwart job of weathering the Reagan administration, while public radio founders. PBS in the past three years has managed to strengthen its programming and, not coincidentally, broadened its viewer appeal. Consider, as examples, the additions of the *Frontline* documentary series and *American Playhouse* to PBS' core schedule.

PBS itself doesn't produce programs, but it does offer itself as the clearinghouse for the financial and creative efforts of its member stations.

But the aches and pains of money shortages are present almost everywhere within the system.

We were told here about the inability to buy into the network pool for political convention coverage, about potentially important series that lie dormant for lack of developmental financing, about the lack of a budget to promote shows. Christensen said the entire program fund of the Corporation for Public Broadcasting is equal to what ABC spent merely to advertise *The Winds of War*.

Several of PBS' new fall series have reached the starting blocks in fits and spurts. Production of a nine-part, $9.5 million series about the history of the Jewish people and culture was halted several times while fresh grants were sought. A few times, production crews cooled their heels because there wasn't enough money to send them on location to film.

PBS is a chaotic system because of its decentralized, noncommercial nature, but it has rumbled along with considerable distinction. The real disgrace would be for PBS to consolidate itself in the service of the Madison Avenue godhead. Let the Froot Loops in, and there goes Mr. Rogers' neighborhood.

GOP makes test pattern look lively

AUGUST 23, 1984

Political junkies began to whoop and holler at the TV networks as soon as the echoes cleared last month from San Francisco's Moscone Center.

Time magazine harrumphed that the networks "cover tennis matches with more fidelity to the action" than they had the Democratic convention and lamented the trim coverage expected for the Republicans this week in Dallas.

The editors of *New Republic* magazine were angrier, insisting that a political convention is "a mammoth combination of the *Tonight Show,* the evening news, *Dynasty, Queen for a Day, People's Court, This Is Your Life, Saturday Night Live* and the biggest Phil Donahue show imaginable."

ABC's David Brinkley, who has been publicly amused by politicians for 28 years, contravened the network line this week with his observation that any political convention is "essentially crazy, which is one reason it's so interesting."

Bill Moyers of CBS also reacted to an ABC executive's now-famous remark that the conventions are dinosaurs. Anyone who thinks they're dull, Moyers said on the *CBS Evening News* this week, suffers from "terminal cynicism."

Gasp.

Before I keel over from incurable cynicism, I would like to say that the Republican convention has afforded the dullest, the most insufferably boring, the most torturous hours of TV viewing I have been forced to endure since public TV invented pledge week.

Television should cover the conventions. Americans have scant opportunity to watch their democracy function in any form, let alone its most extravagant manifestation. It's not too much to ask the networks to lay it out on the screen every four years.

But this year's sleek coverage is enough. This week has been more than enough. You can absorb the flavor of the event and catch the main acts. It doesn't take gavel-to-gavel galvanization to understand that the Republican Party is content with itself, confident of its nominee and brimming with conservative fervor.

The Republicans are, NBC's Tom Brokaw said, "putting on an electric happy face."

People who think the networks are shortchanging them should take a closer look at the Republican coverage. How about that platform plank that would have given Republican-controlled states extra delegates to future conventions? Some kind of news story, huh? But it was the best story the networks could find three nights ago in Dallas.

NBC's Roger Mudd called it "one small bit of news tonight in a convention that doesn't have much." CBS' Bruce Morton more colorfully termed it a "tiny tempest in a teensy teapot."

Gazing up from the floor to Dan Rather in the CBS anchor booth, Morton added, "It's a real small fight, Dan, but of course it's the only one we have."

I don't know whether the Republicans adopted the measure or not. I don't care, either. As the convention wore on Monday and Tuesday nights, the news crews turned their attention to 1988, asking whether the Republican allure would fade with Ronald Reagan's personal magnetism.

ABC's Brinkley and Peter Jennings hosted a parade of guests. Rating them on a z-scale, for sleep-induction effectiveness, Sen. John Tower of Texas gets a zzzzz rating (the equivalent of gulping an entire bottle of sleeping pills). Transportation Secretary Elizabeth Dole rates a zzz, and her husband, Sen. Robert Dole of Kansas, was practically Bob Hope with a single z.

Jennings, Brokaw, Rather and their colleagues handled it all with low-key polish. I've never seen a convention quite like this, even in the Nixon years. The style of coverage, befitting the occasion, was a little like watching the hushed BBC coverage of a pastoral cricket match.

But give CBS a black mark for a sardonic camera shot Tuesday night. As former President Gerald Ford spoke, CBS briefly trained a camera on one of the exits at the hall. The implicit suggestion was that delegates were toddling back to their hotels. In fact, a steady stream of people come and go during any large gathering.

And Robert Novak, a newspaper columnist who was so churlish during the Democratic convention, scored points for honesty Monday on the Cable News Network.

Novak is anything but an enemy of Republicans. But he managed a straightforward assessment of U.S. Treasurer Katherine Ortega's keynote speech, which was given in the sickly sweet style of a homecoming queen, as boring and dully delivered. (ABC's Brinkley, the man who loves craziness, somehow found it "effective.")

Daniel Schorr, more in evidence in Dallas than in San Francisco, was CNN's chief asset. After a colleague blithely said that Mrs. Ortega and U.N. Ambassador Jeane Kirkpatrick represented the Republicans' attempt to address women's issues, Schorr quickly noted that they had done no such thing.

CNN's weak link is Mary Alice Williams. The evidence at two conventions is that she's out of her element and isn't thinking quickly on her tush. For example, she blandly paraphrased the old saying that it is easier to be standing outside attacking someone else's public record than to be stationed inside on defense.

No remark could have been more ill-fitting. The fact is that Americans who cared to watch the Republican convention have seen a self-satisfied political party that appears quite eager to defend the Reagan record.

Tarnished 'Glitter' is typical Spelling

SEPTEMBER 13, 1984

ABC asked Aaron Spelling to produce a show that weighed in between the flyweight schmaltz of the *Love Boat* and the lightweight drama of *Hotel.*

Voila, *Glitter.* If *Entertainment Tonight* could be rendered as fiction rather than mere fatuousness, it would look just like this new series.

Glitter is a magazine in Los Angeles. Everyone reads it, because everyone is fascinated by human-interest stories about the rich, the famous and the weird.

Ace reporters like David Birney and Morgan Brittany devote their energies to stories such as "Sex and the Sunset Years" and to keeping tabs on the private lives of box-office bozos.

It's a convenient format for a series, because the magazine milieu enables the show to be sprinkled with guest stars and their teeny-tiny stories. On tonight's two-hour premiere, we have Mike Connors, Juliet Prowse, Ken Howard (whose TV career seems to be circling the drain), Patricia Neal and Teri Copley.

Connors and Miss Prowse are involved in one of the modular story lines as a pair of one-time lovers who are reunited for a movie called *Palm Springs Holiday. Glitter* magazine editor Van Johnson assigns a pair of world-beaters (series regulars Dianne Kay and Christopher Mayer) to chronicle that breaking story.

Miss Copley, who may be recalled as the blithering dizzard of a dizzy blonde on last season's *We Got It Made,* is in Palm Springs too, scheming to get a break in the movie as a dancer. She's pretending, see, that she and her dance partner are young lovers, not sister and brother.

Howard is once again a Kennedyesque politician. He's hiding a secret that involves the dying Miss Neal, who plays a brothel operator named Madame Lil. Birney and Miss Brittany are pursuing that story, a la Woodward and Bernstein.

Well, these Aaron Spelling shows for ABC have a way of getting the creases ironed out before the closing credits. The characters are warm human beings, one and all, who are caught in the act of becoming close personal friends.

I give Spelling some credit. His shows on ABC, led by *Dynasty,* have as their hallmark a rich, satiny gloss. If Spelling ever got into the business of manufacturing interior paint, I'd buy it.

With *Love Boat, Hotel, Glitter* and another new ABC series, *Finder of Lost Loves,* Spelling has refined a form of television that probably can trace its roots to *Love, American Style.*

These shows are pure TV. They have no narrative distinction. They don't tax the brain—in fact, they don't really even try to penetrate the mind. They are narcotically pretty, moving color pictures that can be watched after a hard day, while you flip through the paper or fix Junior's broken toy. They are the network equivalent of an aquarium.

Spelling, 56, television's most successful producer, says this of his show business idol: "Walt Disney was my total God." With *Love Boat* and its sibling shows, Spelling has created entertainment for a nation weaned on Disney's Fantasyland.

But not today; back now to our regularly scheduled programming. *Glitter* has undergone minor surgery in that the light laugh track, like that heard on the *Love Boat,* has been removed. The plucky musical score, heavy on strings, has been retained.

Of course, *Glitter* is also an example of what's wrong with TV. Its Never Never Land reduces life and love to cliches made of NutraSweet. It forces old questions about the proper function of the nation's most powerful communications medium.

Glitter has been accorded a regular time slot of 9 to 10 p.m. Thursdays. That means a precariously close encounter with CBS' *Simon & Simon.* At the end of that confrontation, ABC may find all that glitters is not gold.

Jim Murray
Los Angeles Times
Finalist, Commentary

Jim Murray, 65, is widely considered as the dean of American sports columnists. He was born in Hartford, Conn., was graduated from Trinity College and began his writing career at the *New Haven Register*. He joined the staff of the *Los Angeles Examiner* in 1944 and in 1953 was one of the founders of *Sports Illustrated.* In 1961 he became the ace sports columnist of the *Los Angeles Times.* His daily syndicated column reached millions of readers across the country. Murray was named "America's Best Sportswriter" 14 times by the National Association of Sportscasters and Sportswriters.

Murray continues to write some of the country's most elegant and humorous sports commentary in spite of the obstacles imposed upon him by failing eyesight. He writes about athletes as a way of writing about human values and aspirations. His columns about South African runner Zola Budd and the murder of Israeli athletes at Munich reflect the perspective of a writer who sees sports as emblematic pageants that embody dreams, achievements and failures. Murray's voice comes through most powerfully in his most personal column, a poignant celebration of his late wife, Gerry.

She took the magic and happy summer with her

APRIL 3, 1984

This is the column I never wanted to write, the story I never wanted to live to tell.

I lost my lovely Gerry the other day. I lost the sunshine and roses, all right, the laughter in the other room. I lost the smile that lit up my life.

God loved Gerry. Everybody loved Gerry. She never went 40 seconds without smiling in her life. She smiled when she was dying. She smiled at life and all the people in it. When you thought of Gerry, you smiled.

She had these big gorgeous brown eyes and they were merry all the time and they looked at you with such trust and happiness. She never looked down or away. She never did anything to be ashamed of. Nothing. Never. She never did anything she didn't think God wanted her to do. She was in charge of smiling for Him.

She never grew old and now, she never will. She wouldn't have anyway. She had four children, this rogue husband, a loving family and this great wisdom and great heart, but I always saw her as this little girl running across a field with a swimming suit on her arm, on a summer day on the way to the gravel pit for an afternoon of swimming and laughing. Life just bubbled out of Gerry. We cry for ourselves. Wherever she is today they can't believe their good luck.

I don't mean to inflict my grief on you, but she deserves to be known by anyone who knows me. She has a right to this space more than any athlete who ever lived. I would not be here if it weren't for her. I feel like half a person without Gerry. For once, I don't exaggerate. No hyperbole. If there was a Hall of Fame for people, she would be No. 1. She was a champion at living.

She never told a lie in her life. And she didn't think anyone else did. Deceit puzzled her. Dishonesty dismayed her. She thought people were good. Around her, surprisingly, they were. Her kindness was legendary.

She loved God. I mean, He made the trees, the flowers, He made children, didn't He? And color and song and, above all, babies. She knew He'd take care of her.

She loved babies. Anybody's. She played the piano like a dream. Ask any of the football coaches, the basketball players, baseball pitchers or just newspapermen who leaned across their drinks and implored her for one more chorus of "Melancholy Baby." She played "Galway Bay" every St. Patrick's Day for a maudlin husband who wept over a moonrise he'd never seen or a sunset that existed only in a glass and an ice cube. She was fun.

She wasn't afraid to die. She didn't want to. But she knew she'd see the mother she lost, the son she lost. In a place where she could never lose them again.

You have funny ways of remembering things. The thing I remember clearest today, for some reason, is the habit she had of leaving notes for the kids when she was only going to be gone for the shortest times, the briefest moments. She would leave these notes on a table in this huge lettering, for her handwriting was like her heart, large and overflowing and joyous. "Gone to store," it would say. "Be right back, Love, Mom." She didn't want the kids to think they were without her love even for a few minutes.

She has left no notes this time. But she has, as usual, left her love.

There is a line at the end of *Alice In Wonderland* that always hurt me to read because it reminded me of my Gerry. Alice's sister is dreaming of Alice: "Lastly, she pictures to herself how this same little sister of hers would, in the aftertime, be herself a grown woman; and how she would keep, through all her riper years, the simple and loving heart of her childhood; and how she would gather about her other little children, and make *their* eyes bright and eager with many a strange tale, perhaps even a dream of Wonderland of long ago; and how she would feel with all their simple sorrows, and find a pleasure in all their simple joys, remembering her own child life, and the happy summer days."

Gerry took the magic and the summer with her. It wasn't supposed to be this way. I was supposed to die first. We would have been married 39 years this year and we thought that was just the natural order of things. I had my speech all ready. I was going to look into her brown eyes and tell her something I should have long ago. I was going to tell her: "It was a privilege just to have known you."

I never got to say it. But it was too true.

Remember Munich? The IOC won't

JULY 22, 1984

On Sept. 5, 1972, at the Olympic Games in Munich, West Germany—while Teofilo Stevenson, the mastodonic Cuban, was systematically dismantling the American, Duane Bobick, while fencers fenced and basketballers took free throws and the children of sport enjoyed the camaraderie of the Olympic Village malt shops and jukebox—nine Jewish athletes lay slumped in a room at 31 Connollystrasse, bound hand and foot and blindfolded, with Kalashnikov machine guns held at their heads by eight heavily armed Arabs. Two comrades lay dead on the floor. None of the nine would see sunrise.

It was, and is, a shocking intrusion of deadly world politics into the toyland of sports.

And the International Olympic Committee has never forgiven the Jews for it.

At least, so it would seem. Consider what has been done by the Olympic movement to commemorate that terrible day.

First of all, on the day of the attack, it was business as usual. The Games went on. The government of West Germany sealed off the Olympic Village—24 hours too late—and, having let armed guerrillas in at 4 a.m., then attempted to keep accredited journalists out in broad daylight. Some of us managed to elude the secret cops, but what we saw in the village was indifference bordering on callousness. Irritation, even.

It was not until nightfall that IOC President Avery Brundage's stubborn fiat that the Games must go on was overruled.

A 24-hour suspension of the sports was ordained, no more and no less. A memorial service was permitted. Beethoven was played. Speeches were made. The Russians and Arabs boycotted the service. So, to tell the truth, did a lot of Americans. Brundage seized the occasion to equate the issue with another "savage attack" on the Olympic Games, the threat of African neighbors to boycott if white Rhodesia were admitted.

Governments had fought to save the lives of the hostages. Sadat of Egypt was pleaded with to intervene. German lives were sacrificed. German officials offered to substitute themselves for the Israeli Olympians.

Books were written about it. Movies were made of it. Songs were sung, poems read.

But the Olympian response of the IOC was to sweep it under the rug. It's never mentioned in polite circles at cocktail parties around Lausanne, Switzerland, home of the IOC. The monocles focus on more chic subjects. It was as if it had all been just another breach of protocol which the IOC, like the Sun King of France, is big on.

The IOC is also big on the past, given to ancestor worship. Statues of Discobolous abound. So do Grecian urns, or amphora. Founder Baron de Coubertin's picture and utterances are everywhere.

But that one day in 1972 seems to have been dropped from the Olympic calendar.

It can't be that the IOC is trying to forget the terrorists. Several of them were even released from prison, if you can believe it. No, it must be the Israelis. They must have committed some monumental gaffe, some unforgivable breach of etiquette.

Because, since that day, the government of Israel has been interested in obtaining some recognition of the sacrifices of their athletes and coaches, slaughtered in a shootout, unprotected, unrescued, unremembered.

Sports commemorates everything. Statues of deceased sluggers dot major-league outfields, plaques recall where a golfer sank a "courageous" two-wood shot, streets are named for football players. But, would you even know who Yosef Gutfreund, Moshe Weinberg, Yaacov Springer, Amitzur Shapira, Joseph Romano, David Berger, Mark Slavin, Eliezer Halfin, Zeev Friedman, Kehat Schorr and Andre Spitzer were? This may be the only place you'll read their names during this Olympics.

Joseph Shane, a Los Angeles businessman; the Southern California Olympians, an organization of ex-Olympic athletes here, headed by Andrew Strenk; and the Israeli consul general in Los Angeles, Gen. Jacob Even of Entebbe fame, have petitioned the IOC for a simple moment of silence in honor of the martyred Israeli athletes at the opening ceremonies of the Los Angeles Games here this week.

It seems a reasonable request. But the IOC reacts as if it were recalling a bad dream. Spokesmen privately point out that the IOC severely curtails all opening-ceremony rites to weed out any "political or national statements." The head of state, be he Hitler or Emperor Hirohito or Ronald Reagan, is restricted to 16 words of opening statement, for example. The IOC not only wants not to honor the 11 dead athletes, it wants to forget them.

Why? They should be on the conscience not only of the Olympic leaders but of society. It isn't as if they were killed in a head-on on the Santa Monica Freeway. They are an ineradicable part of the fabric of the Games forever.

As Gen. Even says, "To forget is to condone—and we must never forget we are in a struggle with terrorism every day of our lives."

If its victims are forgotten, so will be its crimes.

Win or lose, Zola Budd already has her medal

AUGUST 9, 1984

Soviet tanks rumble through Afghan villages, Middle East terrorists bomb busloads of schoolchildren, demagogues seize power in pivotal trouble spots, but to hear some people tell it, the principal threat to world harmony and stability in this Year of Our Lord was a little slip of a girl who wears glasses, carries dolls and hates to wear shoes.

Strong men frothed at the mouth at the sight of her. Editors who should know better wrote stern editorials condemning her. Councils of powerful politicians legislated against her.

If you ever wondered how they could have burned Joan of Arc at the stake, you had only to take a look at the life and times of Zola Budd and the time she ran a simple footrace in the rain one night at London's Crystal Palace. You had only to scan the pictures of the crowd at her event that night. Not since the Luftwaffe has any visitor evoked such contortions of hate on the faces of Londoners. Banners were unfurled, lips were curled, teeth were bared and the shout, "Go home, you South African white trash!" rent the night air. It was an extraordinary study in mob psychology. What they did to this Zola (Budd) called for another Zola (Emile) to properly express the outrage some men felt at this unconscionable abuse of a mere child, this unpretty form of child molestation, a rabble chastising a 5-foot 2-inch, 84-pound schoolgirl. It was enough to make Salem in 1692 perfectly understandable. Not the Empire's finest hour. The Prime Minister herself decried it as "appalling."

Who are these people and why were they doing these terrible things to Zola Budd? Well, one of them was the Greater London City Council, others what one late gubernatorial candidate of the State of California called "the implacables of our civilization." People with a, God help us, cause. People who would fire into lifeboats if someone told them it would advance it.

The cause, it so happens, is laudable enough. What it sets out to do is quarantine South Africa, remove it from the polite company of civilized societies and bring down its unacceptable policy of apartheid or racial superiority.

It's the methods that want examining.

Blaming Zola Budd for apartheid is like blaming Shirley Temple for the Johnstown Flood. First of all, she's 18 years old. She has a constituency of one. She's a farmgirl, not an activist; an athlete, not a provocateur.

She happens to be a great runner who chanced to be born in South Africa. So is a zebra. Do we hold it responsible for the excesses of its government? Maybe Zola should grow stripes.

In a way, she did. At least, she shed her South African citizenship. She changed her spots. She gave up the land of her forebears, the comfort of her family, the solace of her friends, the things of her childhood and emigrated to a land many thousands of miles and a whole continent away—a child braving the unfamiliar, the hostile, the threatening.

She is as much a victim of apartheid as anyone else in her poor benighted country. A wise man once said, in dealing with the aspects of American apartheid, the then segregation in the South: "The white man in the South has the black man in a barrel and he's sitting on it. As long as he's sitting there, the black man ain't going anywhere. But neither is the white man."

Zola wasn't going anywhere, sitting on the barrel. So she got off it. In its way, that was as harsh an indictment of South African policy as a thousand "Zola, Go Home!" banners or a hundred thundering editorials or resolutions of a county council.

Athletes love to call attention to the sacrifices they make for their sport, the long hours they work, the aches and pains of practice, the time away from their loved ones or family, the pleasures forgone. Zola Budd's sacrifice gave new meaning to the term.

Her strange odyssey brought her to the Games of the XXIII Olympiad in Los Angeles' Coliseum Wednesday night and one of the great sport matchups of these or any Games. Zola was finally running for Queen, country and the London *Daily Mail,* which has bought the rights to her diary. The newest subject of the Queen was finally on a course she could handle—a race track. She didn't have to brave the flower of British home office politics, just Mary Decker.

Mary Decker is a case study in her own right. Mary has no trouble with her citizenship, her spectators generally are ruly, even sympathetic, but with Mary, you wish somehow she looked more like she was enjoying herself. Mary approaches a race as if she were hoping for a call from the warden. Her eyes seem to be desperate, staring at something she doesn't really want to see. It's as if she fears the worst, or as if she just got the worst news she ever heard in her life.

It's not easy to tell what she's worried about. She usually wins her 3,000-meter races by zip codes, and she did again in the heat Wednesday night.

Citizen Budd, new of Her Majesty's loyal minions, was less fortunate. Running barefoot in a high fog, she faded to third in her heat. But a race she came through three continents, several time zones and a storm of jeering abuse to take part in Friday evening was finally hers to win or lose—and not some politician's. You still get the feeling she didn't come this far through this much to settle for anything sub-gold or not to give Mary Decker finally something to look that unhappy about. Even if she loses, she won't.

Howard Goodman

Howard Goodman, 36, has been a metropolitan reporter for the *Philadelphia Inquirer* since December 1984. He received a B.A. from Cornell in 1971 and a master's degree in journalism from Berkeley in 1976. He started as a copy editor at the Salem, Oregon, *Statesman-Journal*, and switched to reporting. In 1981-82, he held an NEH Fellowship for Journalists at the University of Michigan. Later he joined the *Kansas City Times* metropolitan staff, where he wrote "The Jedi Homicide" shortly before moving to Philadelphia.

"The Jedi Homicide" came to the attention of the editors through informal channels outside the contest structure. We liked it, we had space for it, so we printed it, retitled "The 'Jedi' Murder."

Goodman captures the interactions of several complex characters in a thoroughly believable way. He writes very spare prose organized along a chronological thread after the opening five paragraphs. The simplicity of his language and the carefully selected documents keep the reader reading.

The 'Jedi' murder

MAY 26, 1984

Blood was all that Stanford Matz could make out when his sons woke him.

Blood covered Leigh's shirt and dripped from his hand. Dried blood was caked under Jimmy's nose. Leigh spoke.

"Daddy, Ralph's dead."

It was early Saturday morning, last Aug. 27. For weeks afterward, Stanford Matz awoke each Saturday at 2:30 a.m., seeing his teen-age boys in front of him, fresh from murder. "It's when the nightmare began," he said.

Because in the suburban Kansas City night, 16-year-old Leigh, aided by his younger brother Jimmy, killed a 20-year-old science-fiction addict in a stabbing much messier than the way heroes and villains die in the outer-space movies. It was a best-friends killing, so laden with shades of sci-fi sword and sorcery that the detective on the case named it "The Jedi Homicide."

Leigh Metz and Ralph Cochran loved stories, and they loved fantasy. Perhaps the story they would love the most, the fantasy they would find the most fantastic, would be their own, created in a landscape as familiar as the America of fast-food joints and shopping mall cinemas—the divorced, mobile, homesick nation near the interstate that still looks to the movies to make dreams come true.

And what might truly please Leigh and Ralph is that, at last, they managed to impress the minds that mattered most: the makers of *Star Wars*.

"It was one of the strangest items I've seen in the years that I've been in the business, period," said Sidney Ganis, vice president of Lucasfilm, let in on what happened by police.

The authorities learned, when they began to outline the case, that Leigh and Ralph fused a friendship on a passion for film and science fiction. That Leigh idolized the older boy.

That Leigh worked tirelessly in a locked bedroom, trying to penetrate the film world as a writer and director. That Ralph undertook to be the ultimate fan, driving a car with Kansas license plates that read "JEDI."

"Leigh followed Ralph around like a puppy dog," said Ralph M. Cochran, Ralph's father, "because Ralph was very knowledgeable in all the things that Leigh wanted to be."

As the psychiatrists who examined Leigh explain it, Ralph returned the adulation by preying on the younger boy's naiveté. He portrayed himself as an insider with special ties to the reigning geniuses of film fantasy: George Lucas and Steven Spielberg.

To nearly everyone, the deceptions were transparent, even simple-minded. But Leigh believed, ignoring opportunities to see Ralph's games for bunk. Psychiatrists said he fell victim to a mental illness that made the claims seem real.

And the claims were outrageous. At their height, George Lucas himself—the reclusive creator of the *Star Wars* epics—was supposed to be breathlessly awaiting Leigh's writings and drawings.

Leigh skipped school to complete projects he thought destined for Mr. Lucas. He churned out hundreds of pages in a meticulous hand, plot lines and schematic drawings for movies he called *Clone Wars* and *The Lost Tomorrows*. He hung on letters of praise and criticism supposedly from Mr. Lucas, and he stayed home on the off-chance that Mr. Lucas might visit. In one 45-day period, he said, he stayed home for 10.

Then pay dirt.

Mr. Matz said that he called home one afternoon and Leigh told him that Mr. Lucas was there, at their Lenexa apartment. He had come in a limousine and was visiting Leigh in the bedroom. He complimented Leigh on his work. He took time to call director Steven Spielberg in California.

Months after the killing, when Leigh finally was persuaded that it was all a sham, he decided that Ralph simply had hired a bearded actor and a limousine.

For Ralph had been enterprising in creating a fictional George Lucas. After the killing, Johnson County sheriff's Detective Frank Denning found evidence that Ralph had forged Mr. Lucas' signature on phony letters and that he had produced other ersatz sci-fi documents to sell to Leigh.

He did it to taunt Leigh. And to squeeze him. Leigh said he gave Ralph nearly $5,000 over four years—money he saved from part-time jobs, by skipping lunches and by misusing his father's credit card. It went for phony scripts, empty promises of movie-making gold and paltry articles of science-fiction fandom.

The more Detective Denning strove to understand the case, the more he left the everyday world. He was staking out psyches no one could fully explain, areas where mind games spun like spider-webbing, with dependency and paranoia riding the thin lines.

He caught the flavor in the early hours as he interviewed the Matz brothers, who had reported the death. They said they had been with Ralph when three strangers jumped them for reasons they couldn't explain. They escaped, they said. Ralph didn't.

The detective said he didn't buy it. He left the station's interrogation room, and the boys and their father conferred. When he came back, they had another story. This one came in a torrent of words.

Leigh was talking about writing movie scripts and designing intergalactic battle stations and hoping to meet George Lucas.

As he listened, Detective Denning was struck by a feeling that he would experience many times to come. "A sixth sense took over," he said. "I had the feeling he was sitting in front of me, telling me just another movie script."

People liked Ralph Cochran. They liked his sunny disposition and his talkative ways, although at the Taco Bell where he worked the night shift, the talking sometimes got in the way of the service because, as a supervisor, Mark Walters, said, "In a fast-food place you need to be fast."

But it was hard to find another knock against Ralph, a gawky redhead with an early Beatles haircut who stood 6 foot 4 and was rarely heard to say anything bad about anybody.

"When I think of Ralph," said Margaret McClatchy, one of his teachers at Shawnee Mission North High School, "I think of nice."

"Everybody who knew Ralph liked him," said his mother, Linda Cochran.

That was certainly true in the drama department, where Mrs. McClatchy directed plays and Ralph made himself a part of every one of them.

When he wasn't acting, he was painting sets or designing programs or posters or T-shirts. As dramas or musicals went into production, Ralph would be the first to arrive and the last to leave. He acted in *The Threepenny Opera, The King and I* and *Don't Drink the Water.* He worked so hard that "it became a kind of joke," said Frank Robertson, a drama coach. "After he graduated we'd look for the hardest worker and say, 'Who's the next Ralph Cochran going to be?' "

He fell for movies ever harder, working part time for about two years at Trailridge Cinema in Lenexa, selling concessions, taking tickets, working in the projection booth. He wanted to make movies, and if he couldn't do that, he immersed himself in being a fan.

Ralph was among the first in his school to see *Star Wars* when it came out in 1977, Mr. Robertson said. Ralph went on to see it 50 to 60 more times.

He liked science as a youngster and wanted to be an astronaut. Then came the film *Planet of the Apes* in the late 1960s, and he was gone on science fiction. That pleased his father, a longtime science-fiction buff and a laborer on a truck loading dock. His wife buttressed the family income with a delivery route for *The Kansas City Times* and *The Kansas City Star* around their Merriam neighborhood.

They found ways to indulge the oldest of their three children.

When Ralph was in elementary school, his parents said, they invited his friends over to watch 8mm shorts based on the *Apes* movies, converting the living room of their modest ranch-style house to a little movie theater, complete with popcorn. When Ralph was older and spotted a good buy for two old 35mm movie projectors at $1,200, his father put up a family pickup truck for collateral.

He was good at stagecraft. He made foam latex face masks, like Roddy McDowell wore in *Planet of the Apes,* that showed genuine promise. He made them for himself, for Leigh, for Jimmy. "He could have become anything he wanted to become," his mother said.

Ralph had a most unteen-agelike disregard for dress. No one ever knew him to have a romance. He had an aversion to touching other people, said a friend, Jane L. Smith. Still, the personality was a winning one. "How could you not like Ralph?" Mrs. McClatchy asked.

But Mrs. McClatchy worried about Ralph after graduation in 1981, when he was still living at home, working part time at the Taco Bell at 75th Street west of Interstate 35. Most of his classmates had gone to college, and Ralph's parents, whose educations went no further than their own graduations from Shawnee Mission North in the early 1960s, seemed peculiarly immune to the usual suburban pressure for children to succeed academically. Ralph skipped a college entrance examination his senior year, and his parents shrugged it off; he had a play rehearsal that day, they said, and they knew that was more important to him.

Mrs. McClatchy said she tried to get Ralph's life on a better track by attempting to get him an arts-based scholarship to the University of Missouri-Kansas City. But his grades were too low.

He had other blemishes on his record. The Johnson County juvenile court put Ralph on probation for something Leigh described as fraud. Ralph's parents said their son wasn't at fault. He'd been trying to help a friend, they said. Later he was fired from his job at Trailridge Cinema, where he had been suspected of helping another youth steal a print of a film. Theater manager Ken Deeter declined to say why he fired Ralph, and his parents similarly declined to disclose the circumstances. But they said it was another instance in which their son had been framed.

Not that Ralph cared much. His real interest was elsewhere. He summed it up on a business card he had printed by the thousands: "R.C. Collectibles. Buy, Sell, Trade, Movie Memorabilia."

He turned the family basement into a treasure-trove of sci-fi mementos: T-shirts, hats, stills, preview films, models, posters, videos. "You wouldn't believe what he gathered," Detective Denning said. "It would take 10 to 15 days to see what he collected."

Much of the stuff came from fan conventions in Chicago, Denver and Wichita as well as the Kansas City area. Ralph became a fixture of the scene, where it's common for fans to buy and sell the detritus of motion picture production and promotion. Scripts are big items. Most are copies that are bootlegged from movie sets. But if the seller can show that the script in hand was the real thing—or a first-generation copy of an original—or was once used, or even touched by an actor or director, then the pages take on almost totemic importance.

Ralph's first foray into script collecting came at a 1981 Denver convention he attended with Ms. Smith, then a Prairie Village 20-year-old who shared his interest in science fiction. They paid about $50 for a fourth-version working script of *Blade Runner,* a Harrison Ford vehicle that was one of Ms. Smith's favorite films. A representative of the production team confirmed the script's authenticity, and it was a real blow when Ms. Smith misplaced it in her rush to pack the car after the convention. She said that Ralph, distressed, managed to find another script "that was even more legitimate"—this one with a note inside apparently from director Ridley Scott.

Ralph was good at making contacts to produce goods like that, Ms. Smith said. He got better, developing sources who provided him with details about new films months before their release. He wanted to be known as the most avid *Star Wars* fan.

"He was really sharp," said Sherri Thurmond, a 19-year-old friend. "You could ask him just about anything about *Star Wars* and he'd know the answer."

His reputation was so well-known that when a reel of *Return of the Jedi* was stolen last year, he was the natural suspect for Overland Park police, Detective Denning said. The police cleared him of any connection with the theft, the detective said.

Ralph managed to see four advance showings of *Jedi,* the third release in the *Star Wars* series, before its public premiere last May. At one of the screenings, a Variety Club benefit at the Glenwood Theatre in Overland Park, Ralph secured the first six tickets for himself and friends, including Leigh, Jimmy and Ms. Smith, who kept the tickets as souvenirs and posed for snapshots to mark the occasion. Ralph, eager to show off, got interviewed by two television stations and a newspaper. He took his parents to one showing of the movie, and they said they were nearly as excited as he was.

As he stood in line for the film's public opening, he wore a patch that read *Revenge of the Jedi*, prized for being the name first chosen for the film but scrubbed after the film makers determined that the title was out of character. Noble Jedi knights would never seek revenge.

Under his jacket, he wore a T-shirt that read *Blue Harvest II—Horror Beyond Imagination*, the code name, he told anyone within earshot, that was used by the crew when filming in Yuma, Ariz., to keep *Star Wars* groupies off the set.

He boasted of knowing Anthony Daniels, the British actor who played the gold-plated robot C-3PO in the three *Star Wars* films.

They met when Mr. Daniels was a "guest" at KC Con, a fan convention held at the Hilton Plaza Inn in Kansas City. And while to most film goers Mr. Daniels labors anonymously in his robot role, to Ralph he was the real thing, someone who could render firsthand accounts of the making of the *Star Wars* saga. They spoke for several hours and began a correspondence. Mr. Daniels said he had to struggle to remember the details, but he recalled sending Ralph "some odds and ends"—patches and the like from Lucasfilm.

"He was such a charming and good person," Mr. Daniels said by telephone from London. He said he considered Ralph an intelligent and well-mannered young man.

But something made the actor wary: "He was very excited about the film industry, and I've always been nervous of people becoming too over-interested in a subject."

And Mr. Daniels said it made him "terribly sad" to realize, after Ralph's death, that Ralph had worshiped him as he did any artifact in the *Star Wars* movie-making machinery.

"Which is scary," Mr. Daniels said, "when you think of all the worthwhile things that he could do with his life, to set knowing me as a goal."

Leigh Philip Matz could use a hero.

Back in Atlanta, where he'd lived with his mother, the *Battlestar Galactica* television series caught his imagination, and he and a friend made their own Super-8 movies as *Battlestar* characters. But after he moved to Johnson County to be with his father, weeks went by without a movie camera or a friend who understood.

He was not a kid to get in trouble. He'd never been mixed up with drugs or liquor. If people thought that he and his 13-year-old brother, Jimmy, were different—and some did—they put it to the fact that the boys had moved from other places and were living only with their father after their parents' divorce.

Jimmy was the outgoing one, Stanford Matz said, "a lovable boy" who dreamed of becoming a football player. His mother, Barbara Matz, said he once told a psychologist that if he could be anything in the world it would be a deer. "Because then," Jimmy had said, "people would pet me and not hurt me."

He took ridicule for attending a special school because of a learning disability that gave him trouble with reading, Mrs. Matz said. But he was spirited and liked people. College-age youths came to him for tips on new dance steps when he was an 8-year-old, his mother said.

After he moved to Kansas last year, sharing his father's room in the two-bedroom apartment, his sixth-grade teacher noted that he made friends quickly but needed extra help with schoolwork. Some people noticed a scared look in his eye.

He was a follower who looked up to Leigh, his intellectual superior. "Jimmy is a highly protective child to those that he loves," Mrs. Matz said by telephone from Milwaukee, where she now lives.

And Jimmy wanted Leigh's love very much, his father said. But Leigh didn't have much time.

Leigh was too busy thinking about movies. "It was his life," Mr. Matz said. "He wanted to see his name up there with George Lucas' in the *Star Wars* sequels. It's all he thought about."

When he wrote to his mother in Milwaukee, it was to tell her that he'd seen *Flash Gordon* four times or to ask her for a typewriter he needed for screenplays. "May the Force be with you all," he closed. "Love, Leigh."

His hawk-like features contrasted with Jimmy's softer looks. He called himself "kind of a wimp," an outcast even in grade school because he liked science fiction. He compensated by playing high school football though only 5 feet 5 inches tall and 122 pounds.

He was a fourth-string player. "A very quiet, unassuming kid," said his coach, Tony Severino. "He just seemed like your average high school student—a very nice kid."

Leigh joined the Distributive Education Club of America to learn about retailing and became a club officer. He bought presents for a girl he liked.

"He had the braces on, the rock 'n' roll T-shirts. He was well-groomed," said Steven Swagerty, Leigh's marketing teacher and club adviser. "He got good grades. He did everything right. In my opinion, he was a kid who deserved your trust. I would have let him baby-sit for any of my children."

If Leigh found the role of all-American teenager easy to play, it was little more than that: a role. "Being popular was no big deal," he said.

He worked part time at a McDonald's, a Pak 'N' Save grocery and the Trailridge Cinema where Ralph worked. He didn't keep jobs long. The theater manager who fired him said he stole candy by the case. "A challenge," Leigh said.

The movies were a refuge. Mr. Matz, an Army captain, served a year in Vietnam soon after Leigh's birth at Fort Lee Military Hospital in Prince George County, Va. "Vietnam brought a very big wound in the marriage," Mrs. Matz said. "The marriage was not too happy after Vietnam."

When Leigh was 3, the family moved to Atlanta after Mr. Matz went to work with the

J.C. Penney Regional Distribution Center there. His mother, then a schoolteacher, put Leigh in her kindergarten class a year early. From then on he remained a year younger than his classmates, and he took the taunts that children rain down on their smaller peers.

Mr. Matz moved out in 1975, leaving behind Leigh, the oldest son, at 9; Jimmy, 5; and an infant son named David, who still lives with his mother. Two years later, with a transfer to the Penney's distribution center in Lenexa, Mr. Matz moved to Johnson County.

Leigh's situation worsened. His mother, who sometimes tutored in prisons, briefly remarried in 1979, her new husband an ex-convict. He was black, which made Leigh the subject of cruel jibes, and as Mrs. Matz tells it, her new husband was abusive to Leigh and to her and was unscrupulous with the family money.

"It created an absolute disaster for all of us," she said. Leigh turned away from her. It was her fault, she said, for bringing "an intruder" into the house.

"Leigh was a model child in all respects I could ever see," Mrs. Matz said. Still, "he was something of a loner," she said, and he became more that way after she went to work and he stayed home to care for his younger brothers.

"He had no life," Mr. Matz said. "Kids made fun of him because he'd wear hand-me-down clothes and get these cheap haircuts."

Leigh never got over his feelings about his mother. "When I talk to her," he said, "I tell her: 'I love you for a mother, but I don't love you as a person,' which if you think of it, messes you up."

Leigh moved to Kansas to be with his father in June 1979—"due to what my mother married," as he put it in a 1983 chronology titled "The History of Leigh Philip Matz" that listed noteworthy dates in his life. The dates included December 1982, when his brother, James Todd Matz, came to live with him and his father at Fox

Run Apartments, just nine months before the killings.

A key date was August 1977: "I saw *Star Wars* for the first time."

Another key date was this: "1979 (Early August): I met Ralph Cochran, who later became my very best friend."

They met at the movies.

Leigh was 12. Ralph was 16, working at the movie house. Leigh called the theater to ask about new movies and about getting some posters. Ralph invited him to come over.

The two became inseparable. "When those two minds came together, there was a fusion there that we'll probably never understand," Detective Denning said.

Leigh and Ralph went to movies together, to conventions together. They spoke on the phone five to eight hours a day.

"He had that personality," Leigh said. "He'd make friends with you at first. And then...."

It was a friendship that some thought would be better if ended.

Leigh's father didn't like Ralph. He called him "a no-good, worthless son of a bitch—nobody who's 20 is going to hang out with a 16-year-old."

Ralph's parents couldn't stand Leigh. "He was not a good influence," Linda Cochran said, describing him as "lying, deceitful, conniving." Mr. Matz and the Cochran parents had no contact with one another.

Ralph's friend Sherri Thurmond always "pictured Leigh as a little rat." As she put it, "His nose was always where it shouldn't be."

Ralph refused to listen to criticism of Leigh, she said. "Ralph had a very good mind," she said, "but he was dense about some things and blind when it came to Leigh."

Nor could Mr. Matz keep his son from seeing Ralph, although he tried. "Ralph was a svengali, the Rasputin in Leigh's life," he said. "It was Ralph, Ralph, Ralph, morning, noon and night."

No one knows what truly connected them, but psychiatry offered an explanation. Dr. Paul C. Laybourne, University of Kansas professor of psychiatry, told a court: "Ralph Cochran for four years programmed an immature, naive boy of 12 into believing that the world was made up of numerous scams, and that Leigh was a very talented scriptwriter, and that famous movie producers were interested in buying his scripts and drawings."

From Leigh's standpoint, Dr. Laybourne said, "It was an intense experience for him, occupying nearly every waking hour of his time for four years."

Leigh was bright. KU psychologists measured his IQ at 122, putting him in the upper 7 percent of the population. But emotional development was as stunted as his intellect was sharp.

Leigh practically lived in his room, an obsessive's province with a desk, a drawing table and a floor covered with carefully stacked papers by the hundreds—story outlines and drawings for movies.

He worked there by the hour, doing work he thought was destined for Mr. Lucas. In hard plastic cases he kept careful files: "Rough sketches." "Final work, incomplete." "Final work to be redrawn." "Final work to be sent to Lucasfilm."

Posters for *Star Wars, Star Trek* and *Superman* movies covered the walls. The lock on the door shut his father and brother from the room, sealing him in with his picture of himself and Anthony Daniels, his models of star ships and of the character Yoda from *The Empire Strikes Back*.

The outline for just one story, *The Lost Tomorrows*—an epic about a world war fought in outer space during "a time when man's future becomes his own nightmare"—ran 131 pages, and his detailed designs for the contending armies' emblems, warships, rankings, formations and movements ran hundreds of pages more.

The volume of materials and energy was so great that Detective Denning had to telephone Lucasfilm headquarters in northern California and hear official denials before he determined that the real George Lucas had no connection or knowledge of Ralph Cochran or Leigh Matz. "Preposterous," said Mr. Ganis, the film company's vice president.

Ralph's parents said they never heard their son make any mention of knowing Mr. Lucas. "They probably still don't believe Ralph was involved in anything funny," Detective Denning said.

But Leigh's father thought his son had hit on some tie to the movie maker, no matter how exaggerated. It was Mr. Matz who bought Leigh the desk, drawing table and typewriter he would need to develop his career. "I thought Leigh was a very, very bright boy," he said, "and I expected great things from him."

Detective Denning felt sorry for Mr. Matz when he told him about Ralph's schemes. "I said to Stan, 'Do you realize that none of your son's work has ever gone to California, that none of it has ever left Merriam?'" Detective Denning said. "He went slack, like he couldn't believe it. He, I think, was astonished momentarily—that all the work he'd seen his son do, and all the time on the phone had been for nothing."

"There were scams on top of scams," said Jon Willard, Leigh's attorney. "These boys liked to play mind games on each other, until you can't sort out what happened."

Leigh attempted to sort them out after the killing. In Johnson County Jail this year, he wrote a meticulous summary enumerating 14 scams over the four years he knew Ralph. Ever the budding scriptwriter, he gave the summary a title: *My Adventures in Kansas.*

It started small: Leigh paying Ralph $95 for bootlegged sci-fi items that Leigh later figured were worth $33.

Then came the first big hope and disappointment. In October 1980, Leigh said, he paid Ralph $75 for "entry fee, film and props" for a screen test. He believed he was being offered the chance to portray Jedair Skywalker, Luke's son, a new character for *Return of the Jedi*, then in the works.

"The plan was to film me acting in Super-8 and send it to Lucasfilm," Leigh said. After taking the money, Ralph told him the deal was off. The character was being dropped from the story.

Ralph offered to sell Leigh scripts, and he bit. Over the next year, Leigh said, he paid $1,040 for titles that would have been valuable, if real: *Indiana Jones and the Temple of Death, Superman IV: Story Proposal, ET II: Story Treatment, Star Trek III: Return to Genesis*. Leigh later figured their worth at $265.

The commerce picked up after Ralph met Anthony Daniels in August 1982. Leigh said Ralph claimed the actor would provide items. Over the next year, Leigh said, he paid Ralph $2,500 for stuff that sounded like prizes, including the whip Indiana Jones snapped in *Raiders of the Lost Ark*.

Nothing came. "I learned how to be patient," Leigh said. "I waited every day."

As days went on, Leigh acted as if under Ralph's control.

On two occasions, Leigh said, he hid in suburban movie theaters until the show was over, sneaking to the projection room to steal preview films Ralph wanted. He failed once when the projectionist worked overtime, he said. He scored in the other attempt.

"Ralph put me up to it," Leigh said. "Ralph was programming me. He programmed me to become a little terrorist."

When Ralph failed to deliver a script Leigh had paid for, Ralph said it had been stolen by a girl with Mafia connections. If Leigh attempted to get it, Ralph warned, it was only a matter of time before the mob got Leigh.

"At that point I understood my father and I were being monitored by hit men," Leigh told psychiatrists.

Ralph came to the rescue. He claimed that he went to the girl's house and shot the first person who came to the door: her father. Leigh said that he became so alarmed over the report that he called two suburban police departments to turn Ralph in. The police said no such crime had occurred; Leigh concluded Ralph found a way of covering it up.

During that incident, Leigh said, Ralph planted this idea in his head: If somebody is an annoyance, kill him.

☐

Oct. 23, 1982
Dearest Leigh,
It has long been my intention to write you and extend my many thanks for your participation in my Blue Harvest II project ....
I truly find myself more impressed with your visualizations than most of the materials my people are turning out at a snail's pace! My staff is working from your designs and drawings rather than from those of their own. We are relying on the written and drawn material from you and Mr. Cochran to use as a basis from which to work out our final designs. I cannot believe that talent like yours is out there untapped and going to waste!
I look forward to some day meeting you and Ralph as there will be openings on our staff in the future as we get involved in more and more film projects. We hope you consider us first when you decide to pursue professional film careers!
Sincerely yours,
George Lucas,
Founder of Lucasfilm

☐

Leigh said it began when Ralph returned from a science-fiction convention in Chicago in August 1982, saying he had met Lucasfilm Vice

President Sid Ganis and other studio officials.
Ralph was excited.

The bigwigs offered him the chance to submit design work for the next *Star Wars* picture, he proclaimed. He'd be in direct contact with the film company as an apprentice. Leigh could participate, too.

Leigh got right to work. From October to February, he handed more than 300 pages to Ralph to submit to Lucasfilm.

"As time passed, Mr. Lucas himself got involved," Leigh said. "Ralph began flying to California, England, India, and keeping in daily touch with Mr. Lucas."

☐

I simply have to thank you for such an excellent present....
Sincerely,
George Lucas, Founder of LFL.

☐

December 1982
Dear Leigh,
Hello again! I just couldn't wait to tell you just how much an integral part of our organization you and your work has (sic) become. It seems that your involvement has made all the difference in the smoothness of our everyday struggle to file away a chunck (sic) of work on The Clone Wars, since we are going to shelf (sic) the project in a short while to make way for more current films. Don't get me wrong...you, quite honestly, are our most important contributor. My guys here keep asking when you are coming by to punch the ol' time card and shoot the bull. But I myself don't know when you are going to do that....
Sincerely with best wishes,
George Lucas, Founder of LFL

Jan. 2, 1983
Dear Mr. Lucas,
I hope you and your family had a merry Christmas and the happiest of New Year's. I trust your New Year's resolution is to make sure E.T. does not become a bigger money maker than Star Wars....

All I can say is thank you for everything! It is an honor and a privilege to be working for you, and again thank you for this opportunity! I am just surprised that you would take to my work the way you have....

I am planning to fly to California this summer, but I don't know if we can meet due to your involvement in Raiders of the Caverns of Doom....

In regars (sic) to college, I am planning on either going to USC or UCLA. I will be moving to California a year from now.... I have writen (sic) both colleges and recived (sic) no reply as yet. If you could have some information about the requirements to get in, price and film school, I would appreciate it....

Can I buy the Star Wars and Jedi video cartridge from you any time soon?...

This may be the wrong time to ask this question, but could I go to work with Lucasfilm Ltd. in some small position?

Well...that's about it for this installment. I hope you like it! Be prepared for a new rebel base idea in my next package. So until then take care and I hope this new year is a good one for you!
Sincerly (sic),
Leigh Philip Matz

☐

Feb. 4, 1983
Leigh—Please excuse my typing. It is very late and I am very tired. I will be heading to India in a few days and would suggest that if you have any more questions you should give them to Ralph since he and I will be spending more time with one another in the coming days. I will bring you

something special if I am able... so until then keep fit and take care of yourself and give your family my greetings!

*Sincerely,
George*

☐

If Leigh needed any more proof of his importance to Lucasfilm, he found it in *Return of the Jedi.*

That shuttlecraft seen near the film's beginning—it looked like a craft Leigh had designed. So did a fighter ship and some of the weapons.

And when actor Harrison Ford set a bomb to blow up a station on the planet of Endor, Leigh deciphered the alien writing on the side of the bomb. He made out his name in the scribbling.

"Mr. Lucas was thanking me for all the time and effort I did on the drawings," he said.

He owed it all to Ralph. Mr. Lucas had offered this advice in an earlier letter: "Feel free to consult Mr. Cochran as he is in charge of all aspects of production."

He called Ralph more often. Sometimes he made Jimmy do it. Their constant calling at the Taco Bell annoyed Ralph, who often voiced "a general disgust with the Matz brothers," said Cynthia R. Nickel, a co-worker.

But as Ms. Nickel told it to Johnson County Detective Lt. Vincent Werkowitch, "Once Ralph got on the phone with the Matz brothers, he was always very nice with them, as he was with everyone he came in contact with."

The whole Taco Bell seemed to be in on the joke. Sometimes Leigh would drop in, and one of the workers would say, "George Lucas was just here, but you missed him." Or they'd give him a note they said Mr. Lucas had left for him.

Ms. Nickel once telephoned Leigh pretending to be Mr. Lucas' secretary calling long distance. She testified in a hearing that she called to welcome him to the Jedi club and to tell him he'd soon be getting a Jedi patch. Leigh replied by thanking her.

Ralph told co-worker Mark Walters that he "was running little scams" and "liked to play mind games on Leigh."

Harmless games, everybody thought. As Ralph's high school drama teacher, Mrs. McClatchy, saw it, if his high school friends had known what was going on, "everyone would have laughed and cheered—because they're normal people, and they would've known it was joking."

But some quit laughing. "I tried to get away from it when it started getting out of hand," said Chuck Williams, an assistant manager. "They started trying to sell Leigh things. I didn't like Leigh or anything, but I started to feel sorry for him."

The "George Lucas" who took such a liking to Leigh liked his cash as well.

Ralph always handled Leigh's money, explaining that Mr. Lucas worried about his personal security and refused to give his address to anyone but a confidant.

Leigh paid $420 for 11 *Star Wars* scripts in various drafts, supposedly Mr. Lucas' personal copies. The money came from his job at the Pak 'N' Save, from his grandparents, from Jimmy. Nothing came back, he said, except two $10 scripts.

Ralph then told Leigh his work had drawn the attention of another admirer: Steven Spielberg, creator of *E. T.* and *Close Encounters of the Third Kind.*

But Mr. Lucas didn't want to lose Leigh as a contributor. To put a lock on Leigh's talent, Mr. Lucas came up with a five-year plan, deciding that Leigh should write several screenplays by 1988. One of the stories would become a movie.

Then Ralph, acting as Leigh's agent, took control of the stories. "He called them his and indicated he had them copyrighted in his name," Leigh said. Ralph told him he sold *The Lost Tomorrows* to the Ladd Co. for $60,000—and added to the fiction by filling a pocket-size address book with phony entries of names and phone numbers for Mr. Lucas, Mr. Spielberg and other film world household names.

Steven McRoberts, a Taco Bell worker, testified that he offered to sell the notebook to Leigh on the pretext that he had found it. Leigh made photocopies of it.

The address book held bad news. Ralph had scribbled notes hinting that soon he would be moving to California to work for Lucasfilm.

And if Leigh wanted his stories back, Ralph advised, he'd have to pay. He set the price at $1,600, Leigh said.

Ralph put more distance in their friendship. Over Labor Day weekend, they were due to drive to Denver for a convention. They'd be seeing Anthony Daniels. As the day drew closer, Ralph told Leigh that he wanted to ride with his friend Sherri Thurmond. Leigh could ride in another car.

Then the secret leaked.

Mark Willis, a Taco Bell shift manager who was angry with Ralph, thought he'd get even by telling Leigh about the Lucas charade.

Leigh confronted Ralph.

Ralph told him he'd cut off the friendship if he took the manager's word. "I snapped right back into believing Ralph," Leigh said.

About a week before the killing, Ralph told fellow worker Mark Walters that he didn't consider Leigh a friend anymore.

About the same time, in a phone conversation with Jane Smith's mother, Ralph talked about going to film school in California, to enter a movie-making career with Ms. Smith as his partner.

Leigh said he watched it all emotionlessly, mechanically. "I knew something wasn't right with me," he said, "but I couldn't really put my finger on it."

Things had been going wrong all summer. Leigh crashed the family car and began a pattern of fights with his father. Ralph's doing, he thought. "Every job I lost was due to Ralph," he said. "Every girlfriend I lost was due to Ralph."

He acted oddly at the Pak 'N' Save. Fellow workers told Lt. Werkowitch that Leigh struck them "as a strange boy who often would gaze off into the distance when spoken to and appeared to be spacey."

In May, a month after landing the job, he asked for a week's vacation. He said he spent it watching *Return of the Jedi.*

In July he twice hit a female worker with a clipboard. She retaliated by kicking him, and he told her, "This will be the last day for you." Later he posted notes with her name on them. "Kill," they said.

He called in sick Aug. 2 and failed to show up without explanation Aug. 5 and 6. He was fired Aug. 12.

A couple of weeks later, he brought his troubles to Jimmy. Leigh said he told Jimmy that Ralph was planning to murder their father by blowing up his car. It was a resurrection, Leigh said, of threats Ralph had made a year before.

"I needed Jimmy's help," Leigh said. "I knew I couldn't do it myself. I needed something to get me going. I needed a spark."

That night Jimmy woke up his father. The 13-year-old was crying. The boy said: "I love you so much. I never want anything to happen to you."

Mr. Matz said, "I never connected it until 72 hours later."

By then Ralph Cochran was dead.

The brothers are ready.

They wait on the Cochran's porch steps at 2 a.m. for Ralph to come home after closing the night shift. Leigh knows that Ralph expects the $1,600 they've been quarreling over.

Ralph drives up. Leigh opens the passenger door. As he slides into the front seat, he finds an answer to the pressures.

Jimmy leans through the open window on the driver's side. He pulls a knife. It's a kitchen knife. The cardboard sheath is still on it.

"You putz," Leigh shouts at his brother.

Everything is going wrong. Leigh shoves Ralph, and Ralph asks what's going on. Jimmy swings his knife and accidentally stabs Leigh in the hand. Leigh wrestles back. Now the adrenaline is pumping, everything is heightening, and Leigh realizes that the situation has gone to now-or-never. Time to get back to the main business.

The business is Ralph.

The boys stab him more than 35 times, Ralph fighting them with his hands and his wits, trying to make last-minute deals, bargaining for breath.

The knives keep flashing. One pierces the aorta. Ralph slumps over the steering wheel, setting the horn blaring through the quiet Merriam side street, announcing his death at age 20.

Blood soaks through his Taco Bell shirt onto the upholstery of his 1976 gold Chevy Caprice with the "JEDI" plates. Blood covers Leigh's shirt and oozes from Jimmy's nose, which took a blow from an elbow. Blood drips on the Cochrans' porch when Leigh lets himself in the house, sneaking to the basement to grab the hundreds of pages of writings and drawings he thought would go to Lucasfilm.

Ralph's brother and sister are asleep. They hear nothing. Ralph's parents are at work.

The Matz boys have no plan except to go back to their Lenexa apartment. They shove Ralph's body from his car. It falls face down in the dew of a ditch along Craig Road.

A 6-inch butcher knife lies nearby. So does a paperback copy of *Return of the Jedi.*

As the brothers drive away, they run a tire over one of the corpse's shoes.

—as told in court records
and through Leigh's recollections
in a hospital interview.

Shawnee Mission North High School is remembering Ralph with annual honors. The Ralph Eugene Cochran Thespian Memorial Award will go to the senior who comes closest to his record in the drama department. The student will get $100 and his name affixed to a plaque bearing Ralph's picture.

Ralph's parents set up the fund with money that people contributed instead of flowers at the funeral. A long line of cars made up the procession. Ralph's parents recalled that the driver of the limousine said he'd rarely seen so many cars.

Ralph's body lay in an open casket at the visitation, dressed in the *Return of the Jedi* T-shirt he often wore, a scarf around his neck to cover the slash wounds. Over the loudspeaker came John Williams' sound-track score to *Return of the Jedi*.

Everything Ralph collected will stay in the basement of the house at 6502 Craig Road, said his father, until some future grandchild takes an interest. Then maybe the family will part with it.

Ralph's 19-year-old sister Lynna drives the Chevy in which Ralph was killed. The car "is a living memorial to Ralph," his father said. "It would be sacrilegious to get rid of it."

Even if the car should give out, the family will hold on to the license plates.

"As far as I'm concerned, those are his plates," Mr. Cochran said, "and nobody else will ever have those plates in Johnson County."

Eight Questions By Leigh Philip Matz

Below are eight questions that I must answer for myself before I can continue with my life. They are listed in order from greatest to least.

1. Who am I?
2. What in my life is real?
3. Is my life one big mind game?
4. Has anything ever appeared to be as it really is?

5. How many wrongs does it take to make a right?
6. What is time?
7. How can you hold onto things that never existed?
8. Is scam a four-letter word?
— written in a Johnson County Jail cell, January 1984

Clinical examination and psychological testing show an encapsulated delusional system regarding all these events. Leigh still anticipates that he will be exonerated from the charges, and that he will go on to be very successful in science fiction movies. Apparently, the experiences with Ralph have only reinforced his belief that he is a genius in this area rather than giving him pause to contemplate whether he really is as talented as he believes.

In view of all this, it is my opinion that he fits criteria for Paranoid Disorder Atypical Type. That he is mentally ill and in need of psychiatric treatment and that by virtue of personality is extremely immature and inappropriate in his testing of reality for a 16-year-old educated male.

Sincerely,
Paul C. Laybourne Jr., M.D.,
Professor of Psychiatry
Nov. 17, 1983

At court hearings, Leigh kept expecting Ralph to show up.

"I thought it was another scam," he said.

Leigh pleaded guilty to second-degree murder, Jimmy to voluntary manslaughter.

Judge William Gray sentenced Leigh on April 13 to the Larned State Hospital until he is declared cured. Then the court is to determine how much of the second-degree murder sentence Leigh will serve. The minimum is five to 15 years. The maximum is 20 to life.

Jimmy got an indefinite sentence at the Youth Center at Atchison, Kan., where his case is reviewed every four months.

But they were sentences that carry question marks. Explanations for the killing remained vague and contradictory.

Ralph and Linda Cochran said they thought their son died because Leigh was jealous of Ralph's science-fiction connections. And they thought Ralph was outgrowing Leigh. "He wanted to find his own way, and that made Leigh angry," Mrs. Cochran said.

Stanford Matz thought his boys became killers because of Ralph's manipulations. "It takes a naive, immature kid to believe all that stuff was real, but Cochran was working on him for four years. You have a psychopath dealing with a mentally ill boy."

He said his boys were certain Ralph was going to have him killed. "They did it to protect me," Mr. Matz said.

The Johnson County district attorney's office asserted that Leigh Matz became a killer out of rage when he realized that Ralph Cochran's ties to George Lucas were a hoax.

Jon Willard, Leigh's attorney, said that even after the killing, Leigh believed in the George Lucas connection. If Leigh's rage can be traced, the lawyer said, it was that Ralph made moves to cut Leigh off from Mr. Lucas.

Anthony Daniels, the robot-playing actor, knows nothing of the causes, but he plumbed the case for the sorrow left behind. "It strikes me," he said, "that we are talking about two 6-year-old kids who believed each other. It sounds like they were playing games and enjoyed playing them. It's really so sad."

If there is a moral, he said, it may lie in the dangers of fanaticism.

"The films are a piece of fun," he said, "and everyone involved wants fans from all over the world to have fun and not take it too seriously.

"If anything comes out of this, I hope it encourages people to know where reality is. That's what films are for: to lose reality for 2½ hours but then go back out on the street and know where you are."

Mr. Swagerty, Leigh's club adviser, said the killing has left Leigh's classmates saddened, feeling confused and betrayed. "They wonder," he said, "how do you distinguish good guys from bad guys?"

The killing showed a hidden side to Leigh, who could be so adept at getting good grades or persuading club members to elect him to office. Leigh was a salesman, Mr. Swagerty concluded, and a good one. He had explained many of his high school absences by saying he'd traveled to California to meet Mr. Lucas. And Mr. Swagerty said he believed him.

Maybe, Mr. Swagerty said, Leigh will prove as exemplary a mental patient as he did a student. Maybe he'll outsmart his doctors.

"I know one thing," Mr. Swagerty said, "I'll never trust a student the same way again."

After traveling several meters further, Heston blacked out and collapsed. The crash and the thick air of the alien world had taken their toll on him. Within minutes another of the shuttle's engines exploded, creating an eerie gray smoke which drifted over Heston's inert body. A shroud of blackness soon fell over everything.
—from *The Lost Tomorrows*

Leigh soon settled in with his writing at the high-security building at Larned. Aides who have read *The Lost Tomorrows* can't put it down, he said, and they've told him he's got a great future.

In April, when he had been there less than two weeks, he agreed to a newspaper interview and sat in a conference room, holding a copy of the psychiatric report.

He looked young, with acne on his cheeks, and when he talked about himself it sounded as if he meant someone else.

He called the killing "the crime" and said he had no remorse over it. He said he cannot explain why it happened. For months he put everything out of his mind.

He talked about Ralph as if he were both friend and enemy, all-powerful.

"I'd always thought I could handle things. Because I'd dealt with the pressures of waiting for things, of problems that would arise like the screen test for *Jedi*. Every problem I'd had I'd been able to handle. I lived through six months of living with my mother and her husband, and I could handle everything—or I thought I did—but I was just kind of falling apart—everything was happening at once—and I said to myself—I don't know what is the matter—I was getting squished from every direction—and it has to be Ralph—it was weird because I thought, I didn't think, I just knew, I just had a feeling...."

He said that if he had been thinking more clearly he would have gotten away with it.

And if he hadn't killed Ralph, he said, he would have solved his problems another way. He would have killed himself.

He said that the actual killing was harder than he expected. "Ralph always made things seem easier than they were," he said.

Stanford Matz's life is making visiting day.

The drive to Larned State Hospital takes about five hours from Lenexa. Mr. Matz plans to make the trip once a month.

It takes about 80 minutes to get to Atchison. Mr. Matz has visited Jimmy every week.

From the moment he woke up to the killing, he made up his mind to do whatever he had to do for his sons. He found the best lawyers and the best psychiatrist he could. He was willing to keep secrets about the murder if withholding details meant lighter sentences.

"When your kid's life is on the line," he said, "you don't ask the cost."

Co-workers at the Penney's distribution center, where Mr. Matz is accuracy control manager, gave him their support. So did Mr. Willard, the attorney, who became his closest friend. "You get through something like this by having a good attorney," Mr. Matz said, "and by praying a lot."

He spends mostly quiet time with Jimmy when he visits. During the week the boy goes to school—"it's not unlike a private school," Mr. Matz said—and he looks forward to weekends.

"He's a lovable, lovable boy," he said. "He's been stepped on...He's the kind who says, 'Hey, love me, I love you, so please love me in return.'

"When I visit, we sit and hug and eat a sandwich."

It is hard, Mr. Matz said, to know exactly where things went wrong. If he had been smarter, Mr. Matz said, he would have seen trouble in Leigh's obsessions. But, he asked, "Who knows what kids are into anymore?"

Mr. Matz and his sons are closer now. For about a year before the killing, he said, he and Leigh rarely spoke unless Leigh was asking for money. Leigh had drawn $1,400 on credit cards to give to Ralph. "I said you can have the money—but get rid of Cochran," Mr. Matz said.

"I'd say, if Ralph is so talented, why is he still working the night shift at Taco Bell? And Leigh would say it's because he can't bring his friendship with Lucas out in public, he had to keep quiet because he wasn't in the union. I'd say bull.

"But it's like a marriage. Even when you know it's bad, you still want to believe it's all right. You want to believe. You believe. He believed in this, and it consumed him."

Ahead are long drives. To repair the emptiness, Mr. Matz has his cruise control, his tapes, his thoughts.

"It consumed all of us, I guess."

Good newspaper writing

By DON FRY

The confident superlative in the title of this volume suggests that the profession, or at least its contest judges, agree on what constitutes "good" newspaper writing. Most writers and editors support the traditional values: accuracy, balance, fairness, completeness, etc., the characteristics that anchor good writing in good reporting. Our 1984 volume praises clear, effective, and graceful prose.

The 1985 winners meet these tests with ease, although they write in categories with different requirements: Richard Aregood in editorials, Jonathan Bor in deadline newswriting, Murray Kempton in commentary, and Greta Tilley in non-deadline writing. They also share four other qualities of good newswriting: precision, steady advance, focus on content, and specific presence.

Richard Aregood writes with precision in every sense of that word, as in the lead from his editorial entitled "Standing Tall":

> As soon as the smoke cleared and the dead and wounded were taken away after the tragic explosion at the U.S. Embassy in Beirut, the president explained what we should do about it.
> We should stand tall, he said.
> He did not say how it helped to merely stand tall and do nothing else, especially since the blast was the third of its kind to victimize Americans in Lebanon.

The reader can sense the anger behind the simplicity of this passage, kept in check by

---

This article appeared in another form in the May 1985 ASNE Bulletin.

careful selection and honing of words. Aregood mixes long and short sentences, and even the longer ones avoid complex structures. He comments, "The more complicated you make a sentence, the more likely you are not only to confuse the reader, but also to confuse yourself. When I find myself raging forward, with commas and various other connectors, I know I'm going to have trouble understanding that sentence when I reread it." Aregood modestly attributes his short, crisp style to his experience as a rewrite man on a tabloid newspaper. We can attribute it to clarity of thought and short, clear, simple presentation, achieved through deliberate and careful underwriting, the essence of precision.

Jonathan Bor exemplifies what we might call "steady advance," that quality of newswriting that keeps the reader reading. Good newswriting never requires the reader to back up late in a story to recall earlier references. A newspaper is meant to be read once, not savored and mulled over, and the reader must understand a story in one pass. Bor's prize-winning piece describes a heart transplant:

> The beer cooler was opened, and the donor heart was placed inside the patient's chest. The new heart, about as large as a relaxed fist, was attached to the blood vessels.
>
> It jerked and fluttered and became Bruce Murray's.
>
> But for the next two hours, the heart-lung machine continued to do much of the pumping. Because the heart was cold, it could not pump vigorously. But as blood pumped by the heart-lung machine flowed through it, it contracted and expanded and gradually warmed. As it warmed, it pumped with more authority.

Bor's vigorous verbs propel the reader along, and the repetition of key words ("Pump, flow, heart") captures the repetitious rhythms of the procedure. Bor avoids medical jargon which might require him to interrupt the flow for explanations. He carefully anticipates questions which might arise in the reader's mind, and answers them before the reader can think of them. Before the reader can wonder how big a heart is, Bor compares it to a relaxed fist. His tight control of the reader's attention produces a self-contained story. No reader, caught in the steady advance of events and details, would think of putting it down.

Greta Tilley also won the ASNE prize in 1983, the only person to win it twice. Her six-part series on a mental hospital in Raleigh succeeds because of its controlled focus on content and meaning, rather than on style or the writer. Despite the apparent freedom occasioned by the length of her series, she writes with precision and steady advance. She comments, "I think you do your best writing when you really are under the gun. When you have too much time, you try too hard instead of trying to say it the simplest way." The lead of her third installment illustrates how she keeps the reader's attention on places and characters, rather than on her own style:

> The lobby of Hoey Building smells of institutional cleaner and early lunch. People still able to do some things for themselves live here in the largest of the three geriatric units at Dorothea Dix Hospital.
>
> A technician in white pants and jacket waits at the first-floor elevator, and turns a key to start it toward the second floor. Locks clicking open and closed make some of the hospital's less haunting music. Uniforms are optional on Dix Hill. Staff members are the people carrying the keys.

Her quiet tone keeps the reader looking at the scene and not at the writer. Elsewhere in the series, Tilley appears as a character in her own narrative, but only to provoke telling quotations from patients. She says, "I'm writing about them, I'm not writing about me. I'm not trying to show, 'Hey, look how well I can write.' " Reacting to George Orwell's comment that "good writing is like a window pane," she laughs, "Good for George Orwell. I wish I could have said it that way." Greta Tilley's apparently unself-conscious prose results from a conscious awareness of her own voice.

At first glance, the writing of Murray Kempton seems to defy the three qualities discussed above. He writes about his own reactions in involved pieces with long sentences. He quips, "My sentences are so long that I can't even find the first word when I get to the last." But his thoughts and sentences are clear and simple in structure, and he lets the reader view events and characters through the writer's focusing eye, an eye that sees with relentless clarity, as in this vignette from his column on the Republican nominating convention:

> Yesterday morning, the secretary of labor was honored at a breakfast tendered by Jackie Presser, president of the Teamsters Union. It was an occasion pregnant with amiability, the only one so far where no one in attendance had to pass through a metal detector, a discourtesy that the Teamsters may or may not have awhile ago decided was inappropriate, not to say impolitic, for any guest list as gamey as theirs usually is.
>
> Every uncountable inch of Jackie Presser's corpus bubbled with goodwill for every stranger; nothing equals his enthusiasm for clasping any hand as soon as he knows it is unencumbered by a subpoena.

Kempton's work depends on specific presence, that sense conveyed to readers that they are actually present at a described event, mostly achieved through sharply observed detail. The writer serves as the readers' witness on the scene and conveys impressions to their senses.

Jonathan Bor puts it this way: "There's no better way to bring the story and the scene home to the reader than to pick out maybe a dozen or so vivid images." Specific presence requires an escape from the abstract. As Kempton says, "I don't like abstract pieces. I'd much rather work the way a drama critic does: Go find a play and watch it." He reports the local play of persons and their follies screened fine through his critical intelligence.

Since writers like rules and editors like lists, we can boil these four qualities of good writing down into maxims:

* * *

How to get into *Best Newspaper Writing 1986*

1) Write with precision, that is, with brevity, clarity, and simplicity at the levels of word, sentence, paragraph, and story.

2) Write with such control that the reader never deviates from the straight path to the final word.

3) Write first for content, and use style to enhance the telling, not the teller.

4) Write concretely so the reader shares your unique witness.

And never forget the basic values:

5) Write clear, effective, graceful prose which embodies accuracy, balance, fairness, completeness, etc.

Finalists

In addition to the winners and finalists included in this year's edition of *Best Newspaper Writing,* the Writing Awards Board also cited these finalists:

Non-deadline writing: Jeff Lyon, *Chicago Tribune;* Herbert Michelson, *Sacramento Bee;* and Jim Naughton, *The Post-Standard,* Syracuse, N.Y.

Deadline writing: Loretta McLaughlin, *The Boston Globe,* and Robert Perry, Associated Press.

Editorial writing: Marvin Seid, *Los Angeles Times.*

Former ASNE Award Winners

1984

Deadline writing: David Zucchino, *The Philadelphia Inquirer*
Non-deadline writing: James Kindall, *The Kansas City Star*
Commentary: Roger Simon, *The Chicago Sun-Times*
Business writing: Peter Rinearson, *The Seattle Times*

1983

Deadline writing: No awards made in this category.
Non-deadline writing: Greta Tilley, *Greensboro News & Record*
Commentary: Rheta Grimsley Johnson, *Memphis Commercial Appeal*
Business writing: Orland Dodson, *Shreveport Times*

1982

Deadline writing: Patrick Sloyan, *Newsday*
Non-deadline writing: William Blundell, *The Wall Street Journal*
Commentary: Theo Lippman Jr., *The Baltimore Sun*
Sports writing: Tom Archdeacon, *The Miami News*

1981

Deadline writing: Richard Zahler, *The Seattle Times*

Non-deadline writing: Saul Pett, Associated Press
Commentary: Paul Greenberg, *Pine Bluff Commercial*
Sports writing: Thomas Boswell, *The Washington Post*

1980

Deadline writing: Carol McCabe, *Providence Journal-Bulletin*
Non-deadline writing: Cynthia Gorney, *The Washington Post*
Commentary: Ellen Goodman, *The Boston Globe*

1979

Deadline writing: Richard Ben Cramer, *The Philadelphia Inquirer*
Non-deadline writing-News: Thomas Oliphant, *Boston Sunday Globe*
Non-deadline writing-Features: Mary Ellen Corbett, *Fort Wayne News Sentinel*
Grand Prize (Commentary): Everett S. Allen, *New Bedford Standard-Times*